A Call to Compassion

On The Hudson

Jung

BOOK SERIES

The Jung on the Hudson Book Series was instituted by the New York Center for Jungian Studies in 1997. This ongoing series is designed to present books that will be of interest to individuals of all fields, including mental health professionals, who are interested in exploring the relevance of the psychology and ideas of C. G. Jung to their personal lives and professional activities.

For more information about this series, the annual Jung on the Hudson seminars, and the New York Center for Jungian Studies contact: Aryeh Maidenbaum, Ph.D., New York Center for Jungian Studies, 27. N. Chestnut St., Ste. 3, New Paltz, NY 12561-1708, telephone (845) 256-0191, fax (845) 256-0196.

For more information about becoming part of this series contact: Valerie Cooper, Nicolas-Hays, P. O. Box 1126, Berwick, ME 03901-1126, telephone (207) 698-1041, email: info@nicolashays.com.

A CALL TO COMPASSION

Bringing Buddhist Practices of the Heart into the Soul of Psychology

AURA GLASER

NICOLAS-HAYS
BERWICK, MAINE

First published in 2005 by
Nicolas-Hays, Inc.
P. O. Box 1126 * Berwick, ME 03901-1126
www.nicolashays.com
Distributed to the trade by
Red Wheel/Weiser, LLC
P. O. Box 612 * York Beach, ME 03910-0612
www.redwheelweiser.com

Library of Congress Cataloging-in-Publication Data
Glaser, Aura.
A call to compassion : bringing buddhist practices of the heart into the soul of psychology /
Aura Glaser; foreword by Robert. A. F. Thurman.
p. cm. — (Jung on the Hudson book series)
Includes bibliographical references and index.
ISBN 0-89254-116-4 (pbk. : alk. paper)
1. Compassion—Religious aspects—Buddhism. 2. Compassion—Psychological aspects.
3. Psychotherapy—Religious aspects—Buddhism. I. Title. II. Series
BQ4360.G53 2005
294.3'3615--dc22   2004028764
VG

Cover and text design by Kathryn Sky-Peck.
Typeset in Dante
Printed in the United States of America
11 10 09 08 07 06 05
7 6 5 4 3 2 1
The paper used in this publication meets the minimum requirements of the
American National Standard for Information Sciences-Permanence of Paper for
Printed Library Materials Z39.48—1992 (R1997).

To my parents,
Whose hearts brim with loving-kindness.

To my treasured teacher Gehlek Rimpoche,
Who embodies the essence of compassion and wisdom.

TABLE OF CONTENTS

PART I:
THE JOURNEY TO A SELF THAT INCLUDES OTHERS

PART II:
REFRAMING THE DIALOGUE

ACKNOWLEDGMENTS

I am grateful to many people who have given beyond measure:

The numerous spiritual teachers who have so generously shared their knowledge and experience, and whose very presence elucidates the meaning of an awakened heart;

Christine Downing, who served as the first reader of this manuscript, provided indispensable help; her depth of scholarship and sage counsel enriched my understanding of both Freud and Jung;

Ruby Webber, for her steadfast support through all the seasons of this book and for the many long walks and countless hours of conversation and laughter; Sandy Finkel, for a friendship that has woven such rich tapestry, including a journey to India that changed both of our lives; Carolyn Arcure, Leigh Daniels, and Evie Gauthier, for early conversations that helped me clarify the direction of this project; Madonna Gauding, Amy Hertz, Steve Kronenberg, Malka Littman, and Brenda Rosen, for their timely thoughts and encouragement; Tina von Moltke for her comments that led to some refinements of the final draft;

Robert Thurman, for his continued encouragement and support; Valerie Cooper at Nicolas-Hays, for patiently guiding me through the publication process; Aryeh Maidenbaum, at Jung on the Hudson, who first sent Valerie the manuscript and encouraged her to consider it;

Sue Anderson, Susan Golden, Ariana Arlen Haynes, and Robert Slattery, for their unique contributions to this process; all of my patients, who courageously share their inner journeys, and teach me so much; friends and family, too many to name, who have helped in innumerable ways;

Octavio Cianno, who died suddenly while I was writing this book, is fondly remembered. As a writer and a student of depth psychology and Tibetan Buddhism, he enthusiastically supported this project. I know he would celebrate its completion.

And finally, my husband and beloved companion, Stephen, has been a bridge, a boat, a rock, medicine, an ear, an eye, a hand, touch, sparkle, nourishment, a harbor, a witness, a soul mate, and a friend. It is not possible to convey adequately the countless ways he has stood present in the unfoldment of this work, and in the whole of my life.

I bow to the ground in gratitude.

FOREWORD

I t is my privilege and pleasure to introduce Aura Glaser's excellent new work, *A Call to Compassion*. She speaks from a place within an ancient spiritual and scientific tradition of psychology. The great Indian Buddhist philosopher and spiritual master of Nalanda University, Chandrakirti, made the same call long ago, in seventh-century India:

> *First saying "I," beings fix upon the self,*
> *With "that is mine!" they long for things,*
> *Cycling helplessly like buckets of a water wheel—*
> *I bow to One who lives compassion for such beings!*

> *Compassion alone is seed for the crop of buddhas,*
> *It is the water that makes their enlightenment grow,*
> *And it ripens to fruition in eternal happiness—*
> *Thus first of all I praise compassion!*

Following the example of His Holiness the Dalai Lama, I have long urged my fellow Buddhists to think and live their "Buddhism" as a practice and a service, not merely a "religion," something distinguished from the rest of life as a "faith," or system of beliefs, there to provide solace for suffering people. As a practice it is a powerful and effective system of intellectual and spiritual education, usable by anyone, of any religion or nonreligion, starting from where they are and helping them progress toward unprecedented levels of clarity of mind and openness of heart. This education begins by heightening awareness of the effects of actions of mind, speech, and body, spurring one to feel one's impact on others and develop a more ethical or sensitive way of relating to them. It proceeds by deconditioning addictive mental habits such as greed, hate, and delusion, and developing positive attitudes, such as generosity, patience, mindfulness, enthusiasm, love, and openness. It culminates with the release of critical intelligence, focusing sharply on the way things seem to be, stripping away illusions and seeing how they really are. Once realistic awareness reveals our amazing interconnectedness with all others, compassion becomes our natural response to that connection. So the path begins with compassionate awareness, progresses by minimizing hard-hearted alienation and maximizing sensitive connection, and culminates in the full blossoming of selfless, blissful love and compassion.

Once a "Buddhist," whether "religiously" a "Buddhist" or not, graduates to some extent from this education of the heart, their "Buddhism" continues as a service to others, while this also develops them further in postgraduate levels. That service is helping others find the root and source of freedom and happiness in themselves through the same educational process. This is not a matter of indoctrinating others in a "faith," since merely believing in the education does not deliver its benefit. That would be like a graduate cook going out in the restaurant and reading aloud high-flown passages and recipes from the cookbook—to serve others he must cook for them the delicious and healthy food that they will enjoy eating. This service is rather helping others as a therapist, opening for them doors to healing through their own insights into their own situations, dangers, and opportunities. Therefore, Buddhism is more like a deep and far-reaching psychotherapy than a religious conversion.

I predict that decades from now, when more and more individuals have used the Buddhist education to their own relief and satisfaction and have continued with it as a service to others, the whole nature of medicine and healing in our society will have changed. Compassion will have become a working watchword, a constant presence, a *sine qua non*, a powerful stream of life-giving water. And at that time, Aura Glaser's lucid, eloquent, heartfelt, illuminating *A Call to Compassion* will be remembered as a clarion call that awakened our inspiration.

She has spent years educating herself in the stages of the path, from its beginning in the discovery of the true preciousness of our special human life form with its extraordinary liberty and rare opportunity for evolutionary freedom, to its high reaches in the realms of universal bliss, crystal wisdom, and impartial love and compassion. Continuing in her service of others, she avoided religious proselytization and turned instead to the Western traditions of psychotherapy, studied Freud and Jung, and Horney and Winnicott and many others, working through their thought in the context of clinical training, trying her hand and heart and mind at the delicate job of healing others. She graduated from that training and then brought what she had learned into connection with her education in the *lojong*, the profound mind and heart transformation practice of the Tibetan Buddhist spiritual and healing tradition so prominently exemplified by His Holiness the Dalai Lama. All along, through her Western and Eastern development, she learned experientially from living masters of the two traditions. As she puts it so well herself:

> It was their human flesh—the living proof that, with sustained, wholehearted, and committed practice, a human being could have ongoing, enduring access to these higher states—that brought to life what would otherwise have been only engaging ideas. I came to understand why no amount of book learning could substitute for a transmission of living knowledge rooted in direct experience (p. 116).

What she has created for us from these studies and practices is something truly wonderful. Her work, though a book, itself feels undeniably like a "transmission of living knowledge." She achieves a sympathetic reading and understanding of the great pioneers of Western psychology, especially Freud and Jung. Then she carefully and courageously steps out beyond into insightful elucidation of the deep compassion they also aspired to at certain moments in their writings. She shows how they were afraid to reach for in a Western profession that privileged "scientific objectivity" understood as cold detachment from any sensitivity for the patient's heart. She teaches us the wisdom of selflessness, the compassion practice of the equal exchange of self and other, and the amazing practice of giving and taking, giving happiness to others and taking away their suffering. These are the practices of persons we might think remotely of as "saints," especially when we labor under deception and hold ourselves incapable of our own quite natural altruism. But Aura deftly shows us how these insights and practices actually arise from the heart of our truer nature, which drives us to live soulfully for a change— really brings us back to the most realistic normality of the happiness of other and self. She teaches us this with powerful logic and evocative poetry. And she does not hold back her own story, the wisdom of the Holocaust survivors in her family, her own joyful lovingness as a child, some of the hard knocks she weathered to become who she is today— her generosity with her own life make her teachings that much more accessible to us.

Again, in her own words:

> We have to provide soil for knowledge to put down roots and become experiential understanding. Only such knowledge has the power to instruct us when life puts us on the spot. Incorporated knowledge is alive. It affects the way we hear, see, smell, taste, touch—and think. No matter how true something seems, it will not be our truth until it dwells in our hearts and extends into our world. This is why the Buddha encouraged all who listened to use his answers as a springboard to question deeply, not only the teachings, but all their own cherished beliefs and assumptions (p. 121).

I enjoyed this work immensely, learned a lot from it, and will return again and again to its inspiration and insight. I am truly pleased to invite you all to enjoy it to the full.

—ROBERT A. F. THURMAN
Jey Tsong Khapa Professor of
Indo-Tibetan Buddhist Studies, Columbia University
Ganden Dekyi Ling, January 1, 2005

A Call to Compassion

INTRODUCTION

T his book is about bringing heart into the soul of psychology. It is about connecting a psychology of soul with a psychology of compassion. Though much of psychology circles the vale of compassion, nowhere does it make compassion central to the foundation, process, or goal of psychological health and wholeness. Nowhere is compassion the principal context and focus of psychological work. On the contrary, the paradigm of scientific objectivism influenced the field, from its earliest beginnings, to adopt a stance of *dis*-passion. It is time to call compassion out of the shadows and margins and bring it openly into view.

Whereas dispassion suggests a detachment born of distance, compassion suggests a caring born of closeness. Compassion moves toward; dispassion moves away. Compassion connects, dispassion divides. Dispassion separates the observer from the observed; it separates self from world, me from you, and us from them. Such distancing fragments feeling, leaving us capable of only superficial emotion and nostalgic sentimentality. Rather than promoting ease or freedom, this attitude breeds estrangement from others and self-alienation, which, not surprisingly, are among the most pressing problems of our times. Looking to the roots of the word "alien," we find it is related to the word "unlinked." Unlinked and disconnected, we experience ourselves as spectators living on the sidelines of our world.

Our modern perspective as bystanders and spectators has become so extreme that we are now "a species whose condition of distance can allow it to contemplate the nuclear destruction of possibly the entire planet, and in the face of that possibility still continue to program the planet for destruction."[1] In the process of distancing, we have plundered and "de-souled" our bodies, our planet, and, in fact, the entire cosmos. It is no wonder we despair.

The origins of psychology reveal a precarious allegiance to dispassion and distance. Caught in the paradigm of their day, early psychoanalysts embraced the widespread belief that intellectual rigor and critical insight depend upon a singularly objective, dispassionate eye. From this perspective, inter-subjectivity and relatedness defile the pure methods of science. If psychology was to be accepted as a science, it had to promote a dispassionate perspective. Ironically, the field of psychology is itself a response to a *dis*-passionate distancing that had actually severed the connection between the most intimate of companions—mind and body. The mind, in its growing orbits, took flight away from matter. And the body, condemned to silence, retreated to the shadows.

The abandoned body stepped out of the shadows and entered Freud's consulting room, expressing itself in the symptoms of hysteria. The hysteric's symptoms mystified. Hysteria resisted comfortable reduction, because it could not be explained as either a physical malady or a psychiatric illness. Its disquieting emergence directly challenged the prevailing belief that body and mind were fundamentally unrelated. The symptoms of hysteria were neither strictly physical nor exclusively mental, leaving open a third possibility: that body and mind were not separate, independently existing phenomena. Body as machine could never be symbolically symptomatic. Nor could mind separated from matter produce physical symptoms. The symptoms of hysteria were a symbolic communication, "the word 'symbol' being taken to mean the best possible expression for a complex fact not yet clearly apprehended by consciousness."[2] To Freud's credit, he had both the curiosity and the daring to explore the symbolic terrain of body-mind language.

Through probing the subtle inter-relationship of body and mind in symptom and dream, psychology began to emerge from the shadow of the dispassionate mind, but without actually escaping its iron grip. We find the imprint of a dispassionate science throughout the literature, dating back to Freud's injunction that psychoanalysts model themselves upon surgeons, putting aside all feelings, "even human sympathy."[3] Unfortunately, such one-sidedness is just that—one-sided. Dispassion without compassion is like light without warmth, or head without heart. It simply is not enough.

We need to talk about compassion and teach about compassion, because compassion awakens the heart. Compassion educates the heart. The word "education" derives from the Latin *educare*, meaning "to draw forth." No one's education can truly be considered complete without this drawing-forth of the heart, yet well-educated people throughout the world, including those in psychology, receive diplomas, credentials, and all manner of recognition, without ever having studied the value of compassion or how to develop it. Psychologists are expected to diagnose and treat psychic pain, but they are not expected to study or talk about compassion. In a field devoted to working with the suffering soul, we have left the practice of compassion to the winds of chance. To say it may sound unbelievable and absurd, but it is true.

The insight conveyed in consulting rooms, classrooms, books, and training programs needs to draw on a great deal more than a keen intellect, or a wealth of stimulating theories and concepts. It must also call forth the intelligence of the heart. Compassion is key to this intelligence, yet the cultivation of compassion is rarely discussed, and then only timidly and fleetingly at best. As Lewin aptly notes, "Our silence about compassion is a silence about the central possibilities of our own natures."[4] This silence is not golden.

Compassion must be central to a therapy that calls itself a "talking cure," because communication is, at the core, a matter of heart. Paracelsus spoke to this hundreds of years ago when he remarked, "Speech is not of the tongue, but of the heart. The tongue is merely the instrument with which one speaks." Moreover, the heart is the seat of the soul. Depth psychology has grown out of a deep reverence for soul and its searchings, its making, and musings. Soul has persistently and unfailingly goaded analysts to explore the improbable, the unknown, the perplexing, and the difficult. Yet, as I look around, I find soul still searching for its heart, not unlike Psyche searching and longing for Eros. We must bring heart into the soul of psychology.

My own call to compassion grew, as such things often do, in the ground of my personal experience. Born into a family of Holocaust survivors, I experienced the Holocaust as a silent witness to the redemptive miracle of existence. Always hovering in the atmosphere of our home, it seemed for a long time that silence was the only space vast enough to contain the Holocaust's inconceivable landscape of grief and horror. Language faltered in the face of speaking the unspeakable. But no words were needed for me to see the scars of indifference, cruelty, and brutality, and of efficiency wedded to loathing. The numbers tattooed on the arms of those close to me, the screams in the nights, were among innumerable, ever-present reminders.

Questions concerning human nature were never far from my mind. As a child, I wondered about evil—my own and others' capacity for it. I couldn't find a sure and impassable line separating myself from others who were capable of perpetrating or passively permitting such atrocity. These perpetrators of genocide were not an alien species; they were all human beings like me. No matter how much I wished it to be otherwise, I could see that this was true. This awareness had a powerful impact on me, intensifying my desire to understand what it means to be human.

Simultaneously present was the miracle of love in the ruins; love that was stronger than every cruelty; love that bears all things and will not die. My great-uncle Joe often came to visit when I was very young. On one such occasion, as I sat on his lap, he asked me to name the people I loved the most. After pausing for a moment, I responded with confidence, "I love everyone!" My father was present for the exchange, and anyone who has heard him telling stories over the years has certainly heard him recount this one. The light in his eyes, the sparkle of delight as he recalled this moment, seemed to reflect his delight at the sovereignty of love. Perhaps more powerful than the miracle of his own survival was witnessing his child seeing the world with eyes of love.

The trajectory of my life has been deeply influenced by an early and intimate awareness of the pain and suffering we humans can both endure and inflict. Equally influential has been my experience that human beings, even when stripped of all we consider human dignity, even in the wake of a world mercilessly destroyed and left in wreaths of smoke, even when deeply wounded and scarred, can access the greater power of love.

In the teachings of Buddhism I found a path resonant with heart and soul, and an invitation to explore deeply the power of the human heart and the evolutionary possibilities of human life. The practices of the heart introduced in this book come from the soul of this timeless tradition.

This book is organized in two parts. In Part I, I begin by defining terms relevant to the discussion—compassion, love, and altruism. I then explore literature from depth psychology and Tibetan Buddhism. Next, I look in greater depth at the work of Sigmund Freud and Carl Jung. As there is little overt emphasis on compassion by either Freud or Jung, I focus on areas in their writing that pertain to the topic of compassion and the related topic of love. It will become clear that while depth psychology recognizes the necessity of love and compassion, it substantially ignores the relationship between compassion and transformation, and articulates no methodology for developing compassion. Indeed, the subject of compassion is left largely unexplored. Tibetan Buddhism, on the other hand, recognizes the twin facets of love and compassion as the engine and elixir of transformation, and offers a clear methodology for their development.

In Part II, I introduce the *lojong* on the basis of the Seven Points for Training the Mind as a powerful and practical approach to developing great love and compassion. I discuss the preliminary practice of the Four Reminders—contemplating the preciousness of human life, its fleeting nature, the power of action and intent, and the confusion that keeps us from experiencing our true nature. I also explore equanimity as a foundation for great compassion, as well as its relationship to dissolving the projections that keep us stuck in rigid and limiting views. I then focus on the central aim of the lojong—the alchemy of the heart. This is achieved through a love and compassion firmly rooted in wisdom. The development of wisdom is, therefore, also central to this discussion. Included in this section is a detailed description of *tonglen,* a meditation practice that conjoins giving and taking with the breath.

The in-breath becomes the vehicle for breathing in the suffering of ourselves and others, and the out-breath for giving away the goodness we cling to and hoard. The practice of tonglen is the method by which contemplations on love and compassion become immediate and embodied. I conclude the book with a reflection on the relevance of compassion for the field of psychology and a distillation of the essential ingredients for the practice of inner alchemy.

As you begin, it is worth recalling a theme that is threaded throughout both Buddhism and psychology: a willingness to leave behind the insistent and clamorous voice of the collective and open to an exploration of the unknown. Such openness is the gateway to growth and transformation. It brings us to the threshold of mystery and revelation. Its rewards are imparted in these words of the Buddha: "If you go where few have gone, you will find what few have found."

Part I

THE JOURNEY TO A SELF
THAT INCLUDES OTHERS

A human being is a part of the whole called by us "the universe," a part limited in time and space. He experiences himself, his thoughts and feelings, as something separate from the rest—a kind of optical delusion of his consciousness. This delusion is a kind of prison for us, restricting us to our personal desires and affection for a few persons nearest to us. Our task must be to free ourselves from this prison by widening our circle of understanding and compassion to embrace all living creatures and the whole of nature in its beauty.

—ALBERT EINSTEIN

Chapter 1

A PSYCHOLOGY OF COMPASSION

■ ■ ■

Sometimes it is necessary to reteach a thing its loveliness.

—GALWAY KINNELL

C ompassion is the basis of connection, intimacy, openness, kindness, hospitality, and joy. It is an expression of human freedom, flowing from a sound intuition of the unity of life and all living things. "Even when we are physically alone and experiencing loneliness we are still essentially with others; indeed, the very fact that we can feel lonely indicates that participation is a basic structural element in our being."[1] Our connection to others does not negate our aloneness. We are simultaneously separate and in relation, and these two truths are ultimately revealed as coexistent and non-contradictory. We are, in the very midst of our aloneness, inextricably connected to others.

This dimension of being does not derive from external factors. We are by nature embedded in relationship with the world, in all its sorrow and beauty. Jung commented on this, saying, "The individual is not just a single separate being, but by his very existence presupposes a collective relationship."[2]

Compassion is at once both deeply personal and thoroughly social. It is the finest expression of our relationship to self and others. It begins with a willingness to open to ourselves and to life as it is. Instead of rejecting one part of life and grasping at another, compassion moves closer to all of life. It resolves the continual struggle against reality by fostering a willingness to be unconditionally present to the whole range of human experience. Compassion is, in part, a practice of unconditional presence. Being unconditionally present means not only *seeing* ourselves and others, but *feeling* ourselves and others. Unconditional presence is both receptive and penetrating, it is both discerning and tender-hearted. Like the sun, it simultaneously illuminates and warms.

Compassion dissolves barriers and distance. Unlike pity, "compassion has the quality of respect."[3] Respect for others comes from a sure knowledge of both our closeness with others and our likeness to them. The Dalai Lama, in his appeal at the end of *Ethics for the New Millennium*, makes this point by reminding us of the profound similarity we have to others, and the respect we need to cultivate toward those who are downtrodden, impoverished, or beleaguered. "Try not to think of yourself as better than even the humblest beggar," he entreats. "You will look the same in your grave."[4]

Compassion is the foundation, process, and goal of psychological health and wholeness. It grounds and guides us, and is the fruit of psychological work. Joseph Campbell refers to it as "the purpose of the journey." He then adds that "once you have come past the pair of opposites you have reached compassion."[5] Arriving past the pair of opposites marks the apex of Jung's psychological goal of individuation. According to Jung, this goal is achieved through what he called the transcendent function, or a "quality of conjoined opposites."[6] Conjoining the opposites or arriving past them are simply different ways of describing the same thing. In either case, a dynamic unity emerges out of what was before a warring tension. Drawing on Jung's alchemical metaphor for this phenomenon, we could say that compassion is the alchemical vessel holding the turbulent *prima materia*. Compassion transforms the original base substance, and compassion is the purified gold that results.

Freud, Jung, and Depth Psychology

Freud and Jung are towering psychological masters whose explorations and insights shaped the first 100 years of depth psychology. They devoted their lives to studying the multivalent terrain of human nature, and to caring for the suffering soul. While Freud and Jung were both remarkably independent and innovative thinkers, they were still deeply influenced by the cultural milieu in which they lived. The philosophical moorings of depth psychology reveal a dynamic tension between the conflicting perspectives of Enlightenment and Romanticism. Both Freud and Jung developed their psychological theories out of the crosscurrents of these divergent worldviews.

Freud has been called "the last great representative of the Enlightenment" and "the first to demonstrate its limitations."[7] He championed reason as the supreme human endowment, and simultaneously embraced the artistic and imaginative impulse so celebrated by the Romantics. Freud was pulled between the imaginal and the rational, and his theories reflect this. His work is suffused with images of struggle and ultimately irreconcilable conflict between opposing forces.

Freud perceived an innate aggressive streak in human beings that was forever opposed by an equally powerful Eros. These two impulses, one toward life and the other toward death, were engaged in eternal battle within the human psyche. Bruno Bettelheim describes Freud's conviction that "the good life—or, at least the best life available to man, the most enjoyable and most meaningful—consists of being able truly to love not oneself, but others."[8] This belief in the importance of loving others was coupled, however, with Freud's view that positive states such as love and compassion were the result of either the suppression or sublimation of narcissistic, selfish motives, and were therefore always fraught with struggle.[9] For Freud, there was simply no transcending the pull of opposites; there was only learning to manage them skillfully.

Jung's analytic psychology also rests upon a theory of opposites, but unlike Freud, Jung believed these opposites were ultimately reconcilable through the process of individuation. In general, Jung held a more optimistic view of human nature and its potential. Distancing himself from Freud, whom he accused of focusing too narrowly on weird and neurotic states, he said, "For my part, I prefer to look at man in light of what in him is healthy and sound."[10] Furthermore, Jung believed the impulse toward health and wholeness was intrinsic to human life, because "within the soul from its primordial beginnings there has been a desire for light and an irrepressible urge to rise out of the primal darkness."[11]

Yet, despite the intimate connection it has with suffering and its alleviation, neither Freud nor Jung concentrated their far-reaching and formidable intellectual powers on the subject of compassion, or more specifically on methods for developing it.

Tibetan Buddhism and Inner Transformation

While compassion has been largely ignored in the field of depth psychology, it has been the main theme of study and practice in Tibetan Buddhism for over 1000 years. I have never come across a single instruction within this infinitely varied and rich tradition in which compassion and its development are not in some way central.

Protected by geographic remoteness and encircling mountains, Tibet exists in an environment not unlike an alchemical vessel. The contents of this vessel are the concentrated study and cultivation of conjoined compassion and wisdom. Tens of thousands of Tibet's finest minds devoted themselves, over many centuries, to this endeavor. Unlike the modern West, where outer progress and military prowess were pursued with zeal, Tibet's passion was directed toward cultivating the soul of the individual. Robert Thurman observes that this concentration on individuals' evolutionary potential contributed to a "unique social and psychological creation, which I call inner, or spiritual modernity, an exact mirror of the outer, or secular modernity just taking off in the Western Enlightenment" Here, Thurman says, "The soul was thought of as a subtle, relative, totally and inextricably interconnected process, powerfully influencing and influenced by its environment."[12] And the primary therapy for the soul was altruism grown out of love and compassion.

James Hillman notes that the "insights of depth psychology derive from the soul *in extremis*, the sick, suffering, abnormal and fantastic conditions of the psyche."[13] This parallels the insights of Buddhism to a point, but with an important distinction. While the principal insights of Buddhism give significant attention to states of suffering and sorrow, they are not derived from it, "but from those who have achieved the most extreme states of awareness, compassion and health."[14]

Suffering is emphasized in Buddhism because we are caught in it, and we suffer it. The true message of Buddhism, however, is not a message of suffering—it is a proclamation of freedom. Our innate capacity for freedom and joy are the heart of the Buddha's realization and the foundation of his teaching, and they form the basis of Indo-Tibetan Buddhist psychology. In Tibet, all three paths of Buddhist teaching were preserved and practiced as a graded path, with each level transcending and including the other. These three paths, or "vehicles," are commonly referred to as *Theravada*, *Mahayana*, and *Vajrayana*, although there are also other ways of classifying them.

An individual following the Theravadan path focuses on uprooting ignorance—the cause of suffering—and attaining the personal liberation of an Arhat. In the Theravadan tradition, also known as the Way of the Elders, compassion for the suffering of others is certainly cultivated, but the goal is individual liberation from suffering through the realization of wisdom.

The Mahayana, or Great Vehicle, subsumes all the basic principles and practices of the Theravada, but adjusts the focus to others and the aim to total enlightenment. This vehicle stresses the view that we can never be completely free as long as others to whom we are inextricably linked suffer. Mahayana practitioners are not concerned with "ordinary liberation" for themselves, but rather commit themselves to total enlightenment—thereby fulfilling the purpose of both self and other. The lojong text and practice introduced later belong to the Mahayana teachings of Tibetan Buddhism.

The Vajrayana, or Diamond Vehicle, is a Mahayana path that introduces an elaborate combination of meditation and visualization techniques intended to accelerate the process of transformation by which an individual may reach complete enlightenment.

Tibetan Buddhism uses the fully awakened state as a blueprint for optimal health, encouraging those who practice to set their sights here. A vision of totality, of complete awakening for the benefit of all beings, inspires individuals to aim for the development of unconditional and unlimited compassion and wisdom. Methods for deepening insight and developing compassion are inseparable from the committed effort to transform habitually painful states.

In contrast to this approach, the intentional cultivation of innate mental health is not generally found in psychology. Mental illness is far more studied and better understood than mental health. Walsh and Vaughan note that, "whereas conventional Western therapies have excellent techniques for reducing negative emotions, they have virtually none for enhancing positive ones."[15] Jung also noted the unfortunate absence of such methodology in the field of depth psychology, and called for his colleagues to find a "bridge" to "self-development."[16]

Among the obstacles to finding such a bridge has been the distinction made by depth psychologists between the heart and the mind. Western civilization has long separated the spheres of heart and mind, relegating thinking and reason to the mind, and emotion and feeling to the heart. This may, in part, explain the absence of words like compassion from most of the literature of depth psychology. Commitment to an affiliation with science and medicine prompted many of the pioneers in the field to distance themselves from subjects that might suggest a departure from, or contamination of, the "pure" reason applied in the natural sciences. Even Jung, who was accused of being mystical and "unreasonable" by many of his detractors, always defended the scientific empiricism of his work, wanting to be seen by his peers as a man of science.

Despite a movement that had long been underway to distinguish between human/inner science and natural/outer science,[17] Freud and Jung were trained as physicians, and both men sought medical and "outer science" credibility. Following his split with Freud, Otto Rank denounced what he called Freud's excessive preoccupation with reason, saying that the dynamic and creative principle of irrationality is the "basis for the emergence of everything of which mankind is capable in personal and social betterment."[18]

In Tibetan Buddhism, this conflict between inner and outer science does not exist. Inner science is viewed as legitimate and empirically verifiable via inner experience, just as outer science is empirically verified by outer means and measures. The development of compassion is within the domain of inner science and depends, not upon the irrational, but upon sound thinking and reasoning. Thus, the particular strength of the Buddhist teaching is that "it shows you clearly the 'logic' of compassion."[19] The heart, from a Buddhist perspective, is not without reason; it is the "place" of a higher reason. Moreover, the same term—*chitta*—is used for both mind and heart.

In Buddhist teachings, the heart is not an adjunct to thinking. It is "a direct presence that allows a complete attunement with reality."[20] Tibetans touch their chests when referring to the mind. They understand the unified heart/mind to mean our most subtle being, our Buddha-nature, the stainless jewel of our innate freedom. Buddha-nature is primordially pure and unconditionally open.

The heart, in this case, is the basis for cultivating both the wisdom that directly perceives the nature of reality and unconditional compassion. The maturation of these two qualities into an integrated and synchronized wisdom and compassion are the principal characteristics of a fully enlightened being. Every individual-in fact, every living being—is endowed with this pure nature, and human beings with wholehearted commitment and skillful guidance can develop this innate quality to an infinite degree.

Primordially pure mind is our innermost and subtlest being, dwelling much deeper than the conditioned personality. It is present in every living being, but is awakened to different degrees within different individuals. The existence of a naturally pure mind does not, however, negate or trivialize the greed, aggression, dissatisfaction, and cruelty found in human beings throughout time. The tension between Eros and Thanatos (death)—yearning and despondency, attraction and repulsion—is a deeply embedded, instinctive pattern within the psyche. There is a colossal struggle between these forces within us, and attending to this dimension of life is crucial.

In this sense, Buddhism and depth psychology are in accord. Buddhism diverges in its contention that a nondual, primordially pure mind reflects our truest and deepest nature. Because of our fundamentally pure nature, we each have in our hearts the potential for unlimited love and compassion. This is the treasure within. If we suddenly discovered a priceless treasure buried beneath our home, we would not delay a moment digging for it. Yet, all too often, we squander the "wish-fulfilling jewel" of our minds.[21]

Lojong

There are countless texts in the Indo-Tibetan tradition devoted to instructions for developing compassion. I will introduce the Seven Points for Training the Mind, which belongs to a tradition of teachings called *lojong*, or thought transformation. The origin of the Tibetan Buddhist lojong tradition is attributed to the great Indian Buddhist Master, Atisha (982–1054), who brought these teachings to Tibet. The word "lojong" has two parts: *lo* means mind, and *jong* means to train or transform. Lojong trains the mind in practices that induce the qualities of kindness, love, compassion, tolerance, inner strength, and wisdom.

The lojong is a sacred technology—the "technology of peace, the technology to produce love, kindness and open-heartedness."[22] Whereas all the great wisdom traditions teach the value of love and compassion, lojong actually provides a clearly articulated methodology for developing them. It has, thus, been praised as "the most profound form of psychology and the best form of meditation."[23]

For generations, these teachings were passed on in whispered secrecy from master to disciple. Much later, they were written down in a variety of forms, the most widely known being *The Root Verses of Seven-Point Mind Training*, composed by Geshe Chekawa Yeshe Dorje (1101–1175). The lojong is now widely taught in all schools of Tibetan Buddhism. Mind training, or thought transformation, has two primary components: the main instruction, which is given in the form of aphorisms, and the practice of *tonglen*, which combines giving and receiving with the breath cycle. Inhalation becomes a vehicle for breathing in the suffering of ourselves and others; exhalation gives away the goodness we cling to and hoard. Lojong, which identifies selfish desire—the continual chorus of "me, me, me"—as the shrewd underminer of our happiness, is specifically designed to counteract ingrained selfishness and strengthen the nascent force of compassion.

Although at an earlier time, the dissemination of the lojong teachings was secretive and restricted, today many great Tibetan masters speak of the benefits of introducing the lojong to a diverse population. The Dalai Lama has said that, "Many of these . . . methods . . . can be practiced not just by Buddhists, but by anyone with a commitment to developing a good heart. We all need love and compassion, whether we are Buddhist or not, inclined to spiritual practice or not."[24]

Lojong practice encourages individuals to start with the life they have and work, one step at a time, with whatever felicity or hardship they encounter. Lojong can be practiced in times of loneliness or gratitude. It can be practiced in times of sorrow, or rage, or fear. It can be practiced in times of exuberance or despair. There is no need for life to be any different than it is for the lojong practice to be applied beneficially. Even beginning to explore and reflect upon the powerful insights and unique methodology of this teaching will serve the care of soul in the world. Moreover, these teachings may provide an inducement to psychologists to further question their views on mental health, mental illness, and psychological life.

Bodhisattva

Lojong is the practice of an actual or an aspiring *bodhisattva*. The term *bodhisattva* has two parts. The first part, *bodhi*, means awakened mind, or awakened heart, and the second part, *sattva*, means courageous mind, or a mind acting with strength and bravery. A bodhisattva is one who acts with courage and bravery to accomplish full awakening for the benefit all beings. The generation of this awakened mind is called the conception of *bodhicitta* or *bodhimind*—the mind/heart of awakening. This mind is said to be so profound and precious that the Earth herself quakes with joy wherever there is one who conceives it.

Perceiving the interminable pain and sorrow of other living beings who are, like us, caught in a web of suffering, we become filled with a burning impulse to free them. Knowing that we cannot bring freedom to others if we are still bound, we dedicate ourselves to the attainment of total freedom in order to help others find their way to happiness and liberty. The inescapable connection with, and compassion for, the suffering of all living beings in all universes is an inexhaustible wellspring of inspiration for the journey. It is also the source of infinite joy.

> As our empathy and love flow out to embrace all living beings on earth, the galaxies, and beyond, we come up against not only black holes of despair but also vast suns of confidence and determination. By becoming a being of radiant blissfulness, a bodhisattva is a living instrument that can effectively bring about the aim of true love—the happiness of infinite beloved others.[25]

The actualization of blissful, unconditioned compassion does not, however, require actually succeeding in relieving the suffering of every being in the universe. The wish, the resolve, and taking action to make it so become themselves the catalysts of transformation.

A bodhisattva is called a child of the Buddha, a hero or heroine of enlightenment. The bodhisattva is praised as a spiritual warrior, one "who dares to be, like a tiger in the jungle."[26] The bodhisattva is also referred to as the new moon, harbinger of the full moon of Buddhahood. Just as the appearance of the crescent moon assures the arrival of the full moon, generation of the awakening mind is the sure precursor to full awakening.

This aspiration to help living beings transform themselves may, at first, seem extravagantly absurd or wildly quixotic, but "the psychology of the bodhisattva is nothing otherworldly."[27] Bodhisattvas generate a "two-pronged mind," uniting the seemingly irreconcilable aims of self and others. They commit to their own awakening for the benefit of all beings, and they gladly forgo their own enlightenment until all beings are liberated. They are resolutely committed to ultimate freedom in order to benefit others, and they are simultaneously so intent on benefiting other beings that they relinquish any ambition for liberation.

Bodhisattvas uninterruptedly hold two seemingly dissonant thoughts: "May I be fully awakened as swiftly as possible in order to be of greatest service to others" and "May I be the very last to be enlightened, after all living beings are utterly and blissfully free." This paradoxical intent hastens transformation and, ultimately, enlightenment. I have heard it said that bodhisattvas cease to care about their own enlightenment, but are "helplessly" enlightened nevertheless.

Bodhisattvas are the prototype of well-being, whether or not they are clothed in monastic robes or wear the mantle of a spiritual teacher. Whatever domain they inhabit, be it public or private, their every breath is dedicated to the awakening of self and other. Bodhisattvas are citizens of the universe, holding all of existence in their infinite embrace. They are the ultimate alchemists, at work in the laboratory of the heart.

Bodhisattvas exert an evolutionary pull on the world around them. They are omegatypes, calling us to the future and to awakening our deepest potential. Ken Wilber writes about the omega-pull such individuals have on awakening our transpersonal, structural potentials. He also notes that these transpersonal structures and their emergence must be distinguished from past, collective, archetypal wisdom with which many have lost touch, and may later re-contact.

> Lost perhaps, but not from the past . . . the "true archetypes"
> . . . have not been *collectively* manifested anywhere in the past,
> but are nonetheless available to each and every individual as
> *structural potentials*, as future structures attempting to come
> down, not past structures struggling to come up. The great and
> rare mystics of the past . . . were, in fact, ahead of their time,
> and are still ahead of ours. In other words they definitely are
> *not* figures of the past. They are figures of the future. In their
> spirituality they did not tap into yesterday, they tapped into
> tomorrow. In their profound awareness we do not see the setting sun, but the new dawn. They absolutely did not inherit the
> past, they inherited the future.[28]

Bodhisattvas are the new dawn. As "psycho-nauts" tapping into the future, they enter territory few have acknowledged, let alone explored. This is yet another reason why the model of the bodhisattva is so important—it challenges us to envision a world of infinite possibility. I marvel at the spirit of the Tibetan people, who, from a Western materialistic standpoint, were backward, primitive, indolent, and ignorant, and yet had the confidence and courage to embrace a vision of human life that entitled them to its ultimate flower—a fully awakened heart. Many psychologists may look upon such aspirations as flights of fantasy, but I suggest that many would have said the same if told, several hundred years ago, that in the not too distant future, people of the Earth would walk on the Moon.

Chapter 2

THE LITERATURE OF COMPASSION: EXPLORING THE RECORD

■   ▓   ■

It is only with the heart that one can see rightly;
what is essential is invisible to the eye.

—ANTOINE DE SAINT-EXUPÉRY

Three terms—compassion, love, and altruism—are essential to any exploration of the literature of compassion. Let's take a closer look at what these words mean in the context of our present discussion.

The Language of Compassion

Throughout the literature of depth psychology, the meanings of words like love, compassion, and altruism are both variegated and vague. Jung remarks that "Love makes a man better."[1] He does not, however, tell us what it is about love that makes a man better, or what he actually means by love. Melanie Klein points out that compassion, sympathy, and tolerance are attitudes that enrich our experience and make us feel more secure in ourselves,[2] while Hillman characterizes love as an explosion of the imagination and an extraordinarily powerful tool of the psyche.[3]

These words elude precise definition because they are also symbols of themselves, and symbols cannot be reduced to one level of meaning. In this instance, however, defining these terms is not meant to limit our way of thinking about compassion, love, or altruism. Nor is it meant to contradict other perspectives. I define them only so that the meaning I have in mind when using them is clear.

Since my intention here is to introduce the heart of Tibetan Buddhist psychology into the field of psychology, I will define these terms in a way consistent with extensive and well-grounded Buddhist literature on the psychology of compassion. When reviewing the literature of depth psychology, I will explore these subjects as they are elaborated upon there, which may at times diverge from the definitions presented here.

Compassion

The Tibetan Buddhist tradition approaches compassion developmentally. Our English word "compassion" derives from the Latin *compati*, which signifies suffering with another. Compassion in the Buddhist sense is also rooted in an empathic "suffering with," but then extends beyond it. Compassion begins with the wish, grown out of empathic awareness, for others to be free from suffering, and is then developed into a profoundly transformative commitment to work toward helping all beings overcome both their suffering and its causes. This ultimate crescendo of compassion in both body and mind is called "great compassion."

The Dalai Lama defines compassion as "a mental attitude based on the wish for others to be free of their suffering."[4] Chögyam Trungpa describes it as a "pure and fearless openness,"[5] while Pabongka Rinpoche characterizes it as a wish that all be "without every suffering."[6] This understanding of compassion is certainly not unique to the East, as is made evident in the work of Schopenhauer, who describes compassion as an

. . . immediate participation, released from all other considerations, first, in the pain of another, and then in the alleviation or termination of that pain, which alone is the true ground of all autonomous righteousness and of all true human love. . . . The weal and woe of another comes to lie directly in my heart . . . as soon as the sentiment of compassion is aroused, and therewith, the difference between him and me is no longer absolute.[7]

Schopenhauer is describing a facet of compassion that is germane to lojong practice: the difference between self and other "is no longer absolute" when compassion is aroused. The Tibetan tradition in general, and the lojong in particular, encourages individuals to abandon the habitually instinctive and deeply ingrained attitude of self-centeredness in favor of one that extends beyond imagined borders of the self, to include and embrace others.

Love

Love is the wish for others to have every form of happiness. Love generates compassion; compassion can also generate love. Although in Tibetan Buddhist practice, meditation on love precedes meditation on compassion, "they do not have . . . a fixed cause and effect relationship."[8] Whereas compassion brings an awareness of the suffering of others and the wish to separate them from it, love is the wish for others to experience freedom and joy. Love and compassion are not, as sometimes imagined, a fanciful escape from life's harsh reality. In fact, the opposite is true. Together, love and compassion give us the flexibility, resilience, and courage, to embrace life, in all of its splendor and sorrow. Trungpa tells us that, "in order to develop love—universal love, cosmic love, whatever you would like to call it—one must accept the whole situation of life as it is."[9]

In essence, love and compassion are two aspects of one mind. In Tibetan Buddhism this is understood. They are always spoken of together, almost as one word: love-compassion. I recall the story of a great Tibetan adept who, when asked to explain the relationship between love and compassion, lifted the napkin from the table before him and held out one side of the napkin saying, "this is love." He then turned the napkin over displaying its other side saying, "this is compassion." Love and compassion may be distinct, but they cannot be separated, any more than we can separate the two sides of a napkin, or the two sides of our hands. They exist together and act together as one. The outstretched hand both reaches out and draws near. The same is true of love and compassion.

Altruism—Great Love and Compassion

Ordinary love and compassion are concerned with the welfare of others, but they may be limited in scope. We can wish sincerely and deeply for a limited number of beings to experience happiness and be free from suffering. This is certainly compassion, but it is not great compassion. Great love and great compassion focus on all beings, equally. The "greatness" of love and compassion is thus characterized, in part, by its universal scope, but this alone does not define it.

Great love and compassion must be universal in scope and include a commitment to act in order to help suffering beings. This great love and compassion becomes the altruistic mind of universal responsibility—universal in the sense that all living beings are included, and responsibility in the sense that we commit to acting on it. "You develop altruism," according to Pabongka Rinpoche, "when you feel 'the responsibility . . . has fallen on me.'"[10] Great compassion, great love, and altruism are ways of doing *and* ways of being. They are verbs as well as nouns. They unite the infinite vision of the mind with a thousand-armed extension of the body.

Depth Psychology: The Poetics of Psyche

The literature of depth psychology reveals a range of perspectives on the subject of love and compassion. Much of the work of Freud and Jung, as well as Hillman, Kohut, and others, points toward compassion by emphasizing the role of kindness, meeting, empathy, or transparency. In general, the great thinkers and practitioners in the field agree upon the ultimate importance of these qualities for a fulfilled human life. Nevertheless, they give only fleeting attention to compassion and love and its transformative role in the psyche. Furthermore, there seems to be a complete absence of methodology for cultivating, enhancing, and stabilizing these positive states.

Even one genuine encounter with another being reveals that our sense of separateness is an experience that occurs on the surface of our lives. If we appear to be islands, it is only because we have not looked far enough beneath the surface to see the deeper and irrevocable connections we have with each other. This *a priori* connection is what allows us to enter intimately into the experience of another. We now know that even the movement of butterflies in China has a ripple effect throughout the world. There is no absolute separation, anywhere.

In the field of depth psychology, we use terms like "transference," "projective identification," "empathy," and "inter-subjective field" to label this *a priori* fact. These dimensions of human experience did not, however, come about as a result of our naming them. We named them to make sense of dynamics already present in human relationships and in the consulting room. Nevertheless, despite depth psychology's passionate interest in the dynamics of human relationship, and in the experience of suffering and transformation, it leaves the power of compassion and love largely untapped.

Love and compassion take us into ourselves, and beyond ourselves. They take us beyond narrow selfish concerns and fearfully erected barriers, and bring us into contact with the infinite openness of being. Attending to and cultivating this heart of our being needs to be the ground for a psychology that is intent on serving not only a decrease in psychic suffering, but an increase in mental health.

We can, perhaps, learn something from Joseph Campbell, who, after a lifetime of immersion in the world's mythologies and religions, concluded that the fulfillment of human life depended upon tapping the wellspring of compassion within. "The key to the Grail is compassion," he claimed, "suffering with, feeling another's sorrow as if it were your own. The one who finds the dynamo of compassion is the one who has found the Grail."[11] The Grail that has stirred the longing and imagination of the Western mind for centuries is not to be found outside ourselves. It is none other than the infinite power of the human heart released by the alchemical dynamo of compassion. The Grail—the soul's fulfillment—depends upon compassion. If we accept this as true, then compassion must be central to a psychology that strives to serve soul in the world.

Compassion, though widely acknowledged as a vital dimension of psychological maturity and wholeness, has tended to evoke an ambiguous response within the field of psychology from Freud's time on. Words like love and, even more so, compassion are not often found in the literature of clinical psychology, as they tend to evoke images of ineffective therapists consoling patients and preventing them from feeling and working through their pain. Compassion seems to lack intelligence, precision, and savvy. It seems religious. Unscientific. Not rigorous. Weak. Freud, who once likened psychoanalysts to surgeons, contradicted himself a year later, saying one could undermine an analysis "if from the start one takes any standpoint other than that of sympathetic understanding."[12] It is not uncommon to see this kind of pushpull concerning the place of compassion in the field.

Because compassion and love seem unscientific and possibly religious, they threaten psychology's affiliation with the medical model. Although depth psychology has strenuously avoided being characterized as an exclusively medical science, it remains ambivalent about committing to compassion. Psychology has long been dominated by an image of itself borrowed from medicine, and has maintained a precarious position between science and religion. But this tension between religion and scientific medicine is relatively new. Although modern medicine fancies itself a strictly outer science, we need only scratch the surface to discover the religious foundations of medicine, as evidenced in the emblem of the physician: the *caduceus*. The caduceus is "a bricolage of three ancient religious symbols: the snake, the staff, and wings."[13]

According to Emma and Ludwig Edelstein, "Such an antagonism of science and religion may be self-evident to the modern mind, yet it was foreign to ancient thought."[14] In ancient Greece, Asclepius, the personification of divine healing power, was also credited with establishing "scientific medicine."[15] The easy union of science and religion disintegrated over time, however. Ron Leifer notes that, as science gained stature, religion lost it. "The scientific revolution and the decline of religion are reciprocally related events," he points out. "Modern people now rely on science for the knowledge to pave the way towards happiness and to avoid and evade suffering and death."[16]

For some, psychology is a branch of medicine, for others a branch of religion. The branch with which one identifies seems to depend largely on beliefs concerning the nature of the mind and the nature of the soul. "To the extent that one believes that mind and soul are similar, psychotherapy has a religious dimension," Leifer notes. "To the extent that one believes that mind is an epiphenomenon of the brain, psychotherapy will be considered a branch of medicine."[17]

Freud and Psychoanalysis

There is perhaps no one whose work more epitomizes the tension between medicine and religion than Sigmund Freud. In *The Future of an Illusion*, Freud strongly argued for distancing psychoanalysis from religion, calling religion "the universal obsessional neurosis of humanity."[18] He described religion as an illusion, and defined illusion as something "derived from human wishes," which, though it "need not be false," does "disregard its relation to reality."[19] "Science," he claims, on the other hand, "has given us the evidence by its numerous and important successes that it is no illusion."[20] Whereas Freud did not deny other ways of knowing, or humanity's yearning for portals to deeper knowledge, he concluded that the only reasonable and credible path to understanding the human mind was through science. "The contribution of the science of psychoanalysis," he declared, "consists precisely in having extended research to the region of the mind . . . . Any other . . . view of the mind has a purely emotional basis."[21]

Having said this, it is also true that Freud vigorously challenged the rigid adherence to a medical model for psychoanalysis. Freud did not want psychology to be imposed upon or constrained by medical science. He wanted to distinguish psychoanalysis from medicine, and called for it to become an independent branch of scientific knowledge, a "science of the unconscious mind."[22] Although Freud began his work "concerned with certain forms of sickness and their cure," he later "resumed a tradition in which psychology as a study of the soul of man was the theoretical basis for the art of living, for achieving happiness."[23] Freud, in fact, described the analyst-in-training as one "bent upon liberating another from suffering," implicitly suggesting that compassion is the motivation underlying the vocation of psychology. Although he advocated throughout his life for psychoanalysis to be accepted as a science, he held more dear the wish that his psychology of the depths would one day become "indispensable to all the branches of knowledge having to do with the origins and history of human culture . . . such as art, religion, and the social order."[24]

This wish left the door open for the prolific imagination of those who followed to reach beyond medicine and beyond the consulting room. Today, when we see the burgeoning interest and numerous contributions so many in the field bring to art, religion, literature, human history, culture, philosophy, politics, and more, we can appreciate that Freud's vision is being realized.

Many, including Jung, accused Freud of reductionism, and there is certainly ample evidence to defend this view. I wonder, however, whether, in restricting Freud to one level of meaning, we fail to grasp the complexity of his thinking. For example, Freud's insistence on upholding psychoanalysis as a branch of science and his simultaneous rejection of the medical model can, at first glance, appear contradictory. His views begin to make more sense, however, when we examine what he actually meant when he spoke of science.

Freud was a student of Franz Brentano, the founder of phenomenology. Phenomenological science did not rely on experimental hypothesis testing, or the natural science model. Rather, it was a human science model; its insights were based on experience, not speculation, and were open to modification on the basis of further experience. Brentano, who remarked, "experience alone is my teacher,"[25] distinguished between natural and human sciences, as did Freud. It seems the human science advocated by Freud may, in fact, have a lot in common with the inner science practiced in the Tibetan Buddhist tradition.

Bruno Bettelheim suggests, moreover, that Freud is misunderstood because he is misread. He offers as an example Freud's use of the word "soul." Freud extolled the merits of science, yet described himself as an archaeologist of the soul. But the term "soul," or *psyche*, is "full of the richest meaning, endowed with emotion, comprehensively human and unscientific,"[26] as Bettelheim points out. Freud used the word *seele*, or "soul," throughout his work, but in English this has been translated as "mind," giving the reader a very different impression.

Fascinated by Greek mythology, Freud intentionally invoked the Hellenistic myth of Psyche and Eros when he coined the term psychoanalysis. Psyche, often symbolically rendered as a butterfly, is the intangible and indestructible energy of the soul and its transformations. And Freud, from the start, aligned psychoanalysis with the poetics of Psyche. Psyche's journey to herself—in search of love, driven by love, and ultimately united with love—has been the guiding myth for depth psychology since its inception. Beneath mountains of theory, the journey of the soul longing for and uniting with love is found at the very foundation and core of depth psychology.

In his later years, Freud increasingly turned his attention to Eros, the cosmic life-principle, "which holds all living things together,"[27] as well as to Eros' ongoing struggle with Death. In the next chapter, I discuss Freud's reflections on Eros and Death, and how his views directly inform and reveal his beliefs about human nature and human potential. This area of Freud's work also illuminates his views regarding the human capacity for compassion and love.

Otto Rank was an early colleague and follower of Freud who later became a leading dissenter. Rank made a connection between the evolution of human love and stages in soul development, saying that these stages proceed from "the corporeal individualism of the shadow-soul, through the divine soul-collective and the corporeal collectivism of sexual procreation, to the spiritual individualism of a love that unites all elements in harmony."[28] The evolution of love depends upon self-love, or self-acceptance, "for only inasmuch as the individual accepts himself can he accept others as they are and in that sense 'love' them."[29] Our neuroses, according to Rank, make us incapable of love, and "crowd out creative celebration of the soul."[30]

Sandor Ferenczi was among Freud's closest collaborators until theoretical divergences caused him to fall out of Freud's favor. Ferenczi was interested in compassion and love in the context of psychoanalytic work. He experimented with the unorthodox practice of "mutual analysis," wherein the analyst reveals "his own weaknesses and feelings."[31] He engaged in such a controversial practice, despite the disapproval of his peers, because of his "compulsive wish to help," and because of the importance he placed on developing an empathic and sympathetic attitude. Without it, he warned, psychoanalysts would never understand their patients. "The advantage of sympathy," he claimed, "is an ability to penetrate deeply into the feelings of others."[32] Despite the failure of many of Ferenczi's experiments in analysis, some of his discoveries foreshadowed future directions in the field.[33]

In order to facilitate healing, Ferenczi continually searched for ways to bring genuine human sympathy into psychoanalysis. His defense of the merits of this effort—to himself, in his diary—gives a sense of the soul-searching he must have done and the criticism he certainly encountered. "To introduce this healing into psychotherapy in the appropriate manner and where it is required is surely not an entirely unworthy task."[34] Later practitioners have echoed a similar refrain to a somewhat more receptive field, long after Ferenczi first risked his credibility and his career.

Jung, Hillman, and Others

Jung departed from Freud in numerous ways, among them in his conviction that a religious attitude need not conflict with the many insights of natural science. "I attribute a positive value to all religions," Jung explained. "I likewise attribute a positive value to biology, and to the empiricism of natural science in general."[35] The religious attitude was, in Jung's estimation, indispensable to making discoveries about the cosmos from within, whereas the empiricism of science was equally necessary for mapping an understanding of the psyche "from the outer world."[36] These two approaches to psyche—

outer and inner—both fit within the theoretical foundations of Jung's analytic psychology.

Although Jung saw "a play of opposites" in every situation, he considered love a cosmogonic force beyond the influence of these opposites. He believed that love alone was stronger than death, and that individuation depended upon love and would be realized when we "bind the opposites by love."[37] However, despite its unique position in his psychology, Jung rarely wrote of love, and even less of compassion. He believed a discussion of such magnitude exceeded the limits of language. Despite these reservations, Jung ends his autobiography with such a powerful homage to love that it leaves no doubt he embraced it as both the alpha and omega of human life. "I falter before the task of finding the language which might adequately express the incalculable paradoxes of love. . . . Love 'bears all things' and 'endures all things' (1 Cor. 13:7). These words say all there is to be said; nothing can be added to them. For we are in the deepest sense the victims and the instruments of cosmogonic 'love.' . . . Man can try to name love, [but if] he possesses a grain of wisdom, he will lay down his arms and name the unknown by the more unknown, *ignotum per ignotius*—that is by the name of God."[38]

In *The Vision Seminars*, Jung unites the twin facets of love and compassion, borrowing an image from Buddhism. He relates a story found among the many stories of Kwannon (Kwan Yin), the merciful Goddess of Love and Compassion, and illustrates quite beautifully the psychological attitude of real love. This goddess, he observes,

> . . . gives nourishment to all living things, even to the evil spirits in hell, and to do so she must go down to hell; but it would frighten the devils if she were to appear there in her heavenly form and, as the Goddess of Kindness, she cannot permit that to happen; so, having such an extraordinary regard for the feelings of the devils, she transforms herself into an evil spirit and takes the food down in that guise. There is a beautiful traditional painting, where she is represented in hell as a devil among the devils, giving food to them; but there is a fine thread going up from her head to a heavenly being above, who is her-

self in all her splendid fury. That is the psychological attitude which real love suggests.[39]

Clearly, Jung recognized the paramount importance of love and compassion. Nevertheless, like Freud, Jung concentrated little of his attention explicitly on compassion or love, and gave virtually no attention to a methodology for developing these qualities. This dearth of methodology was something Jung particularly lamented, because he felt that all of Western civilization lacked a method for what he believed was the next step in "self-development." He commented on what he called "the psychic insufficiency of Western culture as compared with that of the East," and regretted that, although Western psychology "had learned to tame and subject the psyche, . . . [it] knew nothing about its methodological developments and functions."[40]

Jung knew analysts could not guide patients beyond the limits of their own development, yet he had little confidence that doctors would feel the need to "live up to everything we expect of our patient." Nevertheless, he threw down the gauntlet to analysts. He urged them to take seriously the task of their own self-development, all the while acknowledging that his proposal would likely meet "with scant popular approval." Anticipating the resistance of his peers did not, however, prevent Jung from "challenging the doctor to transform himself in order to effect a change in the patient."[41]

Those who followed and were influenced by Jung share both his appreciation for the transformative power of love and compassion, and his lack of methodology for developing these qualities. Edward Edinger notes the relationship of transpersonal love to wholeness, but never writes about how an individual might develop such love.[42] James Hillman expresses a deep reverence for the relationship between love and soul, and derides the field of depth psychology for what it has done to love, saying that, "psychoanalysis has narrowed love to what goes on between two people."[43] This diminishment of love atrophies soul and diminishes the power of therapy because "therapy is love itself, the whole of it, not some special part of it."[44] Where love is lacking, soul cannot thrive. Hillman entreats those in the field of depth psychology to risk a bolder vision of love. He challenges our limited vision and speaks of a love that is capable of expanding exponentially until ultimately it reveals the self to itself, and "serves as a prism for the world."[45] Given his views, it is not surprising that Hillman says, "We really do need a new critique of depth psychology in terms of what it has done to love in our century."[46] And while his writing on compassion is far less impassioned or prolific, he does reflect upon the development of compassion for oneself.[47]

Helen Luke also took an interest in the development of compassion, for both self and other. In her wise and gentle manner, she points out that, all too often, people try to solve the problems of others, their actions appearing compassionate, when in truth they are strenuously avoiding looking at themselves. Such behavior is not compassionate. Individuals must be willing to engage compassionately with their own darkness if they wish to have a positive effect on the world around them. Without compassion for your own darkness, she claims, "you will never have true compassion. First comes compassion for your own weaknesses and then for the person next to you. . . . You may have to fight, but if you don't fight with forgiveness and compassion, you simply are recreating the same situation."[48] Only compassion that is rooted in compassion for oneself can provide a sound basis for skillful action in the world with others. Truly speaking, actions themselves are less important than *who* is acting. The same action taken with different motivation has a completely different effect. Luke makes this distinction clear.

Empathy, Self-Psychology, and Dialogical Psychotherapy: Buber, Kohut, and Others

The literature on empathy and empathic relationship comes close to describing elements of compassion. The word "empathy" has its equivalent in the German *einfühlung*, meaning the capacity to feel into another's experience.

Wilhelm Dilthey discussed the practice of empathy as an analytic tool. Born in 1831, Dilthey was a powerful and influential German philosopher who advocated for *Geistewissenschaften*—or human sciences—that were distinct from the natural sciences, because he believed human studies called for a different way of knowing. Dilthey argued that the interpretation of human phenomena must be derived from lived experience, and therefore the facts of experience must come from inner life and not extrinsic categories. Whereas natural sciences are designed to explain nature, he noted, "human studies understand expressions of life."[49]

For Dilthey, understanding was germane to the exploration of lived experience and empathy was key to such an approach. "The basis of the human studies is not conceptualization," he asserts, "but total awareness of a mental state and its reconstruction based on empathy."[50] The empathy Dilthey spoke of meant the ability to enter another's experience imaginatively, while simultaneously maintaining awareness that it is the other's experience and not our own.

Dilthey was a teacher to philosopher Martin Buber. Buber's seminal work *I and Thou* has inspired several generations of therapists to remember the holy ground of meeting that is the heart of therapeutic work. In later writings, Buber specifically explored what the insights of a dialogical philosophy could offer the practice of psychotherapy. While he did not negate the reality of individual psychic life, his work was a clarion call for all those who had been swept up in one-sided individualism. Insistent that we become, and are, human because of our relatedness to others, Buber distilled his message into one simple statement: "All real living is meeting."[51]

Buber decried equating humanity with individuality, and believed the greatest tragedy of modern times was the loss of human interconnectedness. Preoccupation with individuality strips life of purpose and meaning. In Buber's view, genuine meeting is the only path that can lead an individual to wholeness. "Human life touches on absoluteness in virtue of its dialogical character . . . . Man can become whole not in virtue of a relation to himself but only in virtue of a relation to another self."[52]

Jungian analyst Hans Trub, following a deeply moving personal meeting with Buber, became one of the early pioneers of a dialogical understanding of psychotherapy.[53] Trub called the approach he developed "healing through meeting." He insisted that any therapeutic process needed to be founded on the "between." Trub did not reject Jung's insight into the intra-psychic, "but rather grounded it in a dialogical orientation."[54] This meant that, rather than hailing individuation as the zenith of psychological life, Trub exhorted therapists not to lose sight of "the one true goal of healing, the unlocking of the locked up person for the meeting with the world."[55]

Always keeping the aim of meeting central, the dialogically oriented therapist focuses on building relationships, meeting his patients "with love and understanding like an elder brother."[56] Whereas trust and positive feelings were valued in traditional analytic circles, they were labeled, analyzed, and interpreted as positive transference. There remains much debate in the field as to whether there is, or should be, a real or an as-if relationship between therapist and patient. In the case of dialogical therapy, real relationship and real meeting are perhaps not immediately possible, but there is no controversy as to their importance. They are held out as the goal of the therapeutic endeavor, while psychopathology is regarded primarily as a "flight from meeting."[57] Maurice Friedman, whose work was also deeply influenced by Buber's dialogical perspective, further distinguishes Buber's goal of dialogical meeting from Jung's goal of individuation, pointing out that, "in contrast to Jung, Buber sees dialogue as the goal and individuation as the stepping-stone and the by-product. When one becomes integrated it is so one can go forth into meeting."[58]

Buber urged therapists to view patients in their wholeness as persons by "stepping into elemental relation with them."[59] The elemental relation comes about through "'imagining the real' which is to imagine to myself what another man is at this very moment wishing, feeling, perceiving, thinking, and not as detached content but in his very reality."[60] As a philosopher, Buber was not seeking clinical credibility, and did not feel obliged to conform to the expectations of the scientific community. He had freedoms those in the field of psychology did not feel they had. This allowed him to explore the human dimension of human relations, and to advocate for an appreciation of the sanctity of life's interconnectedness in a way many psychologists were unable to do.

Heinz Kohut, the analyst most credited with introducing the practice of empathic immersion in the consulting room, was outspoken about the therapeutic value of empathy. He also remained concerned throughout his life that his ideas would be misunderstood and detract from his scientific credibility. Kohut was vehement that no one confuse the tool of empathy with "such fuzzily related meanings as kindness, compassion and sympathy." Such ideas, he maintained, threaten "a replacement of the scientific mode of thought by a quasi-religious or mystical approach."[61] Kohut described empathy as a value-neutral tool used by analysts to understand a patient's experience. At times, he described empathy as "the capacity to think and feel oneself into the inner life of another person," but more often he sterilized it with the term "vicarious introspection."[62]

Empathy, according to Kohut, must be "employed with scientific rigor to gather the data of the human experience."[63] Still, we sense a wobble in Kohut's dispassion when he describes analysts as those who have "devoted their life to helping others with the aid of insights obtained via empathic immersion into their inner life." Moreover, he says that analysts "must behave humanely, warmly, and with appropriate empathic responsiveness."[64] So, although it is true that, in the case of self-psychology, the psychotherapist uses the data gathered via vicarious introspection to facilitate healing, Kohut went to absurd lengths to prevent the scientific "tool" of empathy from being confused with an attitude of compassion.

Determined to leave no room for doubt in this matter, Kohut declared that his theories were meant to provide "an antidote to the sentimentalizing perversions in psychotherapy about curing through love, through compassion, to just being there and being nice."[65] Clearly, love and compassion, in Kohut's mind, do not even come close to being powerfully transformative states of mind, which may or may not at any given time have anything to do with being nice. For him, they are the pathetic equivalent of "sentimentalizing perversions."

To further underscore the value-neutral nature of empathy, Kohut used the example of the Nazis, who, in order to inflict the greatest possible emotional pain, employed empathy to perceive their victims' vulnerability. On the other hand, he did acknowledge that a link with an empathic (in this case not neutral) human environment is necessary for psychological life. To illustrate this point, Kohut recounted the story of astronauts who lost control of their ship and were told they could either orbit forever in space or attempt a return to Earth, risking likely incineration upon reentry. The astronauts decided, without question, to risk a return to Earth. The vision of orbiting forever in uninhabited space was far more terrifying than the prospect of incineration. This decision demonstrated that human beings have a fundamental need for contact with an empathic environment. It appears empathy meant different things to Kohut, depending on the point he was trying to make.

Allen Siegel remarks that Kohut not only spoke of different levels of empathy, but also claimed that empathy serves a different function for analyst and patient. "For the analyst," Kohut tells us, "it is a method of gathering data on different levels of maturity, as well as an informer of appropriate analytic action." For the patient, however, "it is the breath of life."[66] The implication that patients could receive the "breath of life" from analysts who perceive themselves as "gathering data" is simply not plausible. Nevertheless, this was as far as Kohut could go. Kohut made the use of empathy central to the therapeutic process, and this is itself a matter of some significance. Unfortunately, preoccupation with maintaining his stature as a man of science seemed to limit the range of his vision.

Tibetan Buddhism: The Compassionate Revolution

By contrast, Indo-Tibetan Buddhist literature is replete with praise for compassion and its transformative power. Unlike depth psychology, which has been torn since its inception between an affiliation with the materialism of science and the beckoning of inner life, Tibetan Buddhist psychology readily acknowledges the spheres of inner and outer, personal and collective, individual and social, body and mind as deeply interconnected processes.

Tibetan Buddhism unequivocally praises the development of compassion rooted in wisdom as the heart of both individual human endeavor and meaningful social relations. It is the ultimate balm for both personal and collective ills. Society is, after all, a collection of individuals, so the happiness of individuals is the best foundation for felicitous communal life. There is no such thing as a happy society full of miserable individuals. And individuals simply cannot be happy without love and compassion. The Dalai Lama urges humanity to consider the necessity of love and compassion for the good of individuals and for the good of the planet. "Compassion and love are not mere luxuries," he notes. "As the source of both inner and external peace, they are fundamental to the continual survival of our species."[67]

The Myth of Modernity

From the Tibetan Buddhist perspective, a lack of emphasis on love and compassion can, in part, be linked to a general neglect of inner life. Devotion to the gods of comfort and material progress has elevated the stature of science and technology in the last century. As a society, we have placed our confidence in science and technology and their promise to relieve the afflictions of humanity. This has inadvertently caused a growing fissure of alienation from ourselves and others. The myth of modernity does not foster inner life.

The Dalai Lama, the great Buddhist leader and prince of peace, has had a fascination since early childhood with both science and technology. He was eager to encounter and learn more about the ingenious minds behind these innovations. In his travels throughout the Western world, however, he became troubled by some of what he saw. Scientific materialism dominates and overshadows other ways of knowing. Many people seem to believe that science is the ultimate authority, holding the answers to all their questions. Placing so much faith in science, we are, unfortunately, "apt to overlook the limitations of science."[68]

We turn to science to answer questions it is not able to address. Witness an example from the area of consciousness research. Science does not currently have the means to perceive consciousness. As a result, science has yet to understand what consciousness is, much less how it exists or functions. This has prompted many scientists to conclude that consciousness does not actually exist. Given that they have looked for consciousness and can't find it, it must simply be an epiphenomenon of the brain. The crux of this argument is that, if consciousness can't be found by currently available means, it must not be there.

If, however, we concede that some types of knowledge may exceed current scientific means of investigation and measurement, then it is premature to conclude that consciousness doesn't exist simply because it hasn't been found by scientists. Not having the means to perceive something doesn't mean it's not there. The Dalai Lama explains that consciousness "belongs to that category of phenomena without form, substance, or color. It is not susceptible to investigation by external means. But this does not mean such things do not exist, merely that science cannot find them."[69] Furthermore, although material and scientific advances can certainly enrich life, they cannot bring about happiness. Outer modernity is not capable of satisfying inner needs. When we look around for even a moment, it becomes abundantly clear that, for all the conveniences of modern life, we are no happier today than in the past. The more we have, the more we feel we need. In many ways, we are more anxious, stressed, and depressed than ever. The pace of life keeps accelerating and we are driven to keep up. It is increasingly difficult to slow the momentum and to focus on what really matters.

Third-world nations, with their limited scientific and technological achievements and their poor living conditions, are perceived as lagging behind. In one way this is true. There are many things individuals in poorer nations suffer that the majority of us in wealthier nations do not. And yet, it appears that we have traded one set of problems for another. In those countries, we find ailments due mostly to poor sanitation and impoverished conditions. In contrast, modern urban life tends to breed illnesses due to anxiety and alienation. "So instead of water-borne diseases we find stress-born diseases."[70]

The neglect of inner life stems from the misunderstanding that well-being can be achieved by material, or outer, means. In contrast to the gradual process of inner development, outer progress holds out the tantalizing promise of immediate gratification. Whereas outer development brings ephemeral satisfaction, inner development, such as the development of compassion, is the "source of all lasting happiness and joy."[71] This does not mean that individuals must abandon striving for material betterment, but that outer development and inner development need to be properly balanced. In order to bring about this balance, the Dalai Lama suggests, "a revolution is called for, certainly . . . . What I propose is a spiritual revolution."[72]

A spiritual revolution is not a religious revolution. Spirituality is rooted in universal principles that individuals can embrace without recourse to a religious or metaphysical system. A spiritual revolution is not something otherworldly, mystical, or metaphysical. "Rather, it is a . . . radical reorientation away from our habitual preoccupation with self."[73] And the arsenal for this revolution is compassion.

Turning toward a wider community of beings and embracing others' interests along with our own loosens the grip of isolated individualism that plagues modern life. Modern living is structured so that it minimizes our direct dependence on others. Distancing ourselves from others reinforces tendencies like competitiveness and envy, rather than cooperation and appreciation. Instead of depending on one another for support, we increasingly rely upon machines and services. Although many, including those in the field of psychology, have recognized the complex demands and the unique challenges of modern life, Tibetan Buddhist literature sends a clear corrective message: Compassion is the most powerful, stable, and effective basis for transforming both self and society.

The seeds of compassion are found in empathy, or the ability to enter into and know, at least in part, the suffering of another. Tibetan Buddhist teachings say this empathy can be cultivated to such a degree that compassion not only arises spontaneously and effortlessly, it becomes universal in scope, generating "a feeling of intimacy with all other sentient beings, including of course those that would harm us. . . ."[74]

Our capacity for empathy is innate, as is our capacity for reason. These innate capacities are braided together in the cultivation of compassion. Empathy combined with reason is the foundation for a compassion that is both stable and continuous. The Dalai Lama points the way to universal compassion in a disarmingly simple manner: "We need to restrain those factors which inhibit compassion . . . ," and "cultivate those which are conducive to it."[75] This practice of combined restraint and cultivation is referred to as the practice of "mind training." Mind training is not a purely cognitive or intellectual exercise, however. Training the mind involves all factors of consciousness. This includes intellect, imagination, and feeling.

Unconditional Openness

Much of Tibetan Buddhist literature focuses on the transformative power of compassion, but few have spoken to the revolutionary nature of compassion as eloquently and provocatively as Chögyam Trungpa. Trungpa reminds us of the courage and generosity that characterize compassion and of the threat such openness poses to the fearful sovereignty of ego. He says:

> Compassion contains fundamental fearlessness, fearlessness without hesitation. This fearlessness is marked by tremendous generosity, in contrast to the fearlessness of exerting one's power over others . . . . Ego would like to establish its territory, whereas compassion is completely open and welcoming. It is a gesture of generosity which excludes no one.[76]

A traditional image for the unconditional openness and generosity of compassion is one moon shining in the sky with its image reflected equally in 100 or 1,000 bowls of water. The moon does not discriminate between this water and that. It shines equally on all surfaces because its nature is to do so. It is not seeking its reflection in the water. Likewise, a fully developed compassion is without ambition or striving. It simply is.

Geshe Rabten further emphasizes the radical implications of such unconditional compassion. "Compassion makes no distinctions as to whether or not its object is good or bad, beautiful or ugly, pleasing or displeasing."[77] Some reject the image of the moon reflected in the water as an example for unconditioned compassion, saying that such generosity of spirit is easy because the water will not turn against the moon as one person will turn against another. Geshe Rabten counters this by pointing out that, from the point of view of compassion, response is irrelevant. "Love and compassion . . . are willing to give without expectations. And no matter what the reaction of the person to whom we give, they remain steady and sincere."[78]

Compassion is "a bridge to the world outside."[79] It opens us to the tone of another, the texture of another's presence, thereby creating an environment for communication. Our timeworn habit is to be preoccupied with our own lives, sealing ourselves off from matters we deem peripheral to our own interests. We adopt this attitude to enhance our personal well-being, but it perpetuates the knot of self-centered unhappiness around our hearts instead. Lama Yeshe, another contemporary Buddhist master, explains that, "as long as we remain so tightly focused upon our own happiness . . . we will never experience the expansiveness of a truly open heart."[80] We experience an open heart when we are free from self preoccupation. Compassion is the key to that freedom—it loosens the grip that our selfishness has on our heart. Rather than leaving precious moments of openness to chance, we are encouraged to consciously cultivate our compassion, and let it blossom. And if we still doubt the rewards of such effort, Trungpa speaks to us of compassion's bounty.

> We could say that compassion is the ultimate attitude of wealth: an anti-poverty attitude, a war on want. It contains all sorts of heroic, juicy, positive, visionary, expansive qualities. And it implies larger scale thinking, a freer and more expansive way of relating to yourself and the world.[81]

Compassion is characterized by warmth. This warmth is not fabricated or generated; it emerges naturally in the absence of aggression. Compassion is not another way of waging war and harming ourselves or others. It relinquishes the false glory of bloodshed and battle in favor of the true glory of nonaggression. It is a practice of inner disarmament. The warmth of compassion is not a defense against hatred; it is a transformation of hatred. Compassion is none other than the energy of aggression and hatred released from the ego's narrow and fearful grasp.

Compassion is further characterized by intelligence; but this intelligence is not conceptual and intellectual. The intelligence of compassion is an intelligence in harmony with reality, an intelligence that exists behind the veil of our habitual blindness. This intelligence is naturally aware of the interdependent nature of self and other.

Grounds for Compassion

The possibility of developing universal compassion is advanced on three principal grounds. The first of these is that the confused states of mind with which we normally identify do not have a valid or self-existing foundation. Our emotions are undeniably fluid; they are changeable and entirely dependent on conditions. Being dependent on conditions, they lack an absolute, independent essence. We may at one time feel a very strong dislike for someone whom we later come to love. The opposite is also true. Feelings of both closeness and distance are based on changeable conditions, and are therefore not intrinsic to the mind. They come, they stay for a while, and then they go. The mind does not, therefore, depend upon them for its existence.

The second ground for accepting the possibility that confused states of mind can be uprooted is that positive states can act as antidotes to negative ones. This means that the greater our capacity to experience positive states like compassion, the weaker the influence of negative or afflicted states. Positive states of mind can de-potentiate negative tendencies.

The ultimate antidote to confused states of mind is a wisdom that perceives the nature of reality. Such wisdom clears all distortions and negative tendencies, like finding the roots of a poisonous plant and pulling it out of the ground. Uprooting ignorance is intimately connected with the cultivation of great compassion, because "the way to cultivate compassion is through wisdom. In other words, the reason we are not compassionate . . . is that our ignorance makes us try to grab things for ourselves."[82] Ignorance creates the identification with me and mine. It, in turn, depends upon an illusion of separateness and a belief in inherent self-existence. However, because ignorance depends upon an illusion, it is by nature weaker than the true reality that we and all phenomena do not exist absolutely and independently, but as subtly interconnected processes.

The third principal ground supporting the development of universal compassion is the mind's innately pure nature. The subtlest consciousness "has a pure basis."[83] This subtle mind, or consciousness, is untainted by negative emotions; it is like the vast, open sky that is present, even when concealed behind passing clouds and storms. Clouds of self-centered emotions may gather, momentarily obscuring our vision of the sky, but the sky remains ever-spacious and unobstructed. Sky remains sky no matter how violent or stormy the weather. The Dalai Lama provides this metaphor to illustrate our pure nature:

> We can conceive of the nature of mind in terms of water in a lake. When the water is stirred up by a storm, the mud from the lake's bottom clouds it, making it appear opaque. But the nature of the water is not dirty. When the storm passes, the mud settles and the water is left clear once again.[84]

Just as a lake is naturally subject to shifting weather conditions, a continual flow of thoughts and emotions occurs naturally in the mind. And, just as weather and lake are interconnected, yet not one and the same, emotions and mind are interconnected, yet not one and the same. We need, therefore, to distinguish between "consciousness as such and the thoughts and emotions it experiences."[85] The tendency in psychology, and many other Western disciplines, is to perceive negative or afflictive emotions as intrinsic to the mind—something we can therefore do little to change.

In Tibetan Buddhism, painful emotional states are referred to as *nyong mong*, or that which afflicts us from within. Although the fact that we are afflicted by such states does not make them intrinsic, as long as the potential for such emotions is present, they can arise and gather force in our psyches. This is why "although our nature is basically disposed toward kindness and compassion, we are all capable of cruelty and hatred."[86] Under the spell of powerful, self-centered emotions, we are denied our most basic wish—to be happy and avoid suffering. Afflictive emotions mislead us because they promise satisfaction but do not deliver. We are hijacked, captured, buffeted, and blinded by our addiction to a vast array of confused emotions. Greed, resentment, jealousy, hatred, and craving create a whirlwind. Under their influence, we cannot generate compassion for either self or other. "But the existence of this negative potential does not give us grounds to suppose that human nature is inherently violent, or even necessarily disposed toward violence."[87]

Mistaking Compassion

There is much confusion about what compassion is and what it isn't. Tibetan Buddhist literature highlights three chief misunderstandings. The first is mistaking "idiot compassion" for genuine compassion. The second is confusing attachment with love and compassion. The third is believing that compassion is strictly a way of being, and not a way of doing.

Whereas genuine compassion is intelligent and discriminating, "idiot compassion is a compassion with neurosis, a slimy way of trying to fulfill your desires secretly. This is your aim, but you give the appearance of being generous and impersonal."[88] Idiot compassion in the guise of compassion may harm rather than help. Genuine compassion is at times gentle and at other times forceful, whereas idiot compassion is constantly trying to appear kind. Sometimes the kindest response may not appear kind. "To the conventional way of thinking, compassion simply means being kind and warm. . . . But true compassion is ruthless, from ego's point of view, because it does not consider ego's drive to maintain itself."[89] Compassion helps others help themselves. It does not foster conditions of self-serving dependency. It puts the responsibility where it belongs: on the individual. Compassion fearlessly pierces to the heart, whereas "superficial kindness lacks courage and intelligence."[90]

Compassion manifests in whatever way is needed to wake someone up, and this can feel somewhat sharp or painful at times. There are times when reassurance and comfort are not the most compassionate response. The distinction between authentic and counterfeit, or idiot, compassion can readily be found in the consulting room. A compassionate therapist creates a safe environment for patients to open to raw and tender experience, including the experience of psychic pain. Acting out of idiot compassion, therapists may, in a variety of ways, prevent a patient's experience of pain because they themselves cannot tolerate the pain of another, or in order to be seen as kind or to be liked. As a perversion of sympathy, idiot compassion actually blocks compassion. Mistaking idiot compassion for genuine compassion and kindness does a great disservice to real compassion, which is unswerving in its allegiance to freedom from self-deception.

It is also important to differentiate genuine love and compassion from love and compassion grown out of attachment. Attachment is by nature fickle and unstable. Our feelings for others vacillate all the time. Although we are willing to go to great lengths for a current love interest, the intensity of these feelings is fleeting and undependable. Genuine compassion, on the other hand, is much more stable and reliable, making it much sounder in the long run. I can readily recall a time in my life when I could not go a single day without speaking to a friend with whom I now have no contact. If I were to rely on these types of feelings as a basis for generating compassion, I would continuously undermine my own effort—not to mention the sheer impossibility of developing compassion for my enemies.

Attachment is partial by nature, so impartial compassion is not possible under its influence. Attachment-tinged compassion is, in fact, closer to hatred than love because, when attachment evaporates, dislike or hatred often replace it. This is commonly experienced in the aftermath of romance, when we find ourselves despising the person we once adored. Attachment-based compassion is carefully deconstructed in Tibetan Buddhist literature. The impartial compassion emphasized there is stable, because it does not situate itself within the transitory boundaries of personal relationships.

Impartial compassion is not subject to the wild fluctuations of attachment-based compassion. Impartial compassion, free of personal attachment, may arise when we see a fish writhing on a hook or an unknown child howling in distress. In such instances, we spontaneously feel and respond to another's pain. While it is initially helpful to recall the experience of a more distant, impartial compassion, this is only the beginning. The ultimate aim of great compassion far exceeds this. Great compassion perceives other beings with an impartial closeness, not an impartial distance. Great compassion raises our concern for all beings to the level we now have for those who are nearest and dearest. Such compassion is both enduring and impassioned.

Finally, compassion is both a way of being and a way of doing. It is both heart and hands. Compassion is not true compassion unless it is active. Sogyal Rinpoche describes compassion as both "the source and essence of enlightenment, and the heart of enlightened activity."[91] Avalokitesvara, the sublime compassionate one, has both a thousand arms and a thousand eyes. His thousand eyes compassionately behold the pain in all parts of the universe, and his thousand arms reach out to extend relief. This image unites the two-fold nature of being and doing at the heart of compassion.

Compassion and Psychotherapy: A Meeting of Minds

The literature bringing Buddhism and psychotherapy into dialogue has come primarily from Western psychotherapists practicing in the Theravadan tradition, with its emphasis on the practices of meditative stabilization, insight meditation, and ethical discipline. There is far less literature relating the Mahayana Buddhist tradition, with its special emphasis on compassion, to psychotherapy.

As Tibetan Buddhism has migrated West and encountered the practice of psychotherapy, there has been limited reflection from a few Tibetan Buddhist masters on the practice of psychotherapy and its relationship to the practice of compassion. Chögyam Trungpa, with his keen understanding of Western culture and his training in the Tibetan Buddhist tradition, was among the first to comment on the relationship between Buddhism and psychotherapy. He remains, to this day, among the most original and provocative Buddhist thinkers to bridge the worlds of East and West.

Trungpa remarked that one of the problems within the field of psychology was the attempt to "pinpoint, categorize, and pigeonhole mind and its contents very neatly." He called this overzealous approach to codifying and cataloguing human experience and putting it in neat categories "psychological materialism." Psychological materialism leaves little room for spontaneity, creativity, and openness. More important, "it overlooks basic healthiness."[92] Trungpa challenged therapists to uplift their vision of health and see beyond the narrow aim of freedom from sickness. Sickness may be present in an individual, but health is ever-present. Because the Tibetan Buddhist tradition posits a fundamentally pure nature of mind, "health is intrinsic. That is, health comes first: sickness is secondary. *Health is.*"[93] This deceptively simple twist in thinking about health and sickness actually makes for a profoundly different approach to the entire therapeutic process.

Trungpa believed therapists were inclined to hide behind the safe walls of theoretical constructions and diagnostic labels, because the raw texture of human experience was embarrassing to them. But "that embarrassment has to be transformed into compassion." Lowering the volume on incessant theorizing and continual conceptualization leaves room for the emergence of insight. "So the main point in working with people is to appreciate and manifest simplicity . . . the more you appreciate simplicity, the more profound your understanding becomes."[94] Instead of being so preoccupied with the perfection of our theories, Trungpa encouraged us to foster basic warmth, first by developing "warmth towards ourselves, which then expands to others. This is the ground for relating with disturbed people, with one another, and with ourselves all within the same framework."[95] Put another way, "If we can make friends with ourselves, if we are willing to be what we are, without hating parts of ourselves and trying to hide them, then we can begin to open up to others . . . then perhaps we can begin to really help others."[96]

Individuals who suffer profound psychic pain tend to either blame themselves or believe the world is to blame. This compounds the pain they experience and elicits aggression toward themselves and others. Compassion gently penetrates this defense, softening the hardened armor of self-protection. Again and again, Trungpa returns to compassion as both an expression of health and the basis for healing. Therapists bring compassion to the environment, not so much with words, but by being compassionate themselves. "So if there is some compassion radiating from your very presence when you walk in to a room and sit down with people . . . that is the preliminary stage of healing . . . That goes a long way."[97] Whatever the problem, and whatever other skills are called for, compassion is always needed.

Tarthang Tulku Rinpoche has also spoken of the connection between Buddhism and psychotherapy, particularly noting their shared emphasis on compassion.

> Therapy and Buddhism is a natural combination. In therapy the most important thing is compassion—not just giving explanations to the patient but giving yourself to him, trying to open your mind to him fully. Compassion is also the major focus of Buddhist practice.[98]

I certainly agree that compassion needs to be the most important thing in therapy, however, it has yet to be acknowledged as such by those in the field.

The Dalai Lama has not addressed the practice of psychotherapy in any depth, but when asked by psychiatrist Howard Cutler to give a definition of mental health or of a mentally healthy person, he responded, "I regard a compassionate warm-hearted person as healthy." When asked to describe how individuals could become mentally healthier, he replied that "cultivating positive mental states such as kindness and compassion definitely lead to better psychological health and happiness."[99] Everyone benefits from cultivating compassion. The Dalai Lama goes on to suggest that even the intractably self-centered can be persuaded of the benefits of love and compassion,

> . . . on the grounds that it is the best way to fulfill their self-interests. They wish to have good health, live a longer life, and have peace of mind, happiness, and joy. And if these are things they desire, I've heard there is even scientific evidence that these things can be enhanced by feelings of love and compassion.[100]

Teaching people about the physical and emotional benefits of compassion is another way to induce those not otherwise convinced to work toward developing these qualities. There is not a single doctor who would prescribe hatred or ruthless ambition as a cure for any disease, because it is well known that such states harm the body and the mind. Compassion, on the other hand, is known to increase contentment, resilience, flexibility, and joy. Because we stand to gain so much from developing compassion, it behooves us to understand its value and strive to develop it.

Some say that, although compassion and love are certainly worth cultivating, there is no benefit to encouraging unlimited, unconditioned compassion, because its attainment is such a far-flung possibility—if it is a possibility at all. They contend that it is better to focus on more readily achievable goals than to encourage such fanciful notions. Moreover, falling short, as we inevitably do, can be disheartening and can bring about feelings of failure and inadequacy. Tibetan Buddhist literature suggests otherwise.

Engaging the possibility of and aspiring to actualize a vast, limitless compassion is a powerful source of inspiration that can have a significant impact on our outlook and actions, day to day. It is immensely beneficial to plant the seeds of this aspiration in our mind and let them slowly take root in our lives. Over time, as these seeds mature, they will help us cut through ancient patterns of aggression and self-deception and awaken our courage and love. And if we are inclined, as many of us are, to be hard on ourselves when we see our lack of impartial compassion for others, or our lack of compassion at all, we can use that situation to generate compassion for ourselves and our own difficulties along the way. Our hindrances, our heartbreak and pain, can soften us. The limits of our compassion can themselves become a doorway to greater compassion.

The Dalai Lama offers this response to those who question the value of this aspiration:

> So to those who say the Dalai Lama is being unrealistic in advocating this ideal of unconditional love, I urge them to experiment with it nonetheless. They will discover that when we reach beyond the confines of narrow self-interest our hearts become filled with strength. Peace and joy become our con-

stant companion. It breaks down barriers of every kind and in the end destroys the notion of my interest as independent from other's interest.[101]

Whereas Tibetan Buddhism unequivocally posits an innate capacity for unlimited love and compassion, the field of depth psychology either rejects this position, or abstains from comment on the issue. This difference in approach stems from divergent opinions and assumptions about human nature. It is not at all clear, however, that the stance taken in depth psychology rests upon a solid foundation of insight or understanding. It seems, therefore, that there are questions each of us must ask ourselves, and that the field as a whole needs to revisit.

Is the dualistic model of the psyche, the experience of dynamic conflict, the struggle between Eros and Death, the final word? Is duality truly emblematic of our deepest nature? What if we consider the existence of a deeper and more subtle consciousness, one that underlies the dualistic tensions and emotional vicissitudes of which we are so aware? What if we consider the possibility that nondual, primordial purity may, in fact, be the nature of our deepest being? I would suggest that, in a field devoted to caring for the soul, it is worth wondering about the nature of the soul we are serving.

Tibetan Buddhism radically centers its psychology on the principles of compassion and love. This centrality of compassion is why I believe Tibetan Buddhism can make a unique contribution to the field of psychology. The royal road to the unconscious so lauded by depth psychologists has been a road to soul. I believe the path to soul is calling, and yearning, for an embrace of heart.

Chapter 3

SIGMUND FREUD:
TRAVERSING THE FIELDS OF DESIRE

■　　■　　■

*You could not discover the limits of soul, even if you traveled every
road to do so; such is the depth of its meaning.*

−HERACLITUS

Ⓘ n this chapter, we will explore Freud's writings on the opposing forces of Eros and Death, desire, narcissism, the conflict
between individual fulfillment and the restraints of civilization, as well as the central role of sublimation. Through this discussion,
we will attempt to uncover Freud's views on love and compassion.

Eros and Death

Freud's model of the psyche focuses on drives and the conflict between
them. This model, which he refined over many years, directly influenced
his beliefs about the human capacity for both compassion and love.
Freud advanced different theories concerning basic human drives over
the span of his long career. He began with a view that was modified over
the years, as his thinking evolved and changed.

In Freud's original formulation, ego drives were not deemed sexual
in nature, and he in fact proposed a conflict between sexual and ego
drives. Ego drives opposed sexual drives, and were described as instinctual trends lacking an object.

Upon further analysis, Freud determined that the ego could be the object of its own desire, and that ego drives could therefore express a libidinal character. Freud's acceptance of an ego-libido meant that the ego itself could be erotically charged. This new perspective catalyzed a reworking of the drive theory. Ultimately, Freud concluded that, since the ego also appeared to have sexual, libidinal drives, the true opposition must lie between the libidinal (ego and object) drive and the death drive. He readily asserted that his views had "from the very first been dualistic, and today they are even more definitely dualistic than before—now that we describe the opposition as being, not between ego instincts and sexual instincts but between life instincts and death instincts."[1] In Freud's revised drive theory, love and life stand over and against aggression and death.

It is worth noting here that, although the word "instinct" had been widely used to translate the German *Trieb*, Bettelheim challenged this translation, saying it completely misrepresented Freud's use of the term.[2] The word *Trieb* means "drive," and is distinct from the German *Instinkt*, which Freud used when he meant instinct. Bettelheim's view has since gained general acceptance. Although many of the sources I quote use the term "instinct," I will use the word "drive."

These organic drives, according to Freud, are conservative and regressive in nature, tending toward the restoration of an earlier state of things. Freud believed that the "final goal of all organic striving" is a return to an original state of being—a return to the initial state from which one had earlier departed. He described it as "the instinct to return to the inanimate state."[3] Freud was aligned with the materialist view that inanimate life exists prior to, and gives rise to, animate life. In other words, it was Freud's belief that matter preceded and, over a great span of time, gave rise to mind. The inanimate state, being the original state, is therefore at the core of human longing. In fact, the urge to return to this earlier state of things virtually defines what Freud meant by drive.[4]

As life evolves away from its original, inanimate state, the path from life back to a longed-for death becomes increasingly complex and circuitous. The detours on the way become ever more extended and convoluted because, as Freud notes, beings seem to "develop" self-preservative instincts along the way. The life-preserving or erotic drives have not, however, always been in the service of life, because "these guardians of life, too, were originally the myrmidons of death." The new twist in evolution made higher life increasingly dynamic and conflicted, because "the hypothesis of self-preservative instincts, such as we attribute to all living beings, stands in marked opposition to the idea that instinctual life as a whole serves to bring about death."[5] This situation gives rise to an irreducible struggle in which ego drives exercise pressure toward death and sexual or erotic drives advance a prolongation of life. The primal drive or impulse toward destruction and death is engaged in eternal battle with an equally powerful drive or impulse to life.[6]

Freud believed that all psychic life was governed by the two opposing forces of Eros and Death. In *An Outline of Psychoanalysis,* he offers this analysis:

> After long hesitancies and vacillations, we have decided to assume the existence of two basic instincts, Eros and the *destructive instinct.* The aim of the first of these basic instincts is to establish ever greater unities—in short, to bind together. The aim of the second is, on the contrary, to undo connections and so to destroy things. In the case of the destructive instinct we may suppose that its final aim is to lead what is living into an inorganic state [matter]. For this reason we also call it the death instinct.[7]

Eros opens the path of love through which an ever-expanding web of relationships unfolds. This higher and wider identity takes us out of ourselves and into the world of others. Moving from body to mind to soul in search of ultimate communion, Eros is the drive to self-transcendence. It is opposed by Death, forever yearning for regression and dispersion, erosion and fragmentation. Death moves away from connection and toward a dissolved, indistinct state—a state that precedes connection or even consciousness. Freud believed the human soul was caught in the fiery struggle between these two immortal adversaries, and that this conflict generates all the difficulties we endure and suffer throughout life. These two forces transcend personal psychology. They are primordial and cosmological, and Freud referred to Eros and Death as "heavenly powers."

Freud's invocation of Eros is also a reminder that he was transliteral when he spoke of sexuality and libido, as well as when he spoke of the death drive (suggesting its expression in the myth of Narcissus). Although there is a tendency to reduce Freud to one level of meaning, particularly in his discussion of sexuality, his approach to the psyche was not reductive. He perceived a profound relationship between the commonplace experience of sexuality and the transcendent powers of cosmogonic love. This connection is made explicit in these words: "In this way the libido of our sexual instincts would coincide with the Eros of the poets and philosophers which holds all living things together."[8]

Freud insisted that understanding our sexuality was the key to understanding ourselves as human beings, and to promoting social harmony. It was also a gateway leading ultimately to understanding the sexuality pervading all of life, the cosmic sexuality of the universe. The natural evolution of libido moves our psychology from the intra-personal to the inter-personal, and finally to the trans-personal. Sexuality takes us out of ourselves, and turns us toward an ever-widening connection with others. Our continuous openness to arousal separates us from other animals, as we must learn to manage a sexuality that is nonperiodic and lifelong. Unlike other animals, we can choose when and how often we wish to engage in sexual activity.

Humans are drawn to sexual intimacy for reasons other than the biological imperative to procreate. Sex can be a way to connect, and it can also be an escape from connection. Furthermore, sexual desire does not necessarily translate into sexual activity. Arousal can be diverted or put off to a later time, a different place, or it may be sublimated into any number of passionate and creative endeavors. There are even those rare human beings who choose lifelong celibacy, and are able to live this choice without repressing the flow and vitality of Eros.

The energy of human sexuality does not demand literal sexual expression, but it does require a response. Freud understood human sexuality as a symbolic meeting place for body and soul and believed it was "connected to our capacity for metaphorical thinking, for symbolization, for mythmaking." He encouraged us to celebrate the "exuberant inventiveness, the resilience of our imagination,"9 which he believed was an outgrowth of our unique sexual nature.

The Haunted Fields of Desire

Eros seeks increase, success, growth, transformation, connection, and satisfaction, whereas Death yearns to resolve, to disperse, to erode, to numb, to remain forever in the still perfection of unchangeability. Eros seeks pleasure, and Death wishes to avoid pain. Eros seeks happiness, meaning, and fulfillment, and Death seeks relief from disappointment and despair. Whether we call them instincts or drives, both Eros and Death are faces of desire. The word "desire" etymologically conjures a place "from the stars." The numinosity of the word desire itself reminds us of the cosmic nature of both Eros and Death. Desire directs our gaze to the firmament, to the vault of heaven and back again. It threads the earthly and the divine.

We are haunted by desire. Desire fuels our lives in every domain, and desire is so adaptable that it is able to take anything as the object of its yearning. The body's hunger for food, sex, warmth, and comfort, or the heart's longing for release, for boundless compassion, and for infinite freedom are all expressions of desire. Desire can be alternately devouring and capricious. It is both insatiable and easily quieted. Desire can, in one instant, greedily plot and scheme for riches and the power to rule nations, and then momentarily settle for a hot bath, a reassuring glance, or a piece of chocolate. Wanting agitates us like a persistent itch asking to be scratched. But, although scratching does bring momentary relief, the itching grows worse as a result. We are caught in a dilemma because we cannot scratch our desires away, and we can't ignore them either.

At the center of desire, we find deprivation. To want is to lack. We do not seek what we have; we seek what we wish for. Desire is absence. Thirst occurs in the absence of water, cold in the absence of warmth, hunger in the absence of food. The clamorous voices of desire promise the world, but leave us perpetually unsatisfied and wanting. As long as

we desire, we remain dissatisfied. So desire is forever wishing for fulfillment, while remaining forever wedded to discontent.

Life and death desires are paired opposites like yes and no, stop
and go, yin and yang, on and off, and up and down. They can never be
separated, no matter how we attempt to keep them apart. Invariably,
we are torn between the two. And still, we try to hide this knowledge
from ourselves. We don't want to know the futility of our ceaseless
gyrations, don't want to see the yes within the no, the stop within the
go. Freud pierced the veil of our denial, exposing the "secret knowledge" that our agitation, our symptoms, our polymorphous perversions come from the guilt and frustration of our desires. He urged us
to look beyond our chagrin at the problem of desire itself. Bettelheim
reflects upon the impact this realization had on Freud's worldview.

> For Freud, the I was a sphere of tragic conflict. From the
> moment we are born until the moment we die, Eros and
> Thanatos struggle for dominance in shaping our lives, and
> make it difficult for us to be at peace with ourselves for any-
> thing but short periods.[10]

And yet, alongside the tragic consequences of these warring desires,
Freud believed this struggle could, if properly approached, greatly
enrich life. He urged us to resist the temptation to resolve the conflict
between Eros and Death by taking sides, because both represent "a
given direction for the soul."[11] Whereas single-minded preoccupation
with death can prevent a robust engagement with life by inciting paral-
ysis, dullness, and stagnant depression, Eros alone can lead to a repressive and frivolous pursuit of empty ambition and meaningless stimu-
lation, with sorrow and bitter disappointment as the inevitable
outcomes. Awareness of death enhances our appreciation of life and of
each precious moment. Embracing life makes the awareness of death
purposeful. Freud advocated a balanced approach to these warring
opposites. This was the basis of a "good life," a life worthy of the
struggle and strife that is inevitable.[12]

The good life forever eludes us if we persist in denying the painful
and difficult aspects of life and insist on viewing loss as an insult. Eros

must be honored in the clear light of death, and not in the shadows of its denial. The conflict between Eros and the death drive can bring forth either the best or the worst in individuals and nations, as history well illustrates. But Freud felt that, despite the dangers, these warring, primal drives endow life with its beauty and luster.

When Eros is divorced and alienated from the lure of the depths, from the drive to dissolution, individuals live in shame of their own darkness and anxiously try to keep it from surfacing. Resisting the pull of the depths, they struggle vainly to remain above them, with a feigned, plastic smile and a naive "love-and-light" persona. They become "spiritualists" who, fearing the engulfment of Earth, try to keep their feet from touching the ground. A one-sided Eros rejects and alienates the depths for fear of being swallowed by its gaping, dark mouth.

On the other hand, Death alone is a flight from, and a fear of, the higher realm. We crave darkness and dissolution. The yearning for extinction leads to regression, reduction, and fixation at the lowest level. Unable to trust the ascending current of Eros and of generative creativity, the death drive is stuck in the muck of matter, with no spark of spirit to illuminate it. Awareness and relatedness are rejected and feared; the flight of Eros plunged into quicksand. Death extinguishes itself in slumber. Eros alone represses, and Death alone regresses.

These two currents exist in all of us, and Freud found no resolution to the ongoing battle between them. He believed all humans are woefully caught between this Scylla and Charybdis. This left him rather pessimistic about the human condition. In his mind, there was no way to unite the antithetical forces of Eros and Death—to overcome their perpetual strife. There was no way out.

Unable to find or believe in a heart that can unite the ascent of Eros and the descent of Death in a dynamic spiral of redemption and transformation, Freud was like a captain on the high seas informing his crew of the exact coordinates of their location, and of their lack of a motor, sail, or paddle with which to reach home. The only alternative left: Make the most of life at sea, until you die.

Love and Death

Love is essentially elegiac. Orgasm is a "little death." Death and dissolution of boundaries are common themes in most tales of romantic love. It seems that sacrifice and surrender serve the release of love's power. William Blake honored the mysterious relationship between love and letting go when he said, "He who binds to himself a joy does the winged life destroy. He who kisses the joy as it flies lives in eternity's sunrise." Love is fulfilled in letting go and setting free. Despite Freud's insistence that Eros and Death irremediably oppose each other, there are clues in his own work suggesting that the relationship between love and death is more entwined and more enigmatic than he allowed.

Because pleasure appears to peak when excitation is kept as low as possible, Freud concluded that all living substance longs to extinguish itself and return to the slumbering silence of the inorganic world. He advanced a theory suggesting that the desire for pleasure serves the death drive because the greatest pleasure we know is the pleasure of sexual arousal, which, culminating in orgasm, brings momentary extinction of excitation. On the basis of this observation, Freud concluded that, "the pleasure principle seems actually to serve the death instincts."[13]

While it is easy to follow the thread of Freud's logic here, it seems he may have jumped to his conclusion. Although in literal, physical terms, death is the end, in Psyche's terms, it is, in fact, a turning point. Psyche's necessary descent to Death is not the end of the tale. It marks a crossroad in a journey leading to a more complete and generative union with Eros. The "winged life" praised by Blake can be likened to the winged butterfly that is Psyche, or the winged Eros, or both. It follows, then, that death, or letting go, serves love and renewed life. If so, only a love that can forfeit itself is a love congruent with the necessities of Psyche or Eros. I believe it is worth recalling some of the key elements in Apuleius' tale of Psyche and Eros, the myth Freud felt best represented the call to soul at the heart of depth psychology.

Eros loves Psyche, and lacks Psyche. Psyche loves Eros and lacks Eros. The lack in each of them initially draws them together, and later causes a rupture in their bond. And yet, although flawed and incomplete, this fractured union ultimately propels each of them to become fully themselves. Neither Psyche nor Eros is fully embodied as Soul and Love until they marry at the end of the tale. Their sacred union comes about after betrayal, suffering, sacrifice, and ultimately death enter the picture. Psyche's incorporation of death is actually a climactic and pivotal moment in the story, not the conclusion.

After successfully completing the first three nearly impossible tasks given to her by an envious and vengeful Aphrodite, Psyche is given a fourth task—the riskiest of all. Psyche must descend to the Underworld and obtain Persephone's beauty casket for Aphrodite. This casket contains beauty unknown to the senses—a beauty known only to death. This is, then, the ultimate challenge of soul making, a conscious incorporation of death and destruction into flesh and bone. The ever-upward effulgence of Eros must be combined with the ever downward, eternal beauty of Persephone—Death.

It is Psyche—or Soul—that connects the invisible world of death with the visible world of outer forms. Destruction and death are not repressed, nor are they the adversaries of love. Quite the contrary. Psyche consciously and willingly encounters and incorporates death in order to mature as a soul. Her meeting with death precedes, by necessity, her conscious union with Eros. The soul can, and does in the case of Psyche herself, find a way to bring together the seemingly irreconcilable opposites of Eros and Death. Death does not distance Psyche from Eros. It brings her back to him with a wholeness she lacked before. Freud did not believe that a reconciliation of opposites was possible, and yet the myth of Psyche and Eros affirms the possibility.

The myth also speaks of the place of pleasure in psychic life, which Freud, as I mentioned earlier, put in service of death. In the words of the story: "Thus did Psyche with all solemnity become Amor's bride, and soon a daughter was born to them: in the language of mortals she is called Pleasure."[14] Using the lens of this myth, it seems that pleasure does not serve death at all. Psyche passes through the narrow portal of death on her journey of awakening to herself and to a sanctified union with Eros. It is from this union that Pleasure is born. Pleasure does not serve death. Pleasure is the generative expression, the offspring of a soul fulfilled in love.

The Alchemy of Sublimation

One cannot speak of Freud's drive/desire theory and its implications for individuals and society without also speaking of sublimation, because desire, its modification and transformation, is at the heart of sublimation. Sublimation is unique to humans, and it highlights a fundamental distinction between human and animal desires. A metaphor drawn from physics, sublimation refers to the transformation of a solid into a gas, as in the melting of dry ice. This ingenious metaphor is particularly apt, because sublimation is in essence the evaporation of the sensuous physical body into the subtle energy body, of base animal urges into refined human desire, of action into language, of the literal and concrete into the metaphorical and imaginal. Sublimation transforms the desire to kill into a desire to compete, conquer, and defeat; the desire to groom and clean into a desire to make ourselves or another beautiful; the desire to satisfy hunger into a desire to dine and feast; the desire to copulate into a desire to make love. Sublimation transforms a mating call into courtship and poetry.

Sublimation is the transformation, individually and socially, of animal tooth and claw into human ambition and striving. It turns animal submission into human restraint and remorse. It takes grief or rage or fear and turns it into art, music, or dance. Through sublimation, children learn to renounce the instant gratification of the body for the delayed gratification of future achievement and reward. Desire for immediate gratification and sensuous pleasure, once sublimated, becomes desire for future goals like academic excellence, marriage and family, accumulating wealth, or for meaning, purpose, and spiritual maturation. Sublimation allows transcendence of limited identification with the physical body. It transforms the raw *prima materia* of desire. It is a form of alchemical magic.

On Narcissism

It was not Freud, but Havelock Ellis and Paul Nacke, who introduced the term "narcissism" in the late 19th century. Freud believed that the human psyche was narcissistic by nature and that, although narcissistic impulses could be sublimated into prosocial actions, narcissism always remained active within the unconscious of the individual. He writes, "Narcissism is the universal and original state of things, from which object-love is only later developed, without the narcissism necessarily disappearing on that account."[15] Even when an individual is able to invest libido in another, those others "represent, as it were, emanations of the libido which remain with his ego and which can be withdrawn into it."[16] The narcissistic store of libido was also described as desexualized eros.[17]

At birth, Freud claimed, sexual drives serve the drives of the ego, or the drive for self-preservation. In normal development, individuals gradually develop love for others and, in the process, forfeit a portion of their own narcissism. Thereafter, they depend on the love of another for their own self-regard. The more we love others, the more we depend on them to uphold our ego needs. "It is only when a person is completely in love," he remarked, "that the main quota of libido is transferred onto an object and the object to some extent takes the place of the ego."[18] This led Freud to conclude that loving others weakens the ego and lowers self-regard, whereas being loved enriches the ego and increases self-regard. Some individuals, however, do not succeed in diverting their ego-libido to others. Instead, they retreat to an earlier state of being the love object for themselves, thereby developing a narcissistic disorder—a disorder in which they are in love with themselves.

Freud suggested that when children's ability to love others is damaged, they naturally withdraw that love back into themselves. To elucidate this type of response, he used the withdrawal from others commonly experienced during illness as an example saying, "so long as he suffers, he ceases to love."[19] If you suffer a toothache, the world recedes into the background and your awareness narrows to the pain in your tooth. Pain concentrates energy, and energy gathers around pain. Freud described narcissism as a psychological condition in which our libido lodges in us, in the same way that energy gathers and builds around a toothache. Narcissistic people are stuck on themselves, and everywhere seek others as mirrors in which to admire and woo their own images.

This ego-centered condition creates a painful conflict for individuals in its grip, because "a strong egoism is a protection against falling ill, but in the last resort we must begin to love in order to not fall ill, and we are bound to fall ill if, in consequence of frustration, we are unable to love."[20] Narcissists are possessed of a love that makes them ill, not well. Their love for themselves is alienating and toxic, and Freud warned of its horribly crippling consequences. Bettelheim remarks on this, saying, "He knew that caring for oneself is self-defeating, that it alienates one from others and from the real world, and eventually from oneself, too. Narcissus, who looked only at his own reflection, lost touch with humanity, even his own."[21]

A Critique of Freud's Theory of Narcissism

Karen Horney was a savvy and pioneering woman who completed her training as a psychoanalyst in Europe during Freud's life. Her insights into Freud's theories draw upon her deep immersion in the study of psychoanalysis, without sacrificing her capacity to think for herself. She was not afraid to stand apart, even when it was professionally risky to do so. I include her critique of Freud's theory of narcissism because I find her assessment to be both relevant and perspicacious. Her ideas about narcissism bridge the worlds of psychoanalytic theory and Buddhist thought regarding the development of wisdom and compassion.

Freud claimed that self-inflation originated in self-love, and that narcissists are incapable of loving others because they love themselves too much. If one accepts Freud's argument that narcissism is an infatuation with the self, then "on this basis it is conclusive indeed to regard egocentricity as an expression of self-love and also to regard normal self-esteem and ideals as its desexualized derivatives."[22] Horney, however, strongly disagrees with Freud's conclusions, saying that "a person with narcissistic trends is alienated from self as well as from others, and hence to the extent that he is narcissistic he is incapable of loving either himself or anyone else."[23] Narcissism is not, in any way, a condition of excessive self-esteem. It develops when self-esteem has withered and atrophied; it is a neurotic and destructive way of coping with inadequate love. The ghost of admiration so desperately pursued by the narcissist is a defense against an intolerable inner emptiness.

Self-inflation and the craving for undue admiration co-exist in a narcissistic character. The question is: What causes some to aggrandize themselves? "The factor which contributes most fundamentally to the development of narcissistic trends," Horney concludes, "appears to be the child's alienation from others, provoked by grievances and fears. His positive emotional ties with others become thin; he loses the capacity to love."[24] Self-aggrandizement conceals painful feelings of inadequacy and nothingness. When we fear invisibility and feel deeply unloved, self-inflation becomes a compensatory gesture.

Such self-inflation is not a withdrawal from others, as Freud inferred; it is actually a misguided attempt to have positive relations with others. Narcissists are trying to have positive relations with others by appearing to be what they believe others will respect and admire. Incapable of affirming their own value, they look to others to affirm their worth, and are always terrified that they will be found lacking. At their core, narcissists believe they are impostors who will one day be discovered for the nobodies they are. Sometimes, this fear is so overwhelming it overshadows grandiosity, and in place of grandiosity individuals feel condemned to a state of unreality and personal emptiness. In this state, nothing feels real, not themselves and not others.

Although most people depend on others to some extent for a sense of self-worth, for the narcissist, nothing else matters. The gnawing and torturous desire for approval is tragically mixed with a deep mistrust of others. And because they do not believe others really will love them, narcissists substitute a different kind of attention for love. Admiration replaces love and, adding insult to injury, they look for admiration from others for qualities they do not, in their own hearts, believe they possess. Whatever admiration they do receive does not provide real sustenance, because they know others are admiring a false front, an empty image.

The grandiose posturing of the narcissist is a paper tiger. It lacks any real foundation. It is flimsy and easily punctured. It is all pretense and psychic pain.

Alienation can never be the basis for genuine self-esteem, and narcissists are fundamentally alienated, not only from others but from themselves. Nevertheless, their alienation does not bring about withdrawal, as suggested by Freud. "On the contrary," Horney contends, "a person with pronounced narcissistic trends, though incapable of love, nevertheless needs people as a source of admiration and support."[25] Whereas Freud placed self-love and other-love on a continuum, with love of self at one end and love of others at the other end, Horney persuasively counters that our capacity to love others and our capacity to love ourselves are not opposite poles, but concentric circles. Narcissism is, therefore, not an expression of self-love but of self-alienation. In reality, "self-esteem and self-inflation are mutually exclusive."[26]

Horney is also critical of Freud's focus on biological and instinctual factors when developing his theories, and his failure to explore the influence of sociological factors. Narcissistic tendencies, she contends, "are not the derivative of an instinct, but represent a neurotic trend."[27] This trend does not develop in a vacuum. Horney suggests that we must look beyond instincts to factors in the culture prompting narcissism. She notes several. The first of these is the growing fear and hostility pervading contemporary culture, leading to increased social alienation. Another factor is the collective standardization of thoughts, feelings, and behaviors, resulting in an inhibition of spontaneity. If people are continually holding their authentic selves back in order to comply with social norms, they can't feel love and acceptance for who they are. This causes individuals to become mistrustful of who they are, and to believe they are only valued for how well they follow the rules. Alienation from the self is further exacerbated by another factor: the excessive importance that is placed on what people do and not who they are. The combination of these factors creates a climate that, according to Horney, has contributed to a proliferation of narcissism.

A Buddhist Footnote

Since Freud's time, psychology has included "healthy" narcissism and "pathological" narcissism in its vocabulary. This means we have to some degree accepted Freud's view that love for self and love for others exist along a continuum, and that a certain quantity of self-absorption, self-ishness, and self-interest are healthy and normal. Pathological narcissism, on the other hand, describes a self-absorption that exceeds the normal, socially acceptable range. An excess of self-absorption is considered an aberration, and is diagnosed as a mental illness.

In the Buddhist view, self-involvement, selfishness, or narcissism—by whatever name it is called—causes our every suffering; there is no healthy amount of it. Whatever amount of it we have, we will suffer to that degree. Because we perceive the self as an independent and absolute entity, we believe we can best care for this self by fulfilling its selfish desires. We are blind to the fact that this approach arises from, and fosters, an illusion and will inevitably generate more suffering. We do not see that the self can never be fulfilled in the ways we hope to fulfill it, because it doesn't exist in the way we imagine. Mark Epstein, a practicing Buddhist and a psychiatrist, comments on what psychology might gain by looking to Buddhist insights regarding the self and its narcissistic tendencies. He says, "Yet, Buddhism has something essential to teach contemporary psychotherapists: it long ago perfected a technique of confronting and uprooting human narcissism, a goal that Western psychotherapy has only recently begun even to contemplate."[28]

The Buddhist antidote for the chronic misapprehension of the self is wisdom. Wisdom shatters the illusion of an independent self by revealing the truth of interdependent origination. Compassion, then, is the antidote for the self-absorption that comes about as a result of our chronic misapprehension of self. Selfishness and compassion are antithetical and opposite. To whatever degree we generate compassion, the stranglehold of selfishness will diminish in kind. Compassion frees us from the pain of our misguided egocentric strivings. It rests upon a clear analysis of the facts of existence, the development of a keen moral compass, and a renunciation of a selfishness based in ignorance in favor of kinship based in reality. When such compassion is coupled with wisdom, it can uproot the narcissism haunting the lives of living beings.

Alone and Together

Freud thought a great deal about the relationship between the psychology of the individual and the development of civilization. He concluded that there was an irremediable antagonism between the demands of individual instinctive life and the increasing restraints of modern social life. Although he acknowledged that such restrictions were the building blocks for many of the great accomplishments of civilization, he also observed that these same restrictions placed a great burden on instinctive human nature. The effort to conform to social norms produces an excess of guilt and anxiety, as individuals strain to keep repressed drives from asserting themselves. Civilization and its requirements were responsible, according to Freud, for the prevalence of neuroses he discovered in his office in Vienna. Pervasive uneasiness and malaise are the price paid for reaping the rewards of culture.

Christine Downing describes Freud's insights regarding the dual function of civilization and culture. "Society is based on love *and* our fear and hatred of others. We want and resent society; it fulfills and frustrates us; we accept it and rebel against it; part of us adapts to the restrictions it demands, part doesn't."[29] Freud understood that the underpinnings of civilization and communal existence were two-fold—libidinal, erotic attachments coupled with the need to restrain human aggression. He remarked that, "the meaning of civilization is that which exists to protect men against nature and to adjust their mutual relations."[30]

The death drive as pitiless adversary of Eros, forever undermining the movement to greater and greater unities within family, society, and humanity, in fierce conflict with Eros' striving to ward off death and dissolution, was the drama Freud observed through the lens of communal life. Civilization depends upon, and is an outgrowth of, Eros; yet the death drive eternally challenges and opposes it. Civilization is humanity's heroic attempt to rein in its aggressive instincts, and "civilized man has exchanged a portion of his possibilities for happiness for a portion of security."[31] The presence of the death drive is not conspicuous, however. It operates silently and insidiously until conditions conducive to its expression ripen. Then it unleashes its fury and cataclysmic power, doing all it can to thwart the impulses of Eros. Civilization came to represent for Freud the struggle between Eros and Death, because civilization magnifies the titanic battle of life itself. To Freud "this struggle is what all life essentially consists of."[32]

Given the unending struggle of existence, Freud asked himself, "What do people demand of life?" People must be expecting or wanting something from life that eludes them and causes them to suffer. What is it? Without hesitation, Freud answered his own query. "The answer to this can hardly be in doubt. They strive after happiness; they want to become happy and remain so."[33] The wish for happiness spawns a two-fold effort, the seeking of pleasure and the avoidance of pain—the efforts of Eros and Death. This is, perhaps, one of the reasons intoxication is so universally seductive. It fulfills, temporarily, both of these objectives, by anesthetizing pain and enhancing pleasure. For many, this is the extent of the relief they can imagine.

The development of the individual and the development of civilization are both characterized by the conflict between Eros and Death, because both, basically, share the same developmental stages. Civilization and individuals are essentially similar, and Freud noted this similarity saying:

> When, however, we look at the relation between the process of human civilization, and the development or educative process of individual human beings, we shall conclude without much hesitation that the two are very similar in nature, if not the very same process applied to different kinds of object.[34]

There is, however, at least one important difference between individuals and societies. The human community does not assign nearly the same value to individual happiness that individuals assign to their own happiness. Personal happiness may be sacrificed for the collective good. Individual desires may, at times, be regarded as obstructions to social betterment. The two urges—toward personal happiness and toward community and communion—require reconciliation within each individual.

Illusion or Transformation

Freud frequently wondered about the possibility of transcendence and transformation, but remained, throughout his life, unconvinced of the possibility. He did, nevertheless, engage in a brilliant and compelling probing of this issue in *Civilization and Its Discontents*. At one point, he remarked, "There is unquestionably no universal instinct towards higher development observable in the animal or plant world, even though it is undeniable that development does in fact occur in that direction."[35] The urge of human beings for higher development is, according to Freud, actually a function of instinctual repression, a repression that represents the most precious achievement of human civilization. Here again we find Freud insisting that all transformation is no more than the successful sublimation of repressed lower instincts. Acknowledging the longing for wholeness, Freud describes it as a religious attitude that is, at its core, an expression of infantile wishes. "The origin of the religious attitude can be traced back in clear outlines as far as the feeling of infantile helplessness."[36]

Given his belief that genuine transformation of lower energy is not possible, it follows that, under the right conditions, our latent destructive instincts will emerge as powerfully as ever. The energy of Eros conjoined with repression take on the appearance of an "instinct towards perfection." This, however, is illusory. There is nothing more to it. Freud acknowledges that it may be difficult for many to accept this, but he insists this is because of the stubborn hold of our illusions and the longing for "infantile" fusion, not because people may have a deeper than conscious awareness of an innate purity that underlies and precedes all other identity. For Freud, this possibility, however appealing it may be, is simply not supportable.

It may be difficult, too, for many of us, to abandon the belief that there is an instinct towards perfection at work in human beings, which has brought them to their present high level of intellectual achievement and ethical sublimation and which may be expected to watch over their development into super-men. I have no faith, however, in the existence of any such internal instinct and I cannot see how this benevolent illusion is to be preserved.[37]

"Love," he tells us, is "one of the foundations of civilization," and yet love also creates a problematic dependence for individuals on their love object. Inevitably, we suffer the pain of loss, separation, or death. It is for this reason, Freud says, that the wise men of every age warned against relying on a love object. Such reliance is most unstable, and actually dangerous to the psychological well-being of those involved. On the other hand, a tiny minority of people are able to find happiness along the path of love, as a result of "far-reaching mental changes in the function of love."[38]

Individuals achieve this rarefied state by focusing their attention on loving others and not on being loved by others. In doing so, they find that loving others brings a level of fulfillment that is usually experienced only through the love of others for them. For these rare individuals, loving others becomes a source of happiness. They are not subject to the devastation of losing their love object, because their love is directed, not to one or two individuals, "but to all men alike."[39] This type of love, unlike ordinary love, is stable and capable of embracing all of humanity. Freud describes the inner workings of this unusual attitude, and its capacity for bringing transcendent or object-free love.

> What they bring about in themselves in this way is a state of evenly suspended, steadfast, affectionate feeling, which has little external resemblance any more to the stormy agitation of genital love . . . . Perhaps St. Francis of Assisi went furthest in thus exploiting love for the benefit of an inner feeling of happiness.[40]

This kind of love becomes possible when the sharp distinction between ego and its objects is lessened. Freud does not hold much hope for humanity to rise to this level of loving, but he does acknowledge that, "this readiness for a universal love of mankind and the world represents the highest standard which man can reach."[41] Immediately following this statement, as if to take it back or diminish its impact, Freud strings together a scathing litany of objections to his own view. In an effort to disabuse people of their illusions, he walks us through the fraught and guilt-inducing territory of such universal love. And to finish the job, he follows this up with a whopping punch to the solar plexus concerning the menace of human aggression. This portion of Freud's writing is a disturbing and poignant demonstration of the struggle Freud was having with this subject. The retrospective eye provides an arresting vantage point from which to view Freud straining to make sense of evil, treachery, and the growing cloud of darkness in the world.

The first problem with this kind of love, according to Freud, is that it lacks discrimination and is therefore an injustice to the other who is loved. There is nothing special about being loved by someone who loves everyone; in fact, it renders the love rather meaningless. Moreover, he says that "not all men are worthy of love."[42] Clearly, Freud did not believe love was a birthright, but a gift that must be earned, a reward of which people must be worthy. Who is it, then, that decides the worth of another, and whether another is "worthy" of love? How is one who is deprived of love, and therefore struggling with how to love, ever to become worthy? And how does denying someone love do anything more than reinforce and perpetuate an already painful situation, not to mention tightening the knot around our own hearts? These are but a few of the many questions that come to mind, but Freud had his own response to these concerns.

Freud advances two criteria for worthiness. The first is that an individual must be like me in important ways, so I can see myself in him or her and therefore love that person as myself. The other worthy candidate for my love is an individual possessing traits I admire, and I can then love this person as one who is a representative of an ideal to which I aspire myself. It is worth mentioning here that, in my later discussion of the lojong, it will be made clear that, through analysis and contemplation, you can come to see all living beings within the very categories Freud outlines here. Through the lojong, loving others becomes a natural expression of our relationship with them and likeness to them, and as our feelings of love and compassion encompass more and more beings, the force of our compassion increases exponentially.

This, however, is certainly not Freud's view. He strikes a blow at the heart of such lofty notions, especially the axiom: "Thou shalt love thy neighbor as thyself," which he calls both a defense against aggression and a guilt-inducing ideal. Individuals trying to live up to such standards face inevitable failure, because Freud contends that such an attitude is humanly impossible. Moreover, such striving only intensifies anguish and shame. On the one hand, Freud recognizes that Eros betrays its infinitely expansive nature when it is narrowed to the love between two human beings. Eros is naturally given to greater and greater unities and ever-growing connections. This purpose is truncated when love is restricted. Nevertheless, Freud believes we must put a limit on it. Universal love worked for St. Francis, he admits, but it remains utterly unrealistic, impractical, and undesirable for the rest of us. And the idea of extending one's love to a stranger is not only implausible; it is unacceptable.

Freud makes the startling proclamation that a stranger is not only unworthy of his love generally speaking, but "has more claim to my hostility and even my hatred."[43] He then presents the "logic" behind his position. It goes something like this. Strangers have no regard for me, and what's more they are all too willing to injure me if it serves their ambition. A stranger thinks nothing of slandering me, jeering at me, insulting and physically harming me. Why then would I "love" that stranger? Reading Freud's description of the stranger, I felt a welling sadness for his tragic pessimism masquerading as realism, and for the scars of prejudice and persecution that had so clearly left their mark.

The lack of discrimination Freud demonstrates concerning the difference between genuine love and compassion and the "idiot" version of these states is also quite striking. Normally, Freud was capable of trenchant observation, but the dark times he lived in seem to have overwhelmed his remarkable capacity for critical thought. He appears, to borrow Jung's term, to be caught in a complex. Phrases such as "tough love" make the point that love can at times require strong measures. Fierceness can also be found among the many faces of love. Freud left no room for this. In his view, loving a stranger necessarily meant approving of and submitting to their slanderous cruelty and their violent blows.

I am reminded of a Sufi tale in which a poisonous snake has a village in terror's clutch because it has bitten and killed many of its inhabitants. Everyone feared being its next victim, or worse yet, losing a child to the snake's deadly venom. One day, a sage came through the village and, hearing of the snake, looked for him and found him at the edge of town. They sat together for some time and nobody knew what was said, but following their conversation, the snake gave up his biting ways. Some months later, the sage passed through this village again and found the snake lying on the side of the road, mangled, battered, and bruised. "What has happened to you, my friend?" the sage inquired. "Well," the snake moaned, "as soon as the village people realized I was no longer a danger to them, they began abusing me in the worst way. Children take pleasure in taunting and torturing me. It surely won't be long now before one of them kills me. How could I have ever agreed to such a miserable fate?" "I am sorry, dear snake," the sage replied. "Perhaps I should have been clearer. It is true I advised you not to bite, but I never meant for you not to hiss."

Freud believed civilization and humanity would be forever in conflict, because civilization invariably confines human drives. He was especially concerned about the innate aggressive drive overwhelming the drive to love. He says, "I adopt the standpoint, therefore, that the inclination to aggression is an original self-subsisting instinctual disposition in man, and I return to my view that it constitutes the greatest impediment to civilization."[44] Freud's concern over a landslide victory for human aggression is made clear in these chilling remarks:

> The element of truth behind all this, which people are so ready
> to disavow, is that men are not gentle creatures who want to be
> loved, and who at the most can defend themselves if they are
> attacked; they are, on the contrary, creatures among whose

instinctual endowments is to be reckoned a powerful share of aggressiveness. As a result, their neighbor is for them not only a potential helper or sexual object, but also someone who tempts them to satisfy their aggressiveness on him, to exploit his capacity for work without compensation, to use him sexually without his consent, to seize his possessions, to humiliate him, to cause him pain, to torture and to kill him. *Homo homini lupus.*[45]

A cruel and aggressive streak "reveals man as a savage beast to whom consideration toward his own kind is something alien." Freud felt this truth was self-evident, and that anyone reviewing the atrocities of recent as well as distant history would "bow humbly before the truth of this view."[46]

A Critique of Freud's Destructive Instinct

Freud never actually observed infant behavior. He based his theory of a destructive instinct, as he did many of his other theories, on the retrospection of adults. Freud noted that, in the earliest "oral" stage, an infant's tendency is to incorporate an object, thereby annihilating it. In the "anal" stage, an infant's tendency is to overpower and gain control over the object. It is only at the "genital" stage that love and hatred emerge as paired opposites. This led Freud to conclude that "hatred is at the bottom of all relations of affection and love between human beings . . . . Hatred in relation to objects is older than love."[47] It is also true that Freud vacillated on this issue, sometimes suggesting that love precedes hatred, and that hatred is an instinctive response to anything that interferes with love. In either case, he saw hatred as both instinctual and innate, and believed one could never be free of it.

Horney, sounding a bit like the Dalai Lama, questions whether Freud has any proof for his assertions concerning the innate nature of the aggressive drive. She doesn't believe there is evidence to support his conclusion. She contends that hostility always has a reason behind it and, if there is a reason for hostility, there is no basis for positing an innate destructive drive. Horney gives examples from her analytic practice to challenge the theory of innate hostility. Although it is true that patients often express hostility toward their analysts that is clearly disproportionate relative to the encounter taking place in the room, Horney argues that the hostility is, in fact, in direct proportion to the degree of threat and danger inwardly perceived by the patient. The degree of hostility expressed is in proportion to the analyst's behavior, not as it actually is, but as it is subjectively experienced. As the patient's subjective perception of threat lessens, so does the aggression.[48]

Analysts who accept an innate death drive may argue that a person's masochistic tendencies are expressed in the guise of greater self-assertion, which is an "aim-inhibited expression of the destruction instinct." Horney objects to this view, however, saying that it flatly and without valid cause denies the possibility of positive self-assertion, as well as the possibility of a constructive attitude toward life and the self. The destructive drive does not, as Freud envisioned, serve death—it serves life. Our wish to destroy is our wish to protect ourselves; it is for the sake of life, for the sake of wished-for happiness, and not for the sake of destruction itself.

> If we want to injure or kill, we do so because we feel endangered, humiliated, abused . . . That is, if we wish to destroy, it is in order to defend our safety, or our happiness, or what appears to us as such. Generally speaking, it is for the sake of life and not for the sake of destruction.[49]

Unless analysts distinguish between these different motives, they tend to interpret every critical or outspoken word on the part of the patient as a form of subversive hostility. This theory, according to Horney, is both contrary to the facts and harmful in its implications. Destructive behavior always has an inner catalyst and, therefore, cannot be considered innate. The destructive drive arises as a response to unbearable conditions within the psyche. This means that working with the underlying causes of destructive energy can facilitate transformation.

Beyond Freud to a Deeper Union

Freud journeyed a long way, through many worlds. Having looked in some depth at his work, I am astonished by his brilliance, provoked by his certitude, touched by his pain, inspired by his artistry, acutely aware of his complex humanity, and deeply moved by his extraordinary and perduring work. I have developed a greater appreciation for the lineage of depth psychology to which he is so integral, and of which I am a part.

Freud devoted his life to contemplating the pain and struggle characterizing so much of human life, giving us a map and a vocabulary by which to understand it. He shattered our frozen and anxious denial and brought the bright light of awareness—Psyche's lamp—to all spheres of human experience. Having said this, I am also keenly aware of the borders Freud did not cross, and of the places he did not, and could not, go. His vision did not extend to a reality beyond the dramatic, dualistic play of Death and Eros. He was unable to consider that a descent to death might ultimately be a descent to love, in which even the moldering earth is embraced as a radiant manifestation of spirit. He was unable to imagine that ascent and Eros could be an embrace of the empty nature of existence of which all things are a manifestation.

Tibetan Buddhism travels into territory unknown to Freud. The experiential declaration of this tradition is that an integration of these cosmic forces is possible through the union of wisdom and compassion. This union is grounded in an understanding of impermanence, transience, and decay, but arises nevertheless to embrace life and all living beings with the infinite fullness of an empty heart. The heart can contain and transcend all opposites. This is where Freud leaves off and the Buddha enters. Therein lies my conviction that depth psychology is calling for a deeper union of heart and soul, and that the practices of Buddhism have a great deal to offer here.

Freud was skeptical of an evolutionary impulse. He denounced as illusory the possibility of freedom from suffering or of great compassion. The Buddha clearly disagreed. It is not unrealistic or impractical to challenge preconceptions about the self and to work toward developing love and compassion far beyond the limited scope of convention and social norms. It is, in fact, the most realistic and practical thing we can ever do. Nothing serves individual life and liberty more, and nothing provides a sounder basis for civilization.

Chapter 4

CARL JUNG:
THE COURAGE TO BE ONESELF

■   ■   ■

The ultimate questions of psychotherapy are not a private matter—
they represent a sublime responsibility.

−C. G. JUNG

arl Jung's work in several areas relates to the subject of compassion and love. In this chapter we will review Jung's writings on the alchemical nature of transference, the transcendent function and its connection to the psychological goal of individuation, the integration of the shadow, and the relationship between individual and societal transformation. Given Jung's synthetic approach, these subjects are intimately connected in his work. Furthermore, the emphasis on *telos* (or aim), which infuses all aspects of his work, adds layers of meaning and intent to his discussion of these subjects.

The shadow and its integration are particularly germane to a discussion of love and compassion. Shadow work requires a willingness to lower the many veils of pretense and denial and see ourselves with unflinching honesty. This process, which can be both painful and humiliating, requires not only overcoming reactivity and self-deception, but generating love and compassion for our weaknesses and inadequacies and for our hidden cruelties as well. Love and compassion for ourselves and for our rejected and broken places thus becomes the firm foundation upon which we can extend love and compassion to others.

Alchemical Transference

When Freud asked Jung what he thought of his theory of the transference, Jung was quick to respond that transference is the "alpha and omega of the analytical method."[1] Jung later diverged from Freud's primarily reductive and regressive views on the transference, but he never stopped emphasizing the importance of the transference as an intersubjective process in service of individual, and ultimately social, transformation.

The transference is a phenomenon in which unconscious contents are projected—like the gushing of an underground spring—upon persons and situations. Some of these projections are quickly withdrawn back into the individual, as spring water recedes back into earth, but other projections resist reintegration. Within the analytic setting, the free-floating, unintegrated contents of the unconscious attach themselves to the analyst in the form of transference. As a result, the analyst becomes directly and intimately aware of the nature of the patient's suffering and this promotes deeper connection and caring. Jung comments on the development of this sympathetic link saying, "The patient then means something to him personally, and this provides the most favorable basis for treatment."[2] The transfer of unconscious contents from patient to analyst may seem an unwelcome prospect, but Jung viewed it as an indispensable form of communication. Analysts, as a result of experiencing the influence of their patients' inner worlds, are far better able to help them with the integration of emerging unconscious material.

Generally, projection precedes awareness. It takes a great deal of practice and skill to become aware of unconscious contents without projection, "for as a rule the unconscious first appears in projected form."[3] Unconscious material, when projected, can become like a mirror into which we look to see our own reflection. The challenge, in the case of projection, is in knowing it is *our* reflection we see. Otherwise we run the risk of becoming like Narcissus, gazing at his own reflection and not knowing it is himself he sees. The awareness of the analyst mitigates this risk. Analysts know they are receiving the unconscious reflection of their patients; they can, therefore, help them recognize the face in the mirror as their own.

Over time, Jung came to see the transference less as a specifically psychotherapeutic tool and increasingly as a paradigm for relationship in general. He did not limit the transference phenomenon to the consulting room; we are in transference relationship wherever and whenever we connect with others. Transference—the projection of unconscious material—is enacted in all human relationships. The thing that distinguishes the therapeutic setting from other spheres of relationship is that a patient willingly submits to the process of having transference material observed and analyzed, and the analyst willingly submits to receiving the unconscious communication, and to helping the patient integrate these unconscious elements into the personality. Extolling the tremendous benefit the transference relationship has for the patient, Jung remarked, "He is in very truth reborn from this psychological relationship, and his field of consciousness is rounded into a circle."[4]

The metaphor that Jung felt best amplified his theory of the transference and its relationship to the goal of psychological wholeness is alchemy. "Alchemy describes, not merely in general outline but often in the most astonishing detail," he pointed out, "the same psychological phenomenology which can be observed in the analysis of unconscious processes."[5] The bond between analyst and patient generates enormous transformative potential because of the alchemical interaction of unconscious contents aroused in the field of the two individuals. Jung likened the meeting between analyst and patient to the meeting between two chemical substances, saying, "When two chemical substances combine, both are altered. This is precisely what happens in the transference."[6]

Analysts open themselves voluntarily to receive the contents of their patients' unconscious. The patients' unconscious in turn activates their own unconscious, thereby establishing an unconscious link between the two and inducing a fascination in the analyst for the patient. The relationship is therefore "founded on mutual unconsciousness."[7] The magnetism of this mutual unconsciousness stimulates an impulse in the analyst to propitiate these energies, an impulse Jung described in this way: "The activated unconscious appears as a flurry of unleashed opposites and calls forth the attempt to reconcile them, so that in the words of the alchemists, the great panacea, the *medicina catholica* may be born."[8]

Jung flatly rejected Freud's assertion that the transference could be adequately explained as a form of regression. Even though the transference may contain regressive material, Jung considered this view reductive, and maintained that the transference has a *telos* at its core. Patients develop an erotic, libidinal bond with their analysts, not only to relive something, but because they are seeking something. This distinction was vitally important to Jung. It was essential that "the understanding of the transference is . . . sought not in its historical antecedents but in its purpose."[9] Transference is goal seeking, the goal being the withdrawal of projections and the integration of split-off parts into the conscious personality. Ultimately, transference serves the goal of individuation. Jung described the transcendent quality of the transference in this way:

> The transference phenomenon is without doubt one of the most important syndromes in the process of individuation; its wealth of meaning goes far beyond personal likes and dislikes. By virtue of its collective contents and symbols it transcends the individual personality and extends into the social sphere, reminding us of those higher human relationships which are so painfully absent in our present social order, or rather disorder.[10]

The alchemical text *Rosarium Philosophorum* provided Jung with both metaphor and compelling visual imagery for the phenomena of transference, individuation, and the transformative nature of the relationship between patient and analyst. Transference had long been associated with love—with its woundings and its pathos. In the ten woodcuts of the *Rosarium*, Jung found a love story that he believed precisely reflected the progressive stages of the transference relationship.

The purpose of the transference in alchemical terms is fulfilled in the mystic marriage, the *hieros gamos* or the *coniunctio*. The *coniunctio* is the culmination of the alchemical opus and depends upon opposites first being properly differentiated, and then properly integrated. An imperfect union of opposites, resulting from incomplete differentiation, is called the lesser *coniunctio*. The *coniunctio* marks the successful reconciliation and integration of fully differentiated opposites, and love is both its cause and its effect.

The images guiding us through the progressive stages leading to the *coniunctio* are not meant to be taken literally, but rather as symbolic language illustrating two "substances or 'bodies' . . . drawn together by what we call an affinity." The image of the *coniunctio* or *hieros gamos* provided Jung with visual amplification for the archetypal union of opposites. The archetype of the *coniunctio*, like all archetypes, is not derived from external conditions; it is a psychic instinct and therefore belongs to the "non-individual psyche." The non-individual, or collective, psyche "is the precondition of each individual psyche, just as the sea is the carrier of the individual wave."[11] It is not possessed by any one individual, but is nevertheless uniquely experienced by each individual. In this same manner, the archetype of the *coniunctio* is both individually experienced and collectively imprinted in the psyche.

The journey of Psyche and Eros from a relationship that falters to a marriage sanctified by the gods illustrates the distinction between the lesser and greater *coniunctio*. When first united, neither Eros nor Psyche is sufficiently differentiated. They are living a dream of unconscious fusion, a dream that is well described by the lesser *coniunctio*. This cannot last, and things inevitably fall apart. Only after both become conscious of their unique individuality can the higher union, the *hieros gamos*, take place. This shift occurs when the knot of fearful, conditioned love loosens and the heart risks opening further. One of the ways I imagine this shift is as a movement from the lesser "falling in love" to the greater "standing in love."

Falling in love opens new worlds. When we fall in love, we touch the unconditioned, the basic openness of our being. But not trusting this openness, we grasp. Grasping at passion dishonors and cripples its basic nature, leaving it without the breath of inspiration. To fall in love is easy, and to fall out of love equally so. Such love can take shape and then, in a moment, dissolve, like a castle made of sand. It cannot endure. To stand in love amid storm and confusion is the true crucible of Eros and Psyche. Standing in love challenges our inclination to run from adversity and reject discomfort. Standing in love, we do not split apart when the wind picks up; we stand steadfast like the willow, fluid and bending, but not easily broken.

Standing in love also means submitting to, bearing, or enduring love's travails. The apostle Paul said, "love bears all things." Standing in love means we bear witness; we "behold" the full spectrum of life. Standing together, Eros and Psyche bind the opposites—ascent and descent, abduction and deliverance, sublime and mundane, alone and together, mortal and deathless. This union of heaven and earth finds unique expression in the human form. With heads positioned heaven-ward on upright spines and feet firmly planted on the earth, our magnificent bodies hint at the potential for the union of opposites for which our souls yearn. Tolerating the tension of ascending and descending currents by standing in love invites transformation.

Transference, as envisioned by Jung, is ultimately a sacrament of the heart, much like the act of standing in love. Unmasking us, exposing us, rubbing us raw, leeching our wounds, challenging our cherished self-image, it all the while brings us into contact with what is most foreign, most strange, and most compelling—the unknown. Unless we are willing to risk journeying into the unknown, the transference relationship can never lead to love. The choice is ours. We can cling to familiar ground or choose to proceed beyond it.

The goal of the transference is neither the transference itself, nor its historical antecedents. It is the transformative power generated when two individuals enter into alchemical relationship. The healing power of such a relationship is not, by any means, limited to analyst and patient. The therapeutic relationship is one among many possibilities. Any transformative relationship can be a lens through which we see our lives anew. Such relationship opens the way for love, in part by unearthing the debris of treasured old habits and exposing the mess of countless shattered mirrors scattered about like wounded soldiers in a bloody battlefield. A great Sufi master evocatively described the perils and promise of such a path saying, "The path of love is like a bridge of hair over a chasm of fire."

Essentially, the analytic relationship and the entire therapeutic endeavor is an effort to help the patient gain or regain a capacity for love. Transference serves this aim. The sealed vessel of analysis protects and contains the process of transformation, while simultaneously putting the contents under pressure. This both allows chaos and creates it. Chögyam Trungpa often remarked that, contrary to what we may think, "Chaos is good news." In myth, Eros is born of Chaos. Perhaps Eros is the good news Chaos brings into the world, and into the therapy room. Together Eros and Chaos shake up our self-centering habit, challenging us to include the other, not only in imagination and dream, but in the flesh, blood, and sinew of real relationship.

Two elements commingle in the therapeutic relationship—the two individuals in the room. This, more than anything else, influences the course and outcome of treatment. Although Jung focused primarily on the importance of the transferential relationship for the patient, he did acknowledge its implications for the analyst. If indeed the meeting between analyst and patient is like the combining of two chemical substances, therapy must transform the doctor as well as the patient in the process. Analysts cannot help patients if they are fortressed behind a wall of aloof professionalism. Quite simply, "You can exert no influence if you are not susceptible to influence."[12] Jung likened the situation of the analyst to the alchemist in the laboratory, "who no longer knew whether he was melting the mysterious amalgam in the crucible or whether he was the salamander glowing in the fire."[13]

In its early years, psychological theory and methodology conformed to medical and clinical guidelines. Jung believed psychology had outgrown its original form, including its confinement to the consulting room, saying, "What was formerly a method of medical treatment now becomes a method of self-education, and therewith the horizon of our modern psychology is immeasurably widened."[14] Widening this horizon of psychology depended upon widening the analyst's horizon, a prospect Jung anticipated would meet with much resistance. But he pointed to it nevertheless, saying, "The physician, then, is called upon himself to face that task which he wishes the patient to face."[15]

It is neither the medical diploma nor extensive training and impressive credentials that have the greatest bearing on the analytic process; it is the quality of human presence in the room. Analysts must be able to know themselves and see themselves with the same openness they ask of their patients. They must be able to work compassionately with the rejected and split-off dimensions of their own psyches if they hope to skillfully engage the rejected elements in another.

If transference is "the alpha and omega of the analytic method," then it is both *prima materia* and *lapis*, both the beginning and end of the process. The therapy of the soul, guided by love and leading to love, is the deepest *telos* of the transference. And though the meeting takes place between two people, far more than the souls of two individuals are furthered by it. Jung believed the healing power of the transference contributed to the moral and spiritual upliftment of humanity. Every healing encounter between two people, as insignificant as it may seem at the time, is "laying an infinitesimal grain in the scales of humanity's soul."[16]

Despite Jung's preoccupation with the intra-psychic aspects of psychological transformation, he readily acknowledged our innate relatedness to the world of others, and the need to actively engage this dimension of human life in order to experience wholeness.

> The unrelated human being lacks wholeness, for he can achieve wholeness only through soul, and the soul cannot exist without its other side, which is always found in a "You." Wholeness is a combination of I and You, and these show themselves to be part of a transcendent unity whose nature can only be grasped symbolically.[17]

This ground of relatedness, expressed in the transference relationship, has "an extremely important instinctive factor behind it: the kinship libido." The kinship libido is key to both the origin and the *telos* of the entire transference phenomenon. The desire to connect that is so crucial to human beings is propelled by Eros. Eros is behind the transference and it is Eros that is served in the enactment of the transference. Jung claimed that the kinship libido "wants the *human* connection," a connection that was impossible to argue away, "because the relationship to self is at once relationship to our fellow man, and no one can be related to the latter until he is related to himself."[18]

At the end of his autobiography, Jung writes movingly of a kinship that both transcends and includes human relationship. He describes an experience of relaxed self-identification that allows him to feel his profound connection to the cosmos. In words that are as inspired as they are succinct, he says: "Yet there is so much that fills me: plants, animals, clouds, day and night, and the eternal in man. The more uncertain I have felt about myself, the more there has grown up in me a feeling of kinship with all things."[19]

Holding Paradox

Our life is a collection of characteristics and habits that don't fit together neatly. Every one of us is an amalgam of idiosyncratic elements of which we are aware to different degrees. We are perpetually ambushed by the eruption of unexpected and unwanted elements within ourselves. Jung called our capacity to contain and transform all the disparate parts of ourselves the transcendent function. The transcendent function transcends the uncomfortable opposition between conscious and unconscious, between the parts we acknowledge and identify with and the parts we often don't see, or acknowledge. This function, he observes, "arises from the union of conscious and unconscious contents."[20]

The unconscious is always participating in our lives—secretly, as it were. The challenge is to bring the pervasive, hidden influence of the unconscious "other" to conscious awareness so that it may openly contribute to the dialogue. Our inability to do so not only limits our development, it prevents us from being able to hold a dialogical space with others from whom we differ. This blocks understanding and undermines communication and community, because we tend to reject and fear that which we do not understand.

The present day shows with appalling clarity how little able people are to let the other man's argument count, although this capacity is a fundamental and indispensable condition for any human community . . . . For to the degree one does not admit the validity of the other person, he denies the "other" within himself the right to exist—and vice versa. The capacity for inner dialogue is a touchstone for outer objectivity.[21]

Learning to work with the warring elements within us fosters inclusive vision, because previously incompatible elements find a way to co-exist harmoniously. Energy combines in new ways. The transcendent function "is synonymous with a progressive attitude towards a new development."[22] Life is not a neatly packaged set of certainties and absolutes despite our efforts to simplify it by making it seem so. When Jung said, "The world into which we are born is brutal and cruel, and at the same time of divine beauty,"[23] he was expressing his transcendent capacity to contain the dissonant aspects of life, and allow paradox, complexity, and unknowing.

The transcendent function can tolerate "don't know." We don't know, can't pass final and absolute judgment; we suspend certainty, allowing ambiguity and emergent meaning. This is one of the most difficult things for a human being to do. We are hard-wired to yes and no. Our brains are binary; our computers mimic brain function in this way. As we all know, there is no gray zone with a computer. If you enter a command that deviates in the slightest way from the standard, it simply doesn't work. Intention and perspective are irrelevant. What you meant to do doesn't matter to a computer. As human beings, we are capable of more, but we are biologically predisposed to a dualistic yes/no, good/bad perspective. We take sides; we want to know who's right and who's wrong. We want closure, resolution. We want to know what team we're on, and who the opponent is. We suffer from our desire for resolution and certainty, but we want it all the same.

The transcendent function is a transcendent capacity precisely because it transcends this ordinary way of functioning. We transcend the habit of favoring one side of life, without sacrificing our capacity for awareness, discrimination, and decisive action. The ability to hold paradox and simultaneously maintain intelligent discrimination is characteristic of the transcendent function. Life becomes more complex, more uncertain, and more spontaneous and creative at the same time. We no longer know if the good guys are all good and the bad guys all bad; we're not so sure if we're the best or we're the worst; we're no longer certain if we were better off when we failed miserably or when we received cheers and applause. And that not knowing is actually very liberating. Perspective and intention begin to take on enormous meaning. The story is never over; it is ever unfolding, and yesterday's crisis could well become today's gift.

There's an old Chinese fable illustrating this transcendent capacity in action. One day, a farmer's horse runs away. His neighbors, hearing of this misfortune, come over to express their sympathy, saying, "Oh, we're so sorry to hear you lost your horse! How sad. Such bad luck for you." To their surprise, the farmer responds, "Oh, I don't know. Who's to say if it's good or if it's bad?" Soon after, the horse returns, bringing with him seven wild horses. Once again, the neighbors hear this news and come to see the farmer. "Look at your good fortune. You had only one horse, and now you have eight!" Again he responds, "Who's to say if it's good or bad?" The very next day, the farmer's son attempts to ride one of the wild horses and is thrown off, badly breaking his leg. The neighbors gather to console the farmer. "Oh, how terrible this must be! Your only son, your only hand in the field, and now he won't move from his bed for months. This is horrible, horrible! We are so sorry for your bad fortune." And the farmer responds, "Well, who's to say if it's good or bad?" A few days later, the king's army comes through the village to conscript all the young men for a battle on the border. Of course, the farmer's son can't go; he has a broken leg. And once again, the neighbors come by, exclaiming, "You have such luck! Our sons all have to go to battle, but your son gets to stay home!" Of course, we know how the farmer responds to this.

The transcendent function delivers us to the threshold of not knowing, of not freezing life into premature meaning. It does not succumb to the hubris of the conceptual mind. The transcendent function initiates us into night vision, where all of our senses take part in both knowing and unknowing. It invites us into an underground stream, into the mysterious light found in dark waters, without losing the biting clarity of day. The transcendent function is starlight and daylight brought together, sometimes like dusk, other times like dawn, and still other times like something utterly fresh and new. It is rhythm and motion, particle and wave. The transcendent function upholds the radical insight that loss can bring gain, adversity can be opportunity, and upside down can be right side up.

In analysis, we initially hold this transcendent capacity on behalf of the patient, who is not yet able to do so. Analysts hold together the conflicted conscious and unconscious elements that the patient splits off from each other. In doing so, they model for their patients a new way of being that the patients, over time, can develop for themselves. In this way, the transference relationship serves the development of the transcendent function within the patient. Jung spoke of the hope patients invest in their analysts on account of this dynamic, whether or not they are conscious of doing so.[24]

As patients develop the transcendent function within themselves, they become less dependent on their analysts to uphold it on their behalf. They are, consequently, able to accept themselves and be themselves more fully. The transcendent function is a "way of attaining liberation by one's own efforts and of finding the courage to be oneself."[25]

Two comments made by Jung at the end of his autobiography beautifully convey this transcendent attitude. In the first, Jung is surveying the phenomena of life as a whole. He says, "I cannot form any final judgment because the phenomenon of life and the phenomenon of man are too vast." In the second, he is self-reflective: "I am astonished, disappointed, pleased with myself. I am distressed, depressed, rapturous. I am all these things at once, and cannot add up the sum."[26] Together, these remarks sum up Jung's open, ever-fluid, holistic approach to psychic life. The elusive, unpredictable, shape-shifting, intangible energy fluttering and darting about the transferential field was personified for Jung in alchemy "as the wily god of revelation, Hermes or Mercurius."[27] The patron saint of liars and the god of communication are united in the figure of Hermes. He is "both order and chaos, truth and falsehood, the mediator between life and death, between celestial values and terrestrial values."[28] This ambiguous and enigmatic being is endowed with both the highest spiritual qualities and a most dangerously duplicitous, devious nature. His dual nature is that of the unconscious itself. Jung described the unconscious, and the fickle and fluid one who personifies unconscious life, in this way:

> The unconscious is not just evil by nature, it is also the source of the highest good: not only dark but also light, not only bestial, semi-human, and demonic but superhuman, spiritual, and in the classical sense of the word "divine." The Mercurius who personifies the unconscious is essentially "duplex," paradoxically dualistic by nature, fiend, monster, beast, and at the same time panacea, "the philosopher's son," *sapientia Dei*, and *donum Spiritus Sancti*.[29]

Hermes/Mercurius is the connector-between-worlds. He is the celebrated and slippery psychopompos guiding us to the transcendent function and to individuation. Because of an ever-present Hermes, psychology and the psychological are always on shifty ground, forever unsettled and emergent. Hermes presides at the border regions, in no-man's land, and in all uncharted spaces between. There is no place into or out of which he cannot find his way. Crafty, clever, invisible, shimmering quicksilver, trickster Hermes is unlike any other. He can be seen trading in the back alleys of the black market, or delivering a message from the divine. Among the gods, Hermes alone travels freely between the upper world and the Underworld. He freely commutes between conscious and unconscious, between dreaming and waking, between light and shadow.

Mercurius is the divine child born of the golden egg. This philosophical egg is both the birthplace of and container for the new attitude symbolized by the alchemical goal—the union of opposites. The double eagle hatched from this egg wears the spiritual and temporal crown, a nod to the paradoxical nature of the transformation process from conception to manifestation. The golden crown is worn by one who transcends paradox—a nod to Hermes as well.

Exiling, Retrieving, and Redeeming the Shadow

Shadows, shadows everywhere! The shadow of evil empires and holy war, the shadow of bright desire, the shadow of lost love and of love that is found, the long shadow of ashes in my mother's eyes and in my father's voice when he speaks wistfully of his childhood village, the shadow of my womb both empty and full, the shadow of the righteous condemning others in the name of God, the shadow of dogma and vengeance disguised as justice, the shadow of angry gangs on the streets, and of prisons bursting with young lives. The shadow of the reasonable mind in the tangled and tortured body of the hysteric. The shadow, in this moment, on the wall behind me. The shadows dancing and playing beneath my fingers as I type away on my keyboard.

Left in the margins, on the periphery, and in the deeps, the shadow grows, gathers, rests beneath, below, behind, under, within, circling round events, thoughts, words, and flesh. The shadow, if sent off to a netherworld to brood, ruthlessly severs bone from blood. This is why, against all odds, Jung believed humanity was ethically bound to unite the seemingly irreconcilable opposites of light and shadow, bringing them face to face and finding on the distant shore of their worlds the inseparability from which they arise. Such an undertaking is difficult but necessary, because only a journey into our own darkness can bring the spark of consciousness to the lowest, most unredeemed elements of nature and deliver the uncommon jewel of life—wholeness.

It is easy to understand the lure of freedom from the burden of shadow and the reluctance to enter a realm we imagine so distant that it leaves only the faintest trace of scent and print. It took a Herculean effort to escape the dominance of unconscious life, to slay the dragon and abandon the weighty body with its endless gravity. This evolutionary achievement, according to Jung, is celebrated metaphorically in the many myths of the hero's journey that have fascinated humanity. Throughout Western history, the shadow has been imagined as monster, dragon, alien, Frankenstein, or Gorgon. The hero bravely battles with the monster of collective slumber, finally killing it—free at last—free from the tenacious claw of unconscious life, and soaring victoriously to spirit.

In Jung's three stages of individuation, the first, *unio mentalis*, is just this. The soul leaves the body and joins spirit, freeing itself from the yoke of earthly desire and longing. As a unity, soul and spirit rise above the torpor and turpitude of flesh, bringing forth the accomplishments of culture. This stage became confused with the goal itself, and a brazen enthusiasm for mastering nature and separating light from dark and heaven from earth has become the lauded hallmark of modern society. There lurks a menacing hubris in this declaration of victory over matter. It invites collision with the tooth and fang of the unconscious, making us unwitting slaves of its darkness. When the abandoned body of the hysteric entered Freud's consulting room, sending out the clarion call that constellated the entire field of depth psychology, this shadow made its presence known.

Assimilation of the shadow connects us to our animal body; it connects us to the paws and claws, the long tail and wild, soft, flesh of animal life; it connects us to the archaic in our nature; it connects us to the rejected and split-off parts of ourselves. Tending the shadow brings us into contact with pain and darkness; it is like tending a festering, neurotic sore. This festering sore is not only present in the obvious suffering and difficulties of life. As Jung suggests, "even our purest and holiest beliefs can be traced to the crudest origins."[30] And despite our reluctance to acknowledge this, Jung is unequivocal that transformation is not possible unless we become much better acquainted with our own nature.

Jung's psychology centered on his conviction that an innate impulse to wholeness exists as an *a priori* human birthright, and that fulfilling this call is "the goal of life."[31] The question for Jung was not, as it was for Freud, whether or not the impulse to wholeness exists, but whether or not one consciously activates it. The experience of wholeness is the equivalent of becoming oneself. Individuation, or wholeness, comes about by means of integrating conscious and unconscious processes, beginning with the shadow. Incorporating the shadow establishes a dynamic, magnetic, gravitational, erotic field—an ensouled body.

The Sufis tell of a man who was so virtuous that the angels offered him the gift of miracles. They offered him the gift of healing hands, the ability to read minds, the gift of flight, and many others. He refused them all. Finally, they insisted that he choose, or they would choose for him. "Very well," he replied. "I ask that I may be able to do great good in the world without myself or anyone else knowing it." The angels granted this request by deciding that every time the saint's shadow was cast behind him, it would have the power to heal illness, to comfort the inconsolable, and to bring joy in place of sorrow. Wherever he walked, his shadow caused dried rivers to flow, withered plants to flower, and brought gladness to the hearts of men, women, and children. The saint simply went about his life, and all this happened in his wake. After a time, his name was forgotten, and he was simply called the "Holy Shadow."

Although our conscious, reasonable minds are convinced nothing of value can possibly be found in the dung heap of our darkness, we need only recall the name of Ploutos, or Pluto, Lord of the Underworld and giver of wealth and bounty, to recall the fruitful nature of this darkness we fear. To retrieve the shadow is to retrieve our own treasury. The journey of individuation necessitates meeting the black shadow we carry, the *sol niger* of the alchemists, the inferior and hidden parts of the personality, the weak underbelly of our strength.

This process is so difficult, "it verges on the impossible."[32] The shadow is "dangerous, disorderly, and forever in hiding, as if the light of consciousness would steal its very life."[33] But this difficulty and danger must not stop us, for, unless we mine the silver of the unconscious, "the end remains as dark as the beginning." Life will be lived, but its essence will remain untapped, its fullness denied. Conversely, if we consciously embark on a journey to wholeness, willingly meeting the shadow, "so much darkness comes to light that the personality is permeated with light, and consciousness necessarily gains in scope and insight."[34] The opus of individuation ends with the Self—a symbol of wholeness "that resolves all opposition and puts an end to conflict, or at least draws its sting."[35] The *lapis*, or Philosopher's Stone, the once despised and reviled symbol of the Self, transforms into that which is valued above all else. So it is with the shadow and its illumination.

I find it compelling and instructive that Jung also used the image of the orphan to symbolize the wholeness he envisioned. The figure holding out the promise of wholeness is a denizen of margins and shadows. The Indo-European root of the word orphan, *orbh*, means to separate, to pull asunder. The image of the orphan reminds us that separation from comfortable and familiar ground takes us through the heart of darkness to the heart of wholeness. The one who is homeless and alone is, paradoxically, the one who guides us home.

The orphan lives in the uncharted wilderness of world and cosmos, embracing it as bride or groom. Cutting the navel string, not physically or literally, but imaginally and psychologically, is the necessary condition that allows the orphan to commune with all of existence. Not bound by the familiar and limiting identification of tribe, nation, race, or religion, the orphan, in belonging to no one, belongs to all of life. Being nobody, the orphan is everybody.

The image of the orphan is timeless; it evokes the uniqueness and differentiation from collective values that characterize individuation. Resonating deeply within the collective, the orphan stirs in each one of us and reminds us that the cornerstone of our uniqueness is discovered in the shadow of our abandoned and rejected selves. Jung gave homage to the figure of the orphan, carving the following words from alchemy on the face of one of the stone tablets standing outside the tower he built in Bollingen:

> I am an orphan, alone; nevertheless I am found everywhere. I am one, but opposed to myself. I am youth and old man at one and the same time. I have known neither father nor mother, because I have had to be fetched out of the deep like a fish, or fell like a white stone from heaven. In woods and mountains I roam, but I am hidden in the innermost soul of man. I am mortal for everyone, yet I am not touched by the cycle of aeons.[36]

Jung's interest and insights regarding the rejected self lurking in the shadows began with observing his own intra-psychic process. He became aware at a young age of two distinct sides to his personality, which he referred to as No. 1 and No. 2. In his autobiography, Jung recounts a dream he had as a young man that heightened his awareness

of the relationship between light and shadow—between the conscious
and unconscious sides of the personality.

> It was night in some unknown place, and I was making slow
> and painful headway against a mighty wind. Dense fog was fly-
> ing along everywhere. I had my hands cupped around a tiny
> light which threatened to go out at any moment. Everything
> depended on my keeping this little light alive. Suddenly I had
> the feeling that something was coming up behind me. I looked
> back and saw a gigantic black figure following me. But at the
> same moment I was conscious that in spite of my terror that I
> must keep my little light going through the night and wind,
> regardless of all dangers. When I awoke I realized at once that
> the figure was "a specter of the Brocken," my own shadow on
> the swirling mists, brought into being by the little light I was
> carrying. I knew too that this little light was my consciousness,
> the only light I have. My own understanding is the sole treasure
> I possess, and the greatest.[37]

As a result of this dream, Jung gained a deeper appreciation for the
importance of both sides of the personality. Given the threatening
mood of the dream, it is no surprise that we have the impulse to run
when the shadow approaches. Meeting the shadow is a frightening
prospect indeed. But Jung concluded that, despite our fears and reservations, the consequences of avoidance are disastrous for the individual, as
well as for the collective.

Jung compares our effort to avoid the darkness in ourselves to an
ostrich putting its head in the ground, embedding itself in a darkness
greater than the one it is trying to escape. The consequences of such
cowardice condemn people to living haunted half-lives, "foisting everything they dislike on to their neighbours and plaguing them with prejudices and projections."[38]

The projection of our individual shadow accelerates the already
rampant spread of the collective shadow that we hear shouting from
every corner newsstand and every evening telecast. This untethered, collective shadow is like a radio broadcast hailing the myrmidons of dark-

ness. It perverts our systems of justice; it creates weapons of mass destruction; it fuels terrorism; it destroys rainforests and wipes out wilderness and wildlife; it steals from the poor and gives to the rich; it oppresses women and despises the "other"; it silences the voices of freedom; it shamelessly poisons our air, our food, and our water, bringing our planet and all its creatures to the brink of a great yawning abyss. The dangers of this split-off collective shadow are immense, and yet the opportunity for transformation is equally great. Jung commented on the razor's edge we walk: "In one sense this is a catastrophe and a retrogression without parallel, but it is not beyond the bounds of possibility that such an experience also has its positive aspects and might become the seed of a nobler culture in a regenerated age."[39]

As we turn to face the shadow, it pulls us like an irresistible force field into its forbidding depths. It confronts us with our self-deceptions, our rationalizations and lies, and the countless ways we sacrifice others to satisfy our narrow selfish aims. Such realizations make us wince. We feel like jumping out of our skins and destroying this dark twin, this evidence of our horribly imperfect selves. But the shadow cannot be destroyed, and our efforts to do so only feed its dark belly. We come upon the perplexing and paradoxical truth that the transformation we seek can only come about through awareness and openness, and that "condemnation does not liberate, it oppresses."[40]

Facing ourselves, as daunting a task as it may be, is only the beginning. We cannot stop there, because the shadow asks far more of us. It asks for a love that is strong enough to bear our every darkness. Jung tells us not to underestimate the challenge:

> Perhaps this sounds very simple, but simple things are always the most difficult. In actual life it requires the greatest discipline to be simple, and the acceptance of oneself is the essence of a moral problem and the epitome of a whole outlook upon life. That I feed the hungry, that I forgive an insult, that I love my enemy in the name of Christ—all these are undoubtedly great virtues. What I do unto the least of my brethren, that I do unto Christ. But what if I should discover that the least amongst

them all, the poorest of all the beggars, the most impudent of all the offenders, the very enemy himself—that these are within me, and that I myself stand in need of the alms of my own kindness—that I myself am the enemy who must be loved—what then?[41]

The inability to distinguish between genuine self-love and neurotic self-involvement common to a great many people makes this considerable challenge even more difficult. Earlier, I discussed Freud's theory of narcissism and how it both reflected and added to the confusion regarding the difference between these two very different things. Jung saw through this confusion. In fact, he masterfully turned the axiom to "love thy neighbor as thyself" on its head, by reminding us that, while we are busy trying to figure out how to love our neighbors—or the stranger—we forget that the measure of this love can never exceed the love we have for ourselves.

"Love thy neighbour" is wonderful, since we then have nothing to do about ourselves; now when it is a question of "love thy neighbour as thyself" we are no longer so sure, for we think it would be egotism to love ourselves. There was no need to preach "love thyself" to people in olden times, because they did so as a matter of course. But how is it nowadays? It would do us good to take this thing somewhat to heart, especially the phrase "as thyself." How can we be altruistic if we do not treat ourselves decently? But if we treat ourselves decently, if we love ourselves, we make discoveries, and then we see what we are and what we should love. There is nothing for it but to put our foot into the serpents' mouth. He who cannot love can never transform the serpent and then nothing is changed.[42]

There is no other way. Can we extend ourselves to the broken, the wounded, and the weak parts of ourselves? Can we enter the ruin and rubble, the perversions and holy horrors of our lives? Can we find love and compassion for our own sickness and weakness? Love and compassion are the weapons of the post-heroic revolution. There was a time for slaying the dragon, and we did. Now, we must use the gift of consciousness and place our feet in the serpent's mouth. The shadow, like the unconscious itself, is more than a cauldron of darkness; it is also a beacon pointing toward greater light. It is both *prima materia* and *lapis*. The shadow is both the awful monster seeking redemption, and the suffering redeemer leading us on our way.

Retrieving the exiled shadow promotes authenticity, humility, and a sense of relatedness. The humility that comes from "eating the shadow" becomes the ground of friendship, intimacy, and community. It may seem incongruous that individuals who achieve true greatness, not simply fame or power, are also humble. Yet it is so. Such individuals do not flee from their demons; they find a way to relate to them. Breathing in their own darkness, they are both humbled and transformed. The Dalai Lama describes this humility as a "courageous state of mind where you are able to relate to others, fully aware of what ability you have to help."[43]

Nelson Mandela is a paragon of humility and fearlessness. After twenty-seven years of cruel and unjust political imprisonment in a South African jail, he emerged a beacon of freedom, in great measure because of his ability to retain his inner liberty in the face of oppression. He is respected throughout the world for his courage in the face of adversity, the endurance of his principles, and the depth of his humanity. In his case, prison became a hermetic vessel in which the raw substance of his being was refined and transformed. His extraordinariness and his ordinariness appear seamlessly unified. This, also, is a measure of his humility. He is not trying to be someone. He is what he is, and it is the genuineness of his presence that so amplifies his greatness. In a recent interview, I heard him speak about the importance of humility, saying it is the basis of all fruitful human relationship, because the truly humble do not threaten or intimidate others. Humility is the soil of openness, respect, trust, and cooperation.

The word "humility" comes from *humus*, the soil, the dark soil. A humble person does not alienate others, but rather connects with them on the basis of shared human experience. In the presence of such individuals, people come to appreciate their own worth and feel inspired to work toward great and far-reaching goals. Human relationships flourish in humble soil. It appears that one of the reasons "the meek shall inherit the Earth" is because the perfect have no need for others. This understanding was well-articulated by Jung:

> A human relationship is not based on differentiation and perfection, for these only emphasize the differences or call forth the exact opposite; it is based, rather, on imperfection, on what is weak, helpless and in need of support—the very ground and motive of dependence.[44]

We Are the World

Whereas Freud studied the impact culture and civilization had on the psychology of individuals, Jung focused on how the relationship between the individual and collective contents of the psyche was mirrored in the relationship between individuals and society, and on the connection between individual transformation and the transformation of societies and nations. As in all of Jung's work, distinctions between these two ideas are blurred, and at times everything blends together.

Jung noted that the development of a discrete, individual personality had been elevated in Western civilization, and the pursuit of such individuality had been coupled with repression of the collective unconscious. A fantasy of isolated individualism had delivered humanity to a dangerous crossroad, one that Jung believed urgently called for a conscious relationship to the heretofore repressed collective elements of psyche. The relationship that exists between personal and collective unconscious contents is linked fundamentally to the kind of relationship that develops between self and society.

Our lives are situated between these two mighty currents, and the introspection that brings personal contents to consciousness inevitably brings collective contents to awareness as well. As this happens, we become increasingly aware of all the ways we resemble others, and how our profound similarities cut across more superficial constructs of family, tribe, race, or nation. The borders dividing self from other fade as awareness of the collective psyche becomes clearer. As a result, a "sense of solidarity with the world is gradually built up."[45]

Jung characterized an individual influenced by this burgeoning awareness as truly "modern." This is not, however, the condition of the average individual. Most are unwittingly controlled by the unconsciousness or "participation mystique" of the collective. Modern individuals extract themselves from this unconsciousness, and are no longer submerged in the mass mind. They are able to think for themselves. The act of freeing the psyche from the atavistic pull of the collective unconscious allows us to live in the present, but "every step forward means an act of tearing himself loose from that all-embracing pristine unconsciousness which claims the bulk of mankind almost entirely."[46] Transcending the pull of repressive, collective unconsciousness and its weighty burden frees one to focus on a higher stage of development. This development cannot, however, be successfully undertaken unless we are able to live and function effectively within prescribed social norms. As Jung said:

A higher level of consciousness is like a burden of guilt . . . only the man who has outgrown the stages of consciousness belonging to the past and has amply fulfilled the duties appointed for him by the world, can achieve a full consciousness of the present. To do this he must be sound and proficient in the best sense—a man who has achieved as much as other people, and even a little more. It is these qualities that enable him to achieve the next highest level of consciousness.[47]

Freedom from collective unconsciousness imposes a greater personal responsibility for our lives and our futures. Jung believed individuals must be socially proficient before attempting such a break, because otherwise they would not have earned the right to forsake tradition in the way individuation demands. Only those who have achieved social proficiency coupled with inner stability can navigate the steep terrain of transpersonal values. Only a socially adapted and psychologically stable individual can undertake the differentiation process without it degenerating into an escape from life or an evasion of responsibility. Individuals separate from the collective in order to re-enter it at a higher and more differentiated level. Escape was the furthest thing from Jung's mind! Individuality is cultivated and refined in order to serve the greater good. An individual personality that develops this higher level of consciousness becomes capable of a more mature level of relating. Jung described the dual nature of the individuated personality thus:

> Individuation has two principal aspects: in the first place it is an internal and subjective process of integration, and in the second it is an equally indispensable process of objective relationship. Neither can exist without the other, although sometimes the one and sometimes the other predominates.[48]

Because individuals do not exist in isolation, but by their very existence presuppose a relationship to others, Jung believed it naturally followed that individuation would lead toward others, and not toward isolation. Furthermore, he felt it was especially critical at this historic juncture for individuals to understand their effect on society, because the individual human being is the "infinitesimal unit on whom a world depends."[49] Our future survival depends on individuals taking responsibility for their share of darkness, rather than continuing to project wickedness onto the world.

At one time, the consequences of our unconsciousness as a species were less grave. We could inflict a great deal of harm, and we certainly did, but the impact and scope of our collective darkness was limited. Today, we have the power to destroy our world, a power Jung called "superhuman." The question facing us is whether we can find an equally superhuman response within ourselves, a response capable of transforming a simmering cauldron of evil. "The only thing that really matters now is whether man can climb to a higher plane of consciousness, in order to be equal to the superhuman powers which the fallen angels have played into his hands."[50] However difficult it may be, Jung urged individuals to take their responsibility for the greater good seriously, because "everything now depends on man: immense power of destruction is given into his hand, and the question is whether he can resist the will to use it, and can temper his will with the spirit of love and wisdom."[51]

We have become far too dangerous as a species, and the terrifying eruption of our shadow could at any time release an unstoppable firestorm in our world. We live, right now, on the brink of this disaster. The responsibility falls to humanity to claim and redeem its own darkness before unleashing it irrevocably. We can no longer wring our hands in helpless innocence and look to others to do the job.

Our habit upon hearing such things is to assume that we ourselves are not implicated. It can't be us. It must be someone else. It must be those people on the other side of town, the government and big corporations, or those wild-eyed extremists I saw on television. Jung recognized and denounced this tendency when he said, "But still too few look inwards, to their own selves, and still fewer ask themselves whether the ends of humanity might not be best served if each man attempted to abolish the old order within himself." Society is composed of individuals, and consequently, "all the highest achievements of virtue, as well as the blackest villainies are individual."[52]

Change does not occur on a collective level; it happens at the level of individuals. Despite rhetoric to the contrary, the collective interest is the sum interest of individuals—not the other way around. The foundation of the totalitarian state—whether fascist, communist, or fundamentalist—rests upon individual suppression in the guise of liberation of the people. Although these dogmas claim to liberate others, their claims are empty, because the truth is that people aren't liberated; they are oppressed and disheartened by such regimes. Liberation happens within individuals, one by one. There is no collective pill to take or magic wand to wave to liberate society as a whole. Only a respect for the sanctity of individual freedom and the power of individual transformation can bring about collective freedom.

Collective transformation depends upon individual transformation, and Jung believed it was the task of each of us to take this truth to heart and make it our own. Although this may at times feel like too much of a burden to bear, the knowledge that transforming our lives is the basis for transforming our world is actually a taste of freedom. It is both empowering and inspiring. We need not depend on someone else to make it happen; we can actually choose to do something ourselves.

Individuals who recognize the need for personal transformation and act upon it, transforming themselves, exude genuine moral authority and are able to make a considerable difference in the world around them. In Jung's words:

> The psychology of the individual is reflected in the psychology of the nation. What the nation does is also done by each individual, and so long as the individual continues to do it, the nation will do likewise. Only a change in the attitude of the individual can initiate a change in the psychology of the nation. The great problems of humanity were never yet solved by general laws, but only through a regeneration of the attitudes of individuals.[53]

This understanding was truly embodied by Mahatma Gandhi. He continually encouraged the Indian populace to choose a path of personal transformation in order to serve their quest for freedom as a people. He gave the following advice to the multitudes of Indians who were alternately frustrated, restless, demoralized, and enraged by years of British rule: "You must be the change you want to see in the world."

Toward Wholeness

The areas of Jung's work I chose to explore both circle and point to love and compassion. Jung was far less interested in developmental issues than in what we might become if only we found the strength to break free of the pull of our reptilian brain and rouse our true potential. The entirety of Jung's work is influenced by his conviction that human beings are called to wholeness and are innately capable of transformation. This perspective holds all the disparate elements of his work together like a thread holding together a strand of pearls.

The process of transformation requires, among other things, the integration of the shadow, authenticity and individual responsibility, and, finally, love—a love rooted in love for oneself. Jung considered such love indispensable. He also insisted that a transformation of the self is needed in order to transform the world. On general principle, there are parallels here with the teachings of Tibetan Buddhism. In many other important specifics, however, Jung and Tibetan Buddhism part ways. Some of the areas of difference include the nature of the self, whether it is possible to fully overcome suffering, as well as whether enlightenment or wholeness are actually possible or simply an endless horizon pulling us ever onward.

All these issues are relevant to this discussion, but the thing that is especially relevant is that Jung, despite the wide net he cast, did not introduce a method to support the development of love and compassion. He brought us to the threshold of love and its necessity, saying, "where love stops, power begins, and violence and terror."[54] He left us with a call to compassion, but no response. Tibetan Buddhism does respond, and I believe the response given fulfills a need in psychology for a union of heart and soul, and for a methodology that supports the love and compassion so necessary to deeper levels of transformation.

Jung blamed the West for advancing an image of perfection in which light and dark were polarized. This stands in contrast to the vision of the East, where the lotus is an honored symbol of love and compassion precisely because it grows out of the mud and yet bears no trace of mud upon it. The lotus reconciles light and dark without abandoning either. Love and compassion are expressions of human wakefulness, capable of redeeming both the individual and the collective shadow. Love and compassion move through the paradoxes of earth and sky, agony and triumph, beauty and horror, life and death, uniting them in one seamless whole.

Part II

REFRAMING THE DIALOGUE

It is the supreme ambrosia
That overcomes the sovereignty of death.
It is the inexhaustible treasure
That eliminates all poverty in the world.

It is the supreme medicine
That quells the world's disease.
It is the tree that shelters all beings
Wandering and tired on the path of conditioned existence.

It is the universal bridge
That leads to freedom from unhappy states of birth.

It is the dawning moon of the mind
That dispels the torment of disturbing conceptions.

It is the great sun that finally removes
The misty ignorance of the world.

—SHANTIDEVA'S WORDS ON THE AWAKENED HEART OF COMPASSION

Chapter 5

A CALL TO COMPASSION:
THE WAY OF TRANSFORMATION

■   ■   ■

Things are not what they appear to be, Nor are they otherwise.

−LANKAVATARA SUTRA

W hat would therapy look like and what would psychology look like if they were framed as compassionate endeavors? What fresh possibilities might emerge if care of the soul were envisioned as cultivating the heart of compassion? If insight and compassion were paired? If alchemy was of the heart? Joseph Campbell often said that compassion is the purpose of the life journey, and that compassion and the Grail are equivalent. Perhaps, rather than envisioning the central task of human life as the refinement of the ego-Self axis, as suggested by Jung, we would do well to re-vision it with the refinement of the *self-other axis* as the fulcrum of all our efforts.

Yet, for all this vision includes, it too falls short. Taken alone, the self-other axis could, by virtue of its one-sidedness, lead us astray. Its singularity can easily fall prey to our habit of absolutizing and reifying relative truths. Standing alone, it occludes the multivalent complexity of life by advancing still another monolith of meaning. It is not my intention to present yet one more false idol to be worshipped. We already have plenty from which to choose. The self-other axis cannot be separated from the *no-self-no-other axis* if our compassion is to achieve full expression. Both are equally true, but taken alone, each is false. Self and other, and no-self and no-other must be understood as co-existing and interdependent realities if we hope to find the Grail of compassion. Of all things paradoxical, this is perhaps the most mind stopping of all.

Nothing is what it appears to be, and everything is just as it is. Embarking on a path of compassion, we cross the threshold of conventional appearances. Our familiar world begins to recede. New patterns of understanding emerge as certainty is replaced by an openness capable of entertaining impossible truths: When we relinquish chronic self-centeredness, we can become "wisely selfish." When we wish for our own happiness, we suffer—but this suffering can become the broom that sweeps away suffering. When we give away everything we cling to and hold dear, we fulfill our deepest desires. When we welcome everything we reject, we dissolve the ancient armor around our heart. And so it continues. The logic of compassion turns the logic of the ego on its head.

The marriage of such paradoxes arouses the enigmatic and electrifying Black Goddess, Baba Yaga, because "she eats whoever is still thinking oppositionally."[1] In a Russian tale called *The Maiden Czar,* young Ivan sets out in search of lost love and, after wandering from one world to another for a great length of time, stumbles across Baba Yaga's hut. This hut is unlike anything he has ever seen. It continually turns on a single chicken leg, and yet the door always faces the darkest part of the forest. What's more, any traveler immediately notices the twelve stakes around the hut. All but one are topped by a human head. The twelfth stake, conspicuously empty, seems to be waiting just for you. And to make the presence of death loom even larger, everything appears to be made of human bone. A thigh bone holds the door shut; a fence fashioned of human bones encircles the hut—you can well imagine the rest. From somewhere in the forest depths, a high-spirited cackle resounds, and in flies Baba Yaga, riding in her mortar and rowing with her pestle. Traveling to her world is usually a one-way trip; one rarely gets out alive. Ivan, however, manages in a most intriguing way.

Just as the Sphinx poses a "trick" question, a riddle, to those wanting to pass through her gates, Baba Yaga narrows her glittering eyes and asks Ivan a question: "My good youth, are you here of your own free will, or by compulsion?" Baba Yaga's question tricks and treats (treats as in heals). She heals us by freeing us—if we are up to the task—from the bondage of literal and concrete thinking. We know from other tales in which Baba Yaga appears that, if you give her an either-or answer, you're finished. If you answer, "I came here by compulsion," you're eaten on the spot. "I came here by my own free will," and she's got you. So how does Ivan respond in a way that satisfies this Goddess as old as time, this Goddess of time itself? Avoiding the trap of literal-mindedness, he says, "Largely of my own free will, and twice as much by compulsion!" Now here's an answer that pleases Baba Yaga. Rather than devouring the young man in a single mouthful, she amicably guides him to his next destination. He has earned the right to continue on his way.

A journey to love and compassion demands going beyond oppositional thinking. Without this, we can't proceed. So if Baba Yaga were to ask you, "Is there a self or is there no self?" "Do you care for your own needs, or do you care for others?" you become dinner if you respond literally, in an either-or way. Unless we can overthrow the tyranny of either-or and develop the kind of double vision that perceives impossible truths, we will wander endlessly in the swamp of sorrow, in the forest deeps, never finding our way to the clearing.

Embarking

A journey to the Grail of love and compassion is a journey of no return. That is to say, the person who leaves is not the one who returns. There's an old Norwegian fairy tale in which the hero embarks on his journey and soon comes to a crossroad, where he sees three paths with three signs. The first sign reads, "Travel this road and return unharmed." The second sign reads, "Travel this road and you may or may not return." And the third sign reads, "Travel this road and you will never return." Which road does he take? He must take the third road if he's to have a real journey. Otherwise it is just a road like any other, with interesting detours, leading nowhere new.

Gehlek Rimpoche often remarks that a groundhog going underground and coming out the same old groundhog is nothing to be impressed or surprised by. If we want genuine transformation, we need to do better than that. If we intend to embark on a real journey and enter unknown territory, a radical reorientation is necessary. Otherwise, our journey will be no different than that of the groundhog who travels underground and returns unchanged. On the other hand, if you do commit to a path of genuine transformation, be forewarned. "Once you choose a Path, you can't just get off it. That's the price of taking it. The Path is not a passive thing; it too has a will."[2] Trungpa agrees: "If you must begin," he exhorts, "then go all the way, because if you begin and quit, the unfinished business you have left behind begins to haunt you all the time."[3]

The theme of a journey of no return is also found in the movie *The Matrix*. Neo, the young hero of the film, is beginning to see through the veil of illusion shrouding his world; he is becoming aware of another reality. This marks the beginning of his stepping toward his path. He is soon brought to Morpheus, and this meeting is his crossroad. Morpheus presents him with two little pills, one red and the other blue, and tells him he must choose between them. If Neo chooses the blue pill, he will return to his old life and everything he's beginning to understand will be forever erased from memory. He will live his remaining days in ignorance, as do those around him. If he takes the red pill, his old life will be left behind and another world will open up to him. This choice is not without peril. If Neo opts for the red pill, everything will be at stake, all the time. He will be walking a razor's edge rife with danger and opportunity. If he chooses the red path, there is no going back, and there's also no way of knowing how his destiny will unfold. It can only be revealed in the living of it. Of course, there couldn't be a movie if Neo took the blue pill—there would be no story, no journey, and no transformation! He must take the red pill, just as our Norwegian lad must take the path of no return.

Understanding this need for radical departure, the great masters in the Tibetan tradition don't mince words. They begin their discourses on beginning the stages of the path by challenging our most basic assumptions—like believing we know what will make us happy. Look again, they say. Don't assume anything. Question all certainties and absolutes. Being sure of something does not guarantee its veracity. Truly speaking, we are deprived of real freedom and joy because of our basic confusion concerning what is real and what is unreal, about what is happiness and what is misery. Acting on the momentum of our habits, we continually try to grasp things for ourselves, and secure ourselves in relation to a world "out there." We are so busy with this pursuit that we don't see that it brings us continual sorrow. We've been doing it for so long, we don't consider that the whole endeavor could be misguided. Moreover, everyone else seems to be doing the same thing, and they can't all be wrong. Or can they?

During two years in Asia, I lived for some time in Dharamsala—the Himalayan refuge in exile of the Dalai Lama. During this time I came in contact with a number of extraordinary individuals. They were clearly human beings, but their "human nature" seemed to be unlike the nature of any humans I had ever known. It appeared they had tapped a source of unconditioned joy and freedom that allowed them to inhabit the world in an utterly unique way. In a voice of lived experience, they told me that anger, hatred, grasping, and confusion were secondary, impermanent traits, not innate, unalterable characteristics of human nature.

The rarity of such people was far less important to me than the inspiration I derived from encountering these beacons of humanity. I could sense that a freedom I had until then only read about and imagined was actually humanly possible. For me, these individuals were "holy" because of the wholeness I glimpsed in them, and the wholeness I then found reflected in myself. I was, after all, looking into the eyes of another human being. What I saw mirrored back was not only a remarkable evolutionary achievement, but my own unborn face.

I was riveted by the presence of these great Buddhist masters and the teachings they shared on wisdom and compassion. I listened intently to encouragement and methods given to free myself from instinctive bondage to hatred, anger, craving, and all other painful and disturbing states of mind. I held my seat and watched the most cherished icon of an independent, separate, and fixed self-identity skillfully taken apart, bit by bit, until all that was left was a subtle, relative, inextricably connected self suddenly free to experience limitless love and compassion. I was moved to the bottom of my heart with thoughts of suffering beings and the wish to liberate all, without exception.

This, however, would probably have been little more than momentarily galvanizing if not for the atmosphere of wisdom and compassion emanating in the field of these individuals. It was their human flesh—the living proof that, with sustained, wholehearted, and committed practice, a human being could have ongoing, enduring access to these higher states—that brought to life what would otherwise have been only engaging ideas. I came to understand why no amount of book learning could substitute for a transmission of living knowledge rooted in direct experience.

Easy to say, but not so easy to change the course of a mighty river whose current carries us from the time we are born until the moment we die (and again, if we allow the possibility of reincarnation). We are not as free as we would like to be, because it is not easy to overcome the misguided habits of our minds. If we want to redirect the flow, we must learn to remain steadfast and open in the face of myriad difficulties, not the least of which is our own resistance. Pema Chödrön makes the choice clear:

> To lead a life that goes beyond pettiness and prejudice and always wanting to make sure that everything turns out on our own terms, to lead a more passionate, full, and delightful life than that, we must realize that we can endure a lot of pain and pleasure for the sake of finding out who we are and what this world is, how we tick and how our world ticks, how the whole thing just *is*. If we're committed to comfort at any cost, as soon as we come up against the least edge of pain, we're going to run; we'll never know what's beyond that particular barrier or wall or fearful thing.[4]

James Hillman describes soul-making as a journey that demands leaving behind habitual preconceptions and projections. It is "going South," he says. "Venturing South is a journey for explorers . . . . Going South means leaving our psychological territory at the risk of archetypal disorientation . . . . Venturing South may mean departing from all we have come to consider psychology."[5] A journey to compassion enters this uncharted territory beyond East and West through North and South, weaving together paradoxical threads of immanence and transcendence, self and other, relative and absolute. On this journey, we are transported beyond all we have come to consider psychology. The choice is ours. We can refuse. But if we do, the Grail will remain locked in our heart, its transformative power untapped. If we are committed to transformation, we must choose the red pill. We must take that third fork in the road that reads, "Travel this road, and you will never return."

Seven Points for Training the Mind

The lojong instruction introduced here is based on the Seven Points for Training the Mind first recorded by Geshe Chekawa nearly 1000 years ago. These teachings can be traced back to Atisha, "one of the last truly great Indian Buddhist masters to teach in Tibet."[6] Atisha received these teachings from several of his Indian masters, but most important in their transmission was an Indonesian master named Serlingpa, whom Atisha traveled thirteen months by sea to reach. Geshe Chekawa later recorded these heretofore secretly transmitted teachings and made them more widely available.

The Seven Points are enumerated in the following way:

• Training in the preliminaries

• Practicing the cultivation of the two bodhiminds

• Transforming adversity

• Integrating mind-training practice throughout life and in death

• Noting signs of progress

• Honoring the commitments of mind training

• General advice and on-the-spot reminders

The aphorisms included under each of the Points vary slightly, in keeping with variations in the texts used.

In essence, Geshe Tharchin tells us, "Lojong practice consists of two main parts: the first is called *dakshen nyamje*, or Equalizing and Exchanging Self and Others; the second is *tonglen*, or Giving and Taking."[7] Equalizing and exchanging self and others is also a two-part practice. The first part entails recognizing the equality of self and other on the basis of a shared desire to experience happiness and avoid suffering. The second is exchanging positions with others, shifting our focus away from narrow self-concern to a more expansive concern for the welfare of others. The practice of tonglen, or giving and taking, strengthens, reinforces, and empowers this shift in focus. Gehlek Rimpoche describes the constituent elements of the lojong quite succinctly: "[Lojong] shows how to develop bodhimind through the 'exchange' method, plus the give and take technique. These two, combined together, are called lojong. If you're missing one, it doesn't qualify to be lojong."[8]

There are a number of excellent commentaries available in English covering all seven points and each of the aphorisms, which anyone with an interest can read. I have included one version of the text in its entirety in the Appendix. This text is provided as an example, not as a definitive version or translation. The aphorisms I introduce are taken from several different translations, so they differ at times from the text in the Appendix.

In this chapter, I will introduce the first of the Seven Points, which covers the practice of the preliminaries, the foundation for all further practice. In the next chapter, I will discuss the second point, which describes the development of the two bodhiminds: the conventional mind of love and compassion and the ultimate mind of the wisdom of emptiness. This includes the practice of tonglen, which I will discuss in some detail.

The Dalai Lama speaks of the pressing need for practical methodology, saying that "at present the world is not lacking in a technology of war. Our weapons of destruction are everywhere . . . . But what we are lacking is the technology of peace, the technology to produce love, kindness, and open-heartedness."[9] If we lack a method that can be applied in daily life, it is very difficult to actually engage in a process of transformation. The lojong is such a method. It is "purely pragmatic: its subject is how to transform one's every activity into a method of opening the heart toward others."[10]

Instead of always looking to see what we can secure for ourselves, we may begin to notice that continually grabbing for ourselves leaves us miserable and lonely. Much to our chagrin, the happiness we desperately seek through our fervent pursuit of self-centered pleasure never comes. Narrow concern for ourselves, and perhaps a few others, makes it impossible to realize the vast potential of our heart and mind; but this attitude is so deeply ingrained and so widely practiced, that we don't often stop to consider how much it limits our lives. Even if we recognize the problem, we still may feel at a loss as to what to do about it.

Among the gifts of Buddhist practice in general, and of the lojong in particular, are the techniques that address our habitual selfishness. But as with all methods, we must see for ourselves if they are worthwhile and effective. We need to question the claims being made, and the solutions being offered. We need to test these methods in our own lives to see if they work or offer us anything of value. If they do, we take them to heart. If not, we can simply forget about them.

Testing the Gold

In a dream, I am part of a group that will be teaching a huge audience. The lights go on before we have completed preparations for the program. The First Lady, who is part of our group, opens up by introducing me as the first speaker of the evening, informing the audience that I will be answering their questions. On stage, some people are setting me up with a cordless mike so I can move about freely. At first, the light in my eyes is so bright it is nearly blinding. After a short period, my eyes adjust and I open to questions from the audience. There are many questions asked and even more hands are raised, but one exchange stands out. Someone asks, "What is the source of your confidence?" I begin by speaking about the difference between the confidence people feel as a result of adherence to dogma, and genuine confidence. I illustrate my point by relaying the Buddha's message about testing his teachings the same way one would test gold before buying it. Only after melting the teachings with the heat of attention, cutting them with critical analysis, and rubbing them against the touchstone of your own experience should you be satisfied. This promotes real confidence. Such confidence does not depend on blind faith and unreasoned belief. It does not flap wildly with every passing breeze, and it does not require heavy armor to protect it. This confidence has deep roots and supple branches.

Questioning is vital to life. We notice our world and wonder about every imaginable thing. As soon as we are able, the questions begin. How are babies born? What makes birch trees white? Do fish sleep? Are the people in the television really inside that little box? Where do they go when we turn it off? Sometimes, an answer is provided that clears away confusion. New understanding takes root and is incorporated in our life. But then there are other questions—big questions—the kind that lurk in the shadows, murmuring in our ears, always there, silently prodding us. Moment to moment, we feel uncertainty about what is real and what is unreal, what is happiness and what is misery, what is freedom and what is bondage. It is annoying, unsettling, and embarrassing at times to be troubled by such seeming ineffables. Articulating these thoughts never does them justice. We ask, "What is the meaning of life?" and it sounds cliché—a shabby messenger carrying a most urgent communication. We seek answers, but answers alone never untangle the knot at the heart of these questions.

Such questions, if we allow them, do not lie still; they stir flesh and blood, bone and sinew, resonating in our body, remaining alive in our mind. They percolate, agitate, motivate, confuse, consume. Such questions prompted Shakyamuni, 2500 years ago, to devote his life to realizing the fully awakened state of enlightenment. Everything he shared thereafter, every word and gesture, was his experiential response to universally asked, yet personally and uniquely experienced, questions. Oddly enough, someone else's answers don't give us any rest. They don't solve our problems. An answer that seems quite helpful when we hear somebody else speak it, can seem hopelessly inadequate when we're driving home feeling upset and angry over a humiliating encounter at work, and we're pulled over for a speeding ticket. Or when we look in the mirror and see ourselves suddenly old and tired. Or worse. A flickering flame of insight is so easily blown out by the powerful winds of life.

We struggle with the fading promise of ideas so hopefully embraced. A once-vivid answer begins to lose its luster, leaving us with our original dilemma and little hope for respite. Something isn't working. Maybe it's not the right answer after all. Maybe we're so different from anyone who ever lived that we require a special method, something not yet invented. Maybe nothing can help us. We could be beyond help. We feel frustrated and disappointed—but then we remember. The value of an answer comes from our unique experiential realization of its meaning. We can amass a great deal of knowledge without it actually affecting our lives. Knowing something in our head simply doesn't count for much when we're pushed to our edge. Our feet need to know it as well.

If we pick a beautiful flower from the garden and carry it in our hands, it comes as no surprise when, after a short while, it withers and dies. Likewise, it should come as no surprise that, removed from the soil of someone else's insight, answers can't long survive. We have to provide soil for knowledge to put down roots and become experiential understanding. Only such knowledge has the power to instruct us when life puts us on the spot. Incorporated knowledge is alive. It affects the way we hear, see, smell, taste, touch—and think. No matter how true something seems, it will not be our truth until it dwells in our hearts and extends into our world. This is why the Buddha encouraged all who listened to use his answers as a springboard to question deeply, not only the teachings, but all their own cherished beliefs and assumptions. This advice holds true today.

The insights we come to as a result of bringing the guidance we are given into conversation with our own lives, are the insights we breathe in and, over time, embody. This level of integration penetrates the dense and conditioned patterns of both body and mind. This is how we transform our lives.

Four Reminders

The first of the Seven Points for Training the Mind reads: First practice the preliminaries. These preliminaries can be presented in many different ways. I will discuss them by introducing the four reminders and exploring in some depth the cultivation of equanimity. Together, these establish a fertile ground for the development of love and compassion.

The four reminders are essentially "four ways of continually waking yourself up."[11] They are a way of remembering why it is worth making the effort every day to sow the seeds of wakefulness. Why make the effort to cultivate love and compassion? Why undertake such a difficult journey when we are already overburdened with bills to pay, family problems, vocational stress, health concerns, and other life dramas? The teachings on the four reminders remind us why it is worth our while, and why, in fact, it needs to be our ultimate concern. Unless we contemplate these four reminders, our efforts to develop love and compassion will have very limited success.

The first reminder is to embrace the preciousness of our life. The life we have is precious and rare, because it gives us the opportunity to fulfill our eternal longing for real happiness. But we often take life for granted, or feel it has failed us. Gehlek Rimpoche speaks of how we are continually bombarded by a cacophony of voices, distracting us from our inner treasure by telling us what is wrong with our lives. " I am sick, I am weak, I'm too fat, I'm too thin . . . I don't have a companion, I don't have a good job, I don't have money, I don't have a house, I don't have a car, I don't have a plane, I don't have a boat."[12] We feel dissatisfied and deprived, and imagine that having everything we want would make us happy. But having is not the medicine for what ails us. No amount of having or doing can heal a lack of being.

Failing to realize the deeper value of our lives, we become disheartened when things don't turn out as we hoped or planned. In the midst of disappointment, humiliation, and loss, we find it hard to recognize how precious our life is. The sting of insults, illness, and failures can obscure our vision, keeping us from seeing the rare opportunity our life offers. In the beloved classic film *It's a Wonderful Life* George Bailey is so overcome by feelings of failure that he throws himself off a bridge. His guardian angel, Clarence, rescues him from an untimely death by showing him the value of his life. Clarence accompanies George through the town he has lived in all his life and lets him see for himself what the town would be like if he had never been born. George had believed his life was worthless and meaningless, but he comes to see how even a small ripple of kindness can touch and change the lives of so many others. This realization transforms George's outlook, enabling him to see that his life is indeed precious and worth living. Living life well does make a difference.

The opportunity to live life well is available to each of us. This is a gift our precious lives provide. Each moment presents us with another chance to choose; the fork in the road is ever before us. One fork leads to increasing kindness and wakefulness; the other keeps us self-absorbed and asleep. Awakening is possible if we set our hearts on that course. "We have this potential because human beings are endowed with a special intelligence . . . and it is through the power of this intelligence that anything becomes possible."[13] We can, as Suzuki Roshi says, "shine a corner of the world."

Although traditional Buddhist teachings are based on an acceptance of reincarnation, you need not accept this in order to develop appreciation for what you have. You can simply read the newspaper and take a good look around you. There are millions of human beings on the planet who are, at this very moment, experiencing such unremitting misery that they have not even a moment's relief. They are so ravaged by the circumstances of their lives that they can think of nothing but stilling the pain. Millions are born and die in this condition. Moreover, how many of our billions of companions on this planet Earth have access to a wealth of teachings and techniques with which to transform their lives, whatever their circumstances? And among those who do come across such methods, how many aspire to a path of transformation? Most live their lives caught up in plans for success and security, or trying to soothe the sting of disappointment and defeat. To have opportunity, information, and inclination is rare indeed!

Recognizing the preciousness of our lives affects the way we perceive the difficulties we encounter. It changes the way we see. No matter how difficult things get, a deeper current of resiliency and appreciation accompanies us, because we realize we have a way to work with situations, be they bitter or sweet. "Beginning to realize how precious life is becomes one of your most powerful tools. It is like gratitude."[14] If we cultivate gratitude when conditions are more gentle, then, when circumstances become especially difficult, we will find we have the inner resources to handle them. There are those for whom an appreciation of life is so well developed that they remain grateful even in the midst of hell.

Our appreciation for the rarity and preciousness of life intensifies when we contemplate the second reminder: Life is fleeting. Like sand through an hourglass, it is passing every moment. Once you are born, there is no way to stop life from slipping away. Every instant brings you closer to death. No matter how long a life you live, it will be brief. Moreover, the time you have left to live is unknown and cannot be predicted. And life is so vulnerable. There are so many things that threaten it. You can die from the prick of a rose, or a single grain of millet. Your body is fragile. A narrow passage in your throat transports the breath on which your life depends. Every organ system depends on the steady beating of your heart. One day, your heart will stop and all the vital signs on which your body depends will shut down. Death comes without warning; our bodies become corpses. This is inevitable. How many more breaths will you take? How much longer do you have? You may have years; you may only have days or moments. The truth is, you don't know.

My dear friend Octavio died so suddenly that it is still hard at times to comprehend his absence. I catch myself thinking that I will hear his voice on the other end of the telephone line, encouraging me to come to Spain and finish my writing there—luring me with the spice and aroma of the open markets in Madrid, the Egyptian phoenix temple visible from the room he intends for me, and the enticement of Moorish mysteries to explore. I will never see his smiling eyes again, hear the pleasing lilt of his voice, or delight in the gift of his imagination. He was there one day, full of brilliance and zest, kindness and wit, and then came the shock and the irreversible news. He's dead. Finished. Dead. Gone.

In Tibetan, the word for body is *lu*, meaning "something you leave behind." Each time this word is spoken, it carries the message of its impermanence, and of the truth that we are travelers taking temporary shelter in this residence. Gehlek Rimpoche often likens the body to a rented apartment. We can live in it as long as the basic necessities of heat, water, and so forth are provided. But when the roof caves in and the pipes burst, when the gas leaks and the floor crumbles beneath our feet, we have to move out. No body lives forever. In an uncertain world, this is one thing we can be sure of.

We fear old age, but we can't even be sure we will experience it. I heard recently of a woman and her husband who had been trying for years to conceive a child, without success. Finally, they decided to adopt and flew across the country to attend the birth of their adoptive child. The whole family gathered in joyful anticipation. How inconceivably painful it must have been for this woman, after so much struggle, to have this newborn die in her arms moments after birth. These are realities we all live with. Death is part of life. Deny it or avoid it, there is nowhere to hide from it. Everywhere we look, there are dead leaves, dead trees, slimy, rotting foliage, dead animals in the road, insect carcasses, slaughterhouses with their long trail of animal flesh, garbage dumps, cemeteries, hospitals, and funeral processions. Death's presence is inescapable. Stephen Batchelor walks us through a contemplation on the inexorability of death in the following way:

> Think of the beginning of life on this earth: single-celled organisms dividing and evolving; gradual emergence of fish, amphibians, and mammals, until the first human beings appeared around five million years ago; then the billions of men and women who preceded my own birth a mere handful of years ago. Each of them was born; each of them died. They died because they were born. What distinguishes me from any of them?[15]

If we become healed toward dying, we will also be healed toward living. The story of Krishna Gotami speaks to the experience of becoming healed toward death, and how this "can bring a real awakening, a transformation in our whole approach to life."[16] Krishna Gotami was a young woman who lived during the time of the Buddha. Her firstborn child fell ill and died when only a year old. Overcome with grief and clutching his tiny body close to her, she walked the streets in anguish, begging everyone she met for medicine to bring her precious child back to life. Finally, she came across a wise man who told her that the only person capable of performing such a miracle was the Buddha.

Krishna Gotami found her way to the Buddha and laid the tiny corpse at his feet, recounting her tragic tale of loss. The Buddha listened and, with great kindness, responded, "There is a way to heal. Go into the city and bring me a mustard seed from any house in which there has been no death." Krishna Gotami was thrilled and, brimming with hope, she set off for the city. She went from one house to another and, although every house had a mustard seed to offer, she could not find a single house that death had not touched.

After trying every house in the city, something inexplicable happened within her heart. She went to the charnel ground with the body of her precious child and said her good-byes. She then returned to the Buddha. "Have you found a mustard seed for me?" the Buddha inquired. "No," she said. "I am beginning to see that death comes to everyone. It is natural as life. I am here to ask you to teach me the truth about life and death and what might lie beyond them." The Buddha agreed to teach Krishna Gotami the way to freedom, and it is said that, by the end of her life, she was free.

We don't contemplate death to destroy our happiness, but to gain it. The reason for meditating on death is not to become despondent or morbid, but to rethink our priorities and experience an opening in the depths of our heart to the life we have and the vulnerability we all share. And to be able to meet death with preparedness and without regret when it actually arrives. Freud struggled with the issue of death awareness in his masterful essay, "On Transience." Walking with two friends in the "smiling" countryside, he observed their divergent responses to the beauty around them and noted that, "the prognoses to decay of all that is beautiful and perfect, can as we know, give rise to two different impulses in the mind. The one leads to the aching despondency . . . while the other leads to rebellion against the facts asserted." Freud could not dispute the fact of transience; nevertheless, "it was incomprehensible . . . that the thought of the transience of beauty should interfere with our joy in it . . . . A flower that blossoms for a single night does not seem to us on that account any less lovely."[17]

Try as he might, Freud could not convince his friends. He decided that the reason they were unable to take pleasure in the beautiful aspects of life was "a revolt in their minds against mourning."[18] In a way, he was right. An unwillingness to mourn is a refusal of life. And just as a revolt against mourning can shut us down to life, the experience of mourning can become an opening into greater life. Robert Romanyshyn discovered that grief and mourning, when consciously endured, had the unexpected effect of connecting him with the world in ways previously unknown to him. He found that "grief lies in the very marrow of our bones" and that profound transformation is possible when we enter these deep recesses. "It was as if my grief and mourning, having plunged me into depths beyond myself, took me out of myself into the world, amplified my being by making me more sensitive and attuned to the pain and suffering of others."[19]

There is more to it, however—more than a refusal to mourn prevents us from living life fully. Sogyal Rinpoche exposes the bottom layer of our resistance. He says, "Perhaps the deepest reason why we are afraid of death is because we do not know who we are. We believe in a personal, unique, and separate identity . . . . It is on this fragile and transient support that we rely for our security."[20] After taking away everything else, death confronts us with ourselves, a being we have been living with all along whom we still do not know, and whose existence we little understand.

If asked, we all readily acknowledge the inevitability of death, but few of us are penetrated by this awareness in a way that transforms our lives. The traditional image given for the impact of contemplating impermanence is the elephant's footprint, because repeated death meditation leaves a most enduring imprint on the mind. The visceral impact of death realization, coupled with an appreciation for the preciousness of life, arouses tenderness for all of existence. It also means we will not squander our time. We will live as though our hair were on fire, and we will see others with greater compassion, for they too are dying. "It is only by acknowledging impermanence that there is the chance to die and the space to be reborn and the possibility of appreciating life as a creative process."[21]

Appreciating life as a creative process leads to the third reminder: Karma. In Sanskrit, karma simply translates as "action." The action can be physical, verbal, or mental. The third reminder is, in essence, a reminder that how we live makes a difference. We create ourselves and our world by the choices we make, the actions we take. Every deed has an evolutionary, or devolutionary, impact on our lives. We are not the victims of karma; we are the creators of it. Karmic consequences are not like rewards or punishments meted out by an outside agency. They are the direct results of our own actions, in the same way that a photograph is the direct result of first taking a picture and then developing it. "Karma, then, is not fatalistic or predetermined. Karma means our ability to create and to change. It is creative because we can determine how and why we act."[22]

Karma is traditionally discussed in the context of coherently linking the actions of one lifetime to consequences in another lifetime. Once again, I encourage you to consider the possibility that this life may not be your first or last. Whatever certainty you imagine you have about this, the truth is that we don't really know. The Dalai Lama has commented on the problems caused for the field of psychology because of the flat rejection of multiple lifetimes. For one thing, it means that anything not apparent to conscious awareness must be accounted for by the unconscious and within this lifetime.

> It's a bit like you've lost something and you decide that the object is in this room. And once you've decided this, then you've already fixed your parameters; you've precluded the possibility of its being outside the room or in another room. So you keep on searching and searching, but you are not finding it, yet you continue to assume that it is still hidden somewhere in the room![23]

When things don't add up, when we don't find what we're looking for, many still refuse to question their assumptions.

Gehlek Rimpoche also comments on the limitations and potential pitfalls of adhering strictly to the view that everything must have its explanation within the conditions of this life. "Psychology," he says, "looks for the causes of suffering, but the only material accessible to it is what happens in the course of one life . . . This can be very helpful . . . yet it might not reach to the deepest layer of cause, and at times it may even create further problems."[24]

Nevertheless, even if you remain unwilling to consider multiple lives as a working hypothesis, understanding karma can help you assume creative responsibility for the life you have. If you scratch beneath the surface of thoughts and activities, you observe the force of habit in your life. We live our lives in a sea of conditioned patterns that repeat themselves over and over. These patterns and tendencies are often more powerful than our conscious intentions, yet we may barely notice them. We believe we are acting freely but, in truth, we are most often acting out of the force of habit. Continual repetition of actions and reinforcement of attitudes gives rise to our way of being in the world. Having programmed ourselves through habit, these patterns automatically reproduce themselves unless counteracted by another greater force. The greater force comes into play when conscious choice counteracts habit.

The choices we make from moment to moment, whether or not they are visible to others, deepen our habits of body, speech, and mind. We carry the imprint of these habits in our hearts. The unforgettable *Picture of Dorian Gray*, by Oscar Wilde, is a haunting portrayal of the way action and intent imprint themselves upon us. Dorian's exquisite beauty masks the swelling darkness in his heart. His portrait, however, unflinchingly reveals every trace of cunning and cruelty. Initially, Dorian experiences a perverse pleasure watching his portrait grow increasingly grotesque while his own face remains frozen in youthful perfection. The locked room where the portrait is hidden from view draws him to it like a magnet. He cannot resist staring at the loathsome figure looking back. He is like Narcissus captured by his reflection, only it is a reflection of evil, not of beauty, that binds him to himself. Ultimately, the sight of his inner self becomes unbearable. No longer able to abide the monster in the mirror, he attempts to destroy the portrait by lunging at it with a knife, dying in the act. His portrait is then restored to its original beauty and his corpse lies crumpled on the floor beneath it, unbearably hideous. The beast in his own heart, invisible to the world, destroyed him. Similarly, our actions, whether or not they are visible to others, create and destroy us. Tarthang Tulku says, "Karma is action extending outward like an echo."[25] It can haunt us, or wake us up.

Actions plant seeds and, under the right conditions, these seeds grow. "The heart is our garden, and along with each action there is an intention planted like a seed."[26] Every moment of anger waters the seeds of anger, and seeds of anger become the fruits of hatred, conflict, and war. Every moment of compassion waters the seeds of compassion, and seeds of compassion become the fruits of peace, friendship, and joy. Knowing this is our freedom and our responsibility. If we understand karma, we have the key to wise action in our hands. The Buddhist teachings tell us that respecting the workings of karma is the gateway to joy, because we realize that, if we act wisely, we will enjoy greater happiness in our hearts and in our lives. In ancient Greece, the three Fates weave the web of life. I love the image of these three women with spindle, thread, and loom. At times, I think of them as a personification of body, speech, and mind.

The fourth reminder helps us see that we are helplessly spinning through cyclic existence, and turns us toward seeking freedom from this painful state. In Sanskrit, the suffering of cyclic existence is called *samsara*; release from it is called *nirvana*. Cyclic existence is not, however, to be confused with life itself. Samsara is not life, and life is not samsara. Neither is samsara a geographic location. We may live in the same house, or sleep in the same bed, alongside someone who is not in samsara. Samsara is a state of being—a state of mind governed by confusion and fear. Being in samsara means we don't see things as they are. We don't see ourselves as we are. We suffer from a case of mistaken identity and are propelled involuntarily through life (and from life to life) on the basis of our mistaken sense of self. It isn't that we don't exist. It's that we don't exist in the way we imagine. Our perception of self is flawed.

Samsara is fueled by ignorance, but this ignorance is more than simply not knowing. It is *wrong* knowing. It is mis-knowledge. We believe we know who and what we are, but we don't. And we don't want to look too closely at our assumptions, because doing so makes us nervous. Besides, we have been living this way for so long, we tell ourselves it must be true. We are conned moment to moment by a belief about the way things are that simply isn't so. But we are conned nonetheless. "Tricky and clever, samsara twists our thoughts into a pattern of self-deception .... It is very difficult to go against this pattern and persuade the mind that another way of being is not only possible but vastly preferable."[27]

Our self seems solid, concrete, independent, and self-generated, but this appearance is an illusion. The true nature of self—a subtle, relative, and interconnected process—is something entirely different. Nevertheless, we live our lives believing that we are the center of a universe that is separate from us, and revolves around us. To add to the confusion, we are continually running into people who believe that the same is true of themselves. This makes for endless trouble and conflict. We perpetually try to hold things together, and they are forever falling apart.

We march to the drum of the dictator "I," trying to gain happiness for ourselves, but it never seems to work. It is as if we are living on the head of a pin, or on the edge of a razor, trying to relax. The unsettling truth that our image of self could be revealed as the fiction it is threatens to undermine our ongoing effort to uphold it. We respond by getting busier and increasingly distracted, filling in any of the cracks where a glimmer of truth might have a chance of getting through. Sogyal Rinpoche comments on the ways our modern world furthers the pattern of self-deception: "Sometimes I think that the greatest achievement of modern culture is its brilliant selling of samsara and its barren distractions. Modern society seems to me a celebration of all the things that lead away from truth, make the truth hard to live for, and discourage people from even believing it exists."[28]

We want happiness, but our every experience is tinged with dissatisfaction because we bind ourselves to misknowledge. Trying to satisfy our craving for security in ways that are futile leaves us perpetually wanting. We try to satisfy the desires of a phantom. Tibetan teachers say our effort to secure ourselves is like drinking salt water to quench our thirst. Instead of quenching our thirst, we become bloated and more thirsty. We may rail and rage against the insults of samsara, but to no avail. Our suffering is wedded to our confusion. And our confusion creates fear.

Generally speaking, this could be regarded as terrible news, but when the Buddha spoke of suffering, he called it a magical elixir. Suffering is the Philosopher's Stone, capable of transforming our lives. The tricky part is this: As long as we deny suffering, we will suffer. But seeing how we suffer opens the way to freedom from suffering. Our feelings of disappointment, humiliation, anger, jealousy, resentment, greed, and fear can become opportunities to see the ways we are holding back. They show us where we are stuck, and where we need to let go. They can become our best teachers and most trusted friends. In this way, our suffering can guide us to freedom.

If, rather than hardening and shutting down, we allow ourselves to be softened by the force of suffering in our life, it will penetrate our heart and open a doorway to the wisdom and compassion within. We will relax our habitual clinging to existence or non-existence, hope or fear, right or wrong, this or that, and instead notice the anxiety and uncertainty driving the furious machinations of our mind. Our greatest challenge is sticking around long enough, when life pushes all our buttons, to see what is going on. In order to learn from painful conditions, we have to slow the momentum of habitual reactivity and watch our mind at work. If we go beneath the storyline and begin searching for the storyteller, we will come ever closer to uprooting the fear and confusion fueling our samsara.

The four reminders encourage us to cultivate an appreciation for the precious opportunity our human life provides, contemplate the fleeting and fragile nature of life, take responsibility for the creative power of our actions and intentions, and move toward freedom from the mistaken view of self that keeps us bound to an endless round of suffering. They can help us establish a firm foundation for the development of love and compassion for ourselves and others.

Equanimity

Although central to the cultivation of love and compassion, equanimity is largely overlooked in our society. It's rarely mentioned, and notably absent in the literature of depth psychology. Even those who speak of love and compassion rarely speak of equanimity. Yet equanimity is the hospitable and fruitful earth in which the type of love and compassion I am advancing here grows and flourishes.

Equanimity is not a necessary constituent of the compassion we ordinarily feel. To the extent that we think of compassion as a private and exclusive feeling reserved for a special few, we don't need equanimity. If our compassion remains limited in this way, the question of establishing a foundation for unconditioned and unlimited love and compassion does not arise. But if we expand our scope beyond the more limited "me and my lover," "me and my mother or father," "me and my sister," "me and my best friend," "me and my dog," "me and my family," "me and my people" to a far-reaching and encompassing "me and all other living beings," equanimity is key.

Underscoring this point, Gehlek Rimpoche begins his instruction on the lojong by saying that "the first and foremost thing we do, not the preliminary, but the actual foundation, is developing equanimity."[29] If we aspire to open our heart to greater love and compassion, we must provide ground on which it can stand. Otherwise, it is like attempting to build the top level of the Empire State Building before laying the ground floor. Equanimity not only provides ground, it provides level, stable ground. Just as water cannot collect atop a jagged mountain, compassion cannot grow in an uneven mind. Once we develop equanimity, however, we "can cultivate bodhicitta quickly and easily."[30]

There are three levels, or stages, of equanimity. The first is called wishing or motivational equanimity. At this level, we deeply wish for all beings—without exception—to have happiness and be free of suffering. I will not be discussing the development of this level of equanimity, although it is in itself a profound practice. The second and third level of equanimity are specifically emphasized in the lojong, so we will focus our attention there.

The second level of equanimity focuses on dissolving projections of friends, enemies, and neutral persons by investigating and seeing through our attachment, anger, and indifference. As projections are reduced, you "recognize that what you thought was out there in another person is not out there, but inside yourself."[31] The process of dissolving projections is like cleansing layers of hardened dirt and clay that obscure a flawless diamond within.

Marie-Louise von Franz used an alchemical metaphor to illustrate the psychological process of withdrawing projections. The alchemical process compares quite closely with the process of developing this level of equanimity. Von Franz likened the *massa confusa* of projection to the blackness of *nigredo*, which has to be cleansed "over and over again." She commented on the patience and persistence required, saying, "This is not an easy thing to do; it is something very complicated and difficult . . . . it needs a long process of inner development and realization for a projection to come back. When it has been withdrawn the disturbing emotional factor vanishes." Once a projection is withdrawn, "the hard part of the work is done" and "a peace establishes itself."³² At this point, we begin the next stage in the alchemical process, the *albedo*. The *albedo*, or whitening stage, is the basis for completing the opus. The whitening process in alchemy parallels the next stage of developing equanimity once the hard work of withdrawing projections is done.

The third level of equanimity builds upon the other two. At this level, we focus on establishing equality between ourselves and others. By contemplating every being's wish to experience happiness and be free from suffering, we recognize our profound similarity to others. Realizing that all beings are, in this deepest sense, like ourselves, we come to see our equality with them, and we arouse a passionate commitment to work for the benefit of all others, equally and unconditionally. This level of equanimity, coupled with the levels preceding it, provides the foundation for the practice of exchanging self and others introduced later in the lojong.

Equanimity Is Not Indifference

A common misconception concerning equanimity is that it entails becoming subtly indifferent to everyone. We may resist developing equanimity because we imagine it means caring less for our friends and family. We fear equanimity could cause our life to lose its color and depth, and our relationships to become flat and boring. But equanimity is neither neutrality nor indifference.

On the surface, equanimity can be mistaken for indifference when, in fact, it is worlds away. Equanimity relaxes the mind's reactivity, enhancing its clarity and receptivity. Developing equanimity increases our capacity to give and receive love, until ultimately "there is no way we can close our heart to anyone."[33] Equanimity opens the heart wider. The more we limit our love and compassion to the few we deem deserving, the more we limit our experience of love altogether. We do ourselves a disservice by underestimating the heart's capacity. The heart is infinite. There is no such thing as too many people to love. The more we open to others, the more affection we feel for everyone.

The Doors of Perception

Everything we experience is filtered through our personal eye. Everything we perceive is a combination of our knowing of it, and of the thing known. It is so easy to forget this. Our opinions and conclusions about events and individuals seem, in the moment, to be objectively true—especially when others support our observations. Conclusions once drawn are often never questioned. Impressions turn into opinions, and soon become facts. It is so easy to imbue subjectivity with concrete, objective reality.

James Hillman argues that what needs healing isn't people's lives, but the stories they tell themselves. He calls psychological work a work of "healing fiction." I agree. The stories we tell ourselves, about ourselves and our world, are true to the extent that we believe them. As a therapist, I am aware that the stories I am told are subjective truths, psychic realities—true fiction. This doesn't mean I don't believe the stories I hear. I do. Everyone's story is like that, including my own.

The ability to see the fictional nature of memory and subjectivity is actually an expression and measure of sanity. The more sane we are, the less likely we are to concretize and literalize experience. In fact, according to conventional psychological wisdom, the more you believe that your views and perceptions are concretely real, the more "insane" you are. Hillman even suggests that, "To be sane we must recognize our beliefs as fictions, and see through our hypotheses as fantasies. For the difference between madness and sanity depends . . . wholly upon our sense of fiction."[34] Tibetan teachers often give the analogy that a person with jaundice looks upon a yellowed world. Likewise, an angry person sees a hostile world, and a greedy person a world full of things to acquire. We see the world, not as it is, but as we are.

As a young girl, I read a story about a woman named Hannah Senesh. She was born in 1921 and died in 1944. In the venomously anti-Semitic atmosphere of Budapest, she became an ardent Zionist; at the age of 18, she emigrated to Palestine. Her growing concerns about the fate of European Jewry and about her mother, still in Budapest, prompted her to join a group of parachutists organized to rescue Allied prisoners of war and organize Jewish resistance. In March 1944, she parachuted into Yugoslavia. A few months later, at the peak of the deportation of Hungarian Jewry, she crossed the border into Hungary and was arrested by the Hungarian police. Though brutally tortured, she revealed nothing to her inquisitors and, following the fascist takeover in Hungary, was quickly condemned to death by a secret court. On November 7, 1944, she was executed by firing squad in a Budapest prison courtyard.

This warrior woman was one of my early heroes. I thought of her often—of her loyalty, her courage, her passion, and her sacrifice. But the image that imprinted more deeply than the rest came from the description I read of her last moments of life, and the illustration that accompanied it. Taken into the courtyard to face the firing squad, Hannah was asked if she had a final request. Yes. She wanted her blindfold removed. She wanted to die with her eyes open. The story was written for a young audience, and I was probably seven when I read it. There were crude black-and-white illustrations in the book, and I can still see the last, of Hannah standing, her feet firmly planted, fearlessly facing her executioners. At the time, I was absolutely sure her stance was a stance of defiance. There was no doubt about it. In my mind's eye, I saw her looking piercingly into the eyes of her cold-blooded killers. I imagined the fierceness of her gaze as an arrow, piercing their savage hearts.

Many years later I recounted the story of Hannah Senesh to a friend, including my conclusions regarding her final request to have the blindfold removed. "Isn't it possible," my friend asked, "that she wanted to have her blindfold removed so she could behold the vastness of the sky before she died? Might not she have wanted to drink in the vastness of life in her last moments?" I had never considered that! I had drawn my conclusion at the age of seven and never looked back. Of course it was possible. In that moment, it seemed likely. Today, I might perceive it yet another way. Our perception of others often reveals more about us than it does about them. It's important to remember this.

At one time in the life of the Buddha, during a gathering of his disciples, one of his foremost disciples, Shariputra, thought to himself, "If the Buddha is such a great being, why does he live in such an inferior universe, and not in a magnificent buddhaverse like other buddhas?" The Buddha became telepathically aware of Shariputra's thought and, in response, he touched the ground with his big toe. The ground was

> . . . transformed into a huge mass of precious jewels, a magnificent array of many hundred thousands of clusters of precious gems . . . . Everyone in the entire assembly was filled with wonder, each perceiving himself seated on a throne of jeweled lotuses.[35]

When he lifted his toe, the Buddha's blissfully pure perception disappeared. All those assembled realized that, although he was sitting alongside them, the world the Buddha perceived was free of the taints they considered intrinsic. We don't know how even the person alongside us perceives the world.

Equanimity as Hospitality

Equanimity elevates our level of concern to include all beings. The Tibetan Buddhist tradition speaks of cultivating an attitude that welcomes all beings as our guests. When I heard Robert Romanyshyn talk about hospitality, it opened, for me, another way of looking at the relationship between equanimity and compassion. I saw that equanimity and hospitality are kindred ways of being. Both can become thresholds into unconditioned love and compassion.

Generally, when people hear the word equanimity, they imagine a calm, unflustered, but aloof way of being in the world. The word hospitality, on the other hand, naturally evokes a sense of warmth. If we see equanimity as a form of hospitality, as a way of being that welcomes without judgment and without preconception, we may more readily perceive the open heart that fosters equanimity and out of which it grows. We may see how everyday reality can blossom into a thing of divine beauty.

The poet William Blake once said that everything in the world is holy. A story told in Ovid's *Metamorphoses* tells of how we might come to see the world this way. Two gods, Jupiter and Mercury, disguised as poor travelers, wander the Earth looking for a place of welcome. As they live in a time when people no longer recognize the divine, the two gods find no place of refuge. No door opens to welcome them, until they arrive at the humble dwelling of an old couple, Philemon and Baucis. Philemon and Baucis have only the simplest of provisions, but they offer hospitality to the weary strangers, inviting them into their home, and willingly sharing their few things. Baucis even suggests to Philemon that they prepare their fatted goose—their one valuable possession—and serve it to the hungry vagabonds.

Philemon and Baucis have been saving their precious fatted goose for a special occasion as a sacrifice to the gods. They decide these strangers are worthy recipients of such an offering. In this moment of unconditioned openness and generosity, the gods reveal themselves; the humble abode is transformed into a magnificent temple, and Philemon and Baucis become its priest and priestess. At the same moment, a flood destroys the rest of the ungodly human race.

Transformations such as these are not the result of externally divined magic or miracles; they represent a radical transformation of consciousness, a radical shift in perspective. Romanyshyn described hospitality as a "devotion to things as they are."[36] The fatted goose offered by Philemon and Baucis is the bird of Venus, the goddess of love. Love is both the cause and effect of hospitality. This message is further underscored by the names of Philemon and Baucis, meaning "loving one" and "tender one." These two figures, the very personifications of love and tenderness, welcome strangers as guests and, in so doing, transform the world. Such are the workings of hospitality as equanimity, and equanimity as hospitality.

Cracking the Armor

Among our most deeply ingrained habits is that of discriminating between friends, enemies, and strangers. These attitudes arise so effortlessly and continuously that we imbue them with objective reality. We identify with these states of mind, and identify others with their given roles. We need to question this habitual mode of perceiving, because, despite how accurate it seems, it can turn out to be flawed. The unevenness in our response to others may reflect our own fluctuating state of mind and not objective truth. Lama Yeshe describes how emotional and mental addictions flavor, and give rise to, our perceptions of others.

> With our tremendous grasping desire we become attached to and cling to our dear friends, with aversion and hatred we reject those we do not like, and with indifference we turn a blind eye to the countless people who appear to be neither helpful nor harmful to us.[37]

Our perceptions can provide an accurate snapshot of experience in the moment, but nothing more. Some people are friends and others are enemies or strangers, but these relationships are not static; they are forever changing. Temporary friend, enemy, and stranger do exist; however, "there is no such thing as permanent or unchangeable enemy, friend, or neutral person."[38] Someone may be our enemy for the time being, but this does not make him or her a permanent enemy. The same person may later become our closest and dearest friend. This uncertainty also applies to our best friend, who may later become our worst enemy. The transition from friend to enemy happens every day. Our current relationship with someone provides only the thinnest glimpse into a much vaster network of relationship. Since there is no "fixed" relationship between ourselves and others, equanimity regarding the happiness and welfare of others is the attitude of the wise.

In the Tibetan Buddhist tradition, our existence over multiple life-times is a given, opening the field of relationship even wider, because every other being has been in every conceivable relationship with us over countless lives. If someone is kind to you today, and someone else was kind to you ten years ago, or ten lifetimes ago, is one person's kindness more important because it is closer to you in time? We tend to attribute more importance to the one who is there for us now, but there is no real basis for this. A kindness extended toward us many years ago may continue to benefit us today. And, at the time, it was no less significant than the kindness we are benefiting from in the moment. Furthermore, if we consider the possibility of limitless lives, it is quite feasible that everyone has been both kind and cruel to us at different times. This collapses our distinctions even more. Holding to one viewpoint, based on a snapshot of experience, becomes untenable.

Our limited ability to perceive the fluctuating nature of our relationships, especially if we consider multiple lifetimes, can have rather ironic consequences, as illustrated by this brief tale. A clairvoyant adept approaches a young mother who is cradling her beloved child in her lap and feeding the child freshly prepared lamb. She puts the piece of meat down for a moment and, in that instant, a dog runs off with it. The woman immediately hurls a stone at the dog, almost killing it. The adept, through the power of his clairvoyance, sees that the child she holds so dear had, in its previous life, been an enemy of her parents and had been responsible for the destruction of their household. Her murdered father had since taken rebirth as the sheep whose flesh she was eating and feeding to her child. And the woman's own precious mother had taken rebirth as the dog she had nearly killed with a stone.

Three Ways of Seeing

Three types of beings exist in our minds. In truth, there aren't three types of beings, there are three habitual modes of perception. These modes have little to do with others and a great deal to do with ourselves. Interestingly, Karen Horney also notes three kinds of response, or three types of defense, in relation to others. She describes these as moving toward people, moving against people, and moving away from people. These attitudes respectively parallel grasping, hostility, and indifference. Horney asserts that these three stances constitute "the core of neurosis," or more specifically, that these three attitudes are "the dynamic center from which neuroses emanate."[39]

The Buddha made this observation as well. There are those whom we desire and to whom we are attached. We imagine that our happiness depends on them. There are those we dislike or hate and wish to push away or harm. We imagine they are the cause of our agitation and fury. And there are those toward whom we feel indifferent. We imagine their fate means nothing to us.

When we care for someone, we are willing to sacrifice and suffer for them. This transcendence of self-interest can be quite noble, except that it is often done to satisfy our own yearning, rather than out of love or compassion for the other. If we are acting out of our own desire, such "selflessness" brings little joy. Instead, we often end up feeling anguished, disappointed, and embittered. The one who made our heart sing with delight becomes a nightmare vision, a ghost rattling in the attic, and we become martyrs in the name of love. Genuine love and compassion are self-nourishing because, as our hearts open to others, we experience the joy of that openness. Desirous attachment, on the other hand, is always tinged with anxiety and fear of loss. Attachment exaggerates the qualities of the other, whether it be a person or an object, and this inevitably leads to disappointment, when the other fails to fulfill its promise. Most of the time, our love and attachment are intimately entwined, and our relationships to others are an amalgam of the two.

Desire, as previously discussed, comes "from the stars." It is energized presence, pulsating, radiating, and illuminating life. Too often, however, we are hypnotized by the energy of desire, becoming fixated on individuals and objects, and losing sight of the energy of life itself. Unconditioned desire contracts and becomes conditional attachment. We take a force pervading infinite galaxies and universes and try to possess it by squeezing it into a space the size of a phone booth. Is it any wonder if our life overheats and goes up in flames? Desire burns us because we try to narrow and domesticate it. We project the splendor of existence onto another, and then try to control its elusive reflection. Love with projections and conditions always leads to disappointment, restlessness, and displeasure.

Hatred and anger, the attitude we feel toward a second group of beings, is also rooted in self-centeredness. We dislike or hate those who insult and hurt us, or who hurt our loved ones. These people, we decide, are not deserving of happiness. The irony is that, just as attachment inevitably brings pain and disappointment, "as soon as hostility arises in the mind, you're already damaging yourself, and so in a sense you're accomplishing the task of the enemy."[40] Hostility toward others actually inflicts injury upon ourselves. It is like holding a burning coal in our hands with the intention of using it to burn another, and all the while burning ourselves.

When Nelson Mandela was released after decades of political imprisonment, he described his walk past his prison guards into life as a free man. Upon seeing the guards, anger flared for a moment in his mind. In that moment, he made a choice. He realized that these people had imprisoned him for over twenty years and that becoming angry with them would simply delay his freedom further. He was not going to give the guards one more day of his life by becoming a prisoner of anger. Leaving prison behind, he walked into life ahead, truly a free man. This is the way to be wisely selfish. If we care for ourselves and want to be free, we will protect ourselves from the consuming flames of our anger. Although it is very hard to put into practice, I was fortunate to be given the gift of this hard-won insight at a young age.

At the age of thirteen, I was on the threshold of many things, none of which I could have known. A fierce independence was growing stronger day by day. I relied, as many adolescents do, on angry outbursts to release the tension mounting within. A flame of wrath marked my territory. No trespassing. Danger. Do not enter. Land mines. Proceed at your own risk. This territory, passionately staked out, held the illusive Grail of my individuality and freedom. I did not know then that it could also destroy the freedom I was trying so vehemently to protect. Perhaps only my mother, the person from whom I least expected it, could shock me into such recognition.

I came home from school, fuming over an interaction with a teacher. Looking for a place to vent, I sought out my mother. She was in the basement washing clothes. I quickly descended the stairs into the basement; a fitting image for my own abasement. My mother was standing by the washing machine putting the just-washed clothes through the wringer. One by one, each piece of clothing submitted to the wringer, releasing its water into the basin, before being hung to dry on three lines crisscrossing the room. I began raging about my day at school. At first, my mother seemed only half-interested. Her attention was divided. My intensity reached fever pitch. Was it going to be me or that pile of clothes? I was making my case. I had been wronged, and I was shouting it to the world. My mother began to listen more intently.

"I hate my teacher. I hate her!" I shouted. Until this moment, my mother had remained silent. Then, looking at me across the infinite expanse of the human heart, she spoke. "If you hate someone, it is your own life you destroy." I was stopped. Her words, in a moment, disarmed me. My indignant world turned inside out. If hate were ever just, I knew no one who was more entitled to it than my mother. She had watched her life go up in Nazi smoke. Auschwitz. Just uttering this one word is enough to deliver me to unfathomable depths of human hatred and anguish. The Holocaust, a conflagration, destroyed a world. That world lived in my mother, and now she was giving me the golden elixir of her passage through darkness.

Many years later, I became involved in Buddhist practice and first heard about an unbroken lineage of teachers comprising a "living tradition." I understood that this meant that the teachings I was receiving had been passed on continuously since the time of the Buddha by individuals embodying their realization. The uninterrupted flow of realization from one human being to another via body, breath, and heart is what makes a teaching transmission "alive." This was the secret power in my mother's message. It was alive. She was passing on her living truth.

As an adult, I came across the extraordinary diaries of Etty Hillesum. These diaries were written by a young Jewish woman who both witnessed and experienced the growing horrors of the Third Reich. With exquisite lucidity, Etty reveals her rare and moving perspective regarding the scourge of evil flooding the world, and her conviction that it was the duty of each individual to look within for the roots of brutality and ugliness. In one passage, written while reflecting upon the tendency to respond to hatred or injustice with hatred, she observes, "I know that those who hate have good reason to do so. But why should we always choose the cheapest and easiest way? It has been brought home forcibly to me here, how even an atom of hatred added to the world makes it an even more inhospitable place."[41] Hillesum's words complete the circle of understanding begun by my mother. Hatred, however just it may seem, destroys our lives. Moreover, hatred as a response to hatred only fuels the very hatred we are trying to extinguish. "Hatred is never overcome by hatred, but by love alone," the Buddha said. "This is an ancient and eternal law." An "absence of hatred in no way implies the absence of moral indignation, however."[42] An absence of hatred keeps us free. Out of freedom, we act. Love and compassion, as I stated earlier, are expressions of human freedom. Hatred, however empowering it may feel, is an expression of bondage.

Although attachment and anger abound, indifference colors our attitude toward the great majority. Indifference is the third mode of perceiving beings. As with attachment and anger, our indifference toward others is self-centered. Because we feel no relationship to nameless, faceless, numberless other beings, "we are totally unconcerned about them—whether they are unhappy or suffer does not effect [sic] us in the slightest."[43]

Indifference is coolly destructive. We perceive those to whom we are indifferent as non-beings, and hence their suffering is a non-event. Our treatment of those to whom we feel indifferent is also inconsequential. We simply do whatever whim dictates. We may ignore and neglect, or we may harass and harm. It doesn't much matter to us. Geshe Rabten uses an example of hunters and their prey to illustrate the attitude of indifference.

> Usually hunters do not have strong attachment or aversion to their prey; for their own enjoyment they recklessly destroy the lives of others. But if one thinks deeply about this and reflects on how strongly attached one is to one's own life, considering it very precious, one should realize that in just the same way every being, every animal or human, shares this very same kind of attachment, this very same view of its own life. [44]

It is easy to forget or deny that all living beings have feelings. Preoccupied with our own comfort or pleasure, we often treat others in our world, including non-human others, as though they exist for our benefit and not for their own happiness. Of course, we may protest, saying it is hard enough to be considerate of the few beings to whom we are close. But every being deserves consideration. The Buddha goes as far as to say that, over countless lifetimes, all beings have, at one time or another, been our mother, showing us the greatest kindness. Therefore, all beings are not only worthy of our consideration, they are also worthy of our gratitude, love, and compassion.

One hot summer day—I was probably five or six—my parents took me to the zoo. While there, I had an experience that spoke to me of the consideration and liberty all beings wish for. Like most children, I loved seeing all the wild and exotic animals at the zoo. And it was always a special source of delight to watch the playful monkeys swing effortlessly through the air. We were watching the monkeys with a lot of other people. I didn't know what kind of monkeys these were, except to say they were the kind with the bright red bottoms.

There was a big crowd at the zoo that day. I was standing on a nearby bench so I could see over the heads of all the tall people in front of me, and what I saw really upset me. The monkeys were sitting on the ground, and people were throwing all kinds of food at them. The humans wanted to be entertained, and they were harassing the monkeys, trying to get them to perform. Finally, one monkey responded by crossing his arms, turning around, and pointing his bright red rump directly at the crowd. Seeing this, I cheered enthusiastically: "Good for you, monkey! Good for you!" Everybody turned to look at me. Who was this human child cheering for the rights and dignity of a monkey?

Seeing Others through the "I" of the Beholder

The following meditation is recommended as a way to observe your attachment, anger, and indifference, and determine whether they merit the power you give them. It will help you probe these emotions and consider whether they give good counsel as to whether another is worthy of compassion. And it will help reveal the manner in which these feelings are caused by, and give rise to, projection. The meditation begins by focusing on one person at a time. After gaining some stability contemplating different types of people, you can expand your scope to include a wider circle of beings, without diminishing the effectiveness of the practice.

This meditation is not intended to be an intellectual exercise. It is meant "to stimulate the mind on many different emotional levels and extend the force of the practice through those levels—imagination is the key."[45] If you begin with a nameless and faceless "all beings" and not with individual beings, then, when a particular being irritates you, your equanimity will dissolve on the spot. I also recommend that you begin your contemplation of enemies with your least significant enemies, and gradually include your worst enemies. Your worst enemy, if really brought to mind, is initially too volatile a subject for contemplation, and will undermine rather than promote the development of equanimity. If you practice this meditation repeatedly, feelings of attachment, aversion, and indifference will gradually lose their hold, and equanimity will gain ground.

BRING TO MIND SOMEONE FOR WHOM YOU CARE DEEPLY, AND imagine this person as clearly and vividly as possible. Watch as the person walks through the door and into the room. Listen for the sound of a voice, a laugh. Feel his or her presence. You may sense a smile cross your face, a sparkle come into your eyes, or you may experience a rush of warmth. Your skin may soften. Notice whatever it is that you experience when you imagine this person before you. If he or she were to irritate you, you might be temporarily upset, but ultimately you would forgive. If you imagine this person hurt or in pain, what do you feel? How deeply would you wish for him or her to be free of suffering? How far would you go to help?

Reflect on all the reasons for feeling this way about your friend, all the reasons you find that person special. How much of this specialness has to do with a special relationship to you? If you didn't know this person, would he or she be any less special? Recall a time when you did not know this person, when he or she was still a stranger to you, and consider that some years from now, this person may no longer be as special to you. Is your friend really more deserving of love and compassion because of your feelings in this moment? Was your friend less deserving of love and compassion before your acquaintance? Would your friend become less deserving if you were no longer close? Is there any guarantee your feelings will remain as they are right now?

Now think of a neutral person, a stranger. Bring a specific person to mind—perhaps the cashier at the grocery store, the bank teller, or the person sitting in the booth in a public parking lot. Imagine this person as clearly as possible. Notice your feelings when you look at this person. You may feel neither great warmth, nor especially withdrawn. You may experience a removed curiosity. Whatever your inclinations are toward most people, open or suspicious, accepting or critical, you may notice those feelings surface now, since you have little information to draw on. Observe those tendencies.

Notice how quickly you project an image onto someone. Ask yourself why this person means so little to you. If he or she were to be ill or in pain, how much would it bother you? Perhaps you think this stranger means little to you because you share no relationship. This person's existence has no effect on you or your life. Can you be certain it will always be this way? All your friends began as strangers, and this person, who seems unimportant to you, could become your best friend in the future. This person, even as a stranger, may at some future time save your life, or the life of a loved one. Should this stranger's share of happiness and joy depend upon sharing a relationship with you at this moment?

Now bring a third person to mind—a person for whom you feel a measure of dislike or hostility, someone whose pain or suffering would not disturb you, someone in whose experience of misfortune you might even take pleasure. See this person in your mind and feel your dislike, your disapproval, or revulsion. You may find yourself grimacing. Observing your body, you may notice a tightening of the chest, rigidity in your arms or legs, or the hot flush of anger across the back of your neck. Or perhaps you will feel a sharp blade of animosity and hostility in your solar plexus. Think about the basis of these feelings. There was a time when you didn't know this person, a time when his or her image would not particularly have moved you. Or there may have been a time when this person was your most intimate companion for whose presence you pined night and day. Whatever the case, these feelings of hatred or hostility were not always there, and they may be completely gone at some future time. This person may become your most trusted ally. Why should this moment in time determine his or her right to love and compassion?

■   ■   ■

Relationships are like water, yet we try to fashion them as if they were stone. Feelings are fluid and transparent, but we imagine them to be solid and opaque. Things change from day to day. A friend saved me from hypothermia and likely drowning in an early spring lake. The same man, because of his anger, caused a car accident a year later. Refusing to look my way, he didn't check the traffic coming in our direction and, in the flash of a moment, a fast-approaching car filled my window as it crashed into us. How do I decide about this man? Can I suspend judgment? Leave it open? Can I allow, or at least consider, that he is as deserving of compassion when he was causing an accident that could have killed me as when he was saving my life?

It is important to stop equating people with their behavior, be it good or bad. Behavior is temporary, and when we equate people with their behavior, we freeze them in time. I certainly do not want to be frozen in time, and I don't imagine anyone else wants that either. "To equate a person with their behavior is unrealistic, and very harmful to ourselves. The point of the practice is to never equate any person with a form of behavior."[46] If we accept, or at least consider, that every living being has Buddha nature, then we also accept, or at least consider, that there is more to individuals than the loathsome characteristics they may be exhibiting in the moment. If the person afflicted with detestable traits were our own child, how fervently we would wish to free that child from the chains of affliction. How much would we gladly sacrifice to help them?

Another way to observe the constantly fluctuating nature of friends, enemies, and strangers is to look at the world stage and see our current political enemies and how they have changed over the short span of a lifetime. Allies and enemies fluctuate all the time. I recall a time when the Russians were our intractable foes, holding our collective imagination in fear of their cunning. In scores of movies, diabolical Soviets plot the demise and ultimate destruction of the United States. They seem truly alien and evil. Today we see they are people. They are a collection of people facing their own set of challenges. They have fears, desires, and ambitions. They're not really fundamentally different from us. The same holds true if we look at nations throughout the world.

When I visited the Holocaust Memorial Museum in Washington, D.C., this realization was brought home to me poignantly. Looking at photo after photo of children of the Third Reich raising their arms in praise of Hitler, I saw that they looked like any other children. Without the uniforms and chilling collective gesture, these children were indistinguishable from any children wishing for happiness and wishing to avoid suffering. Their behavior and their mental characteristics may be abhorrent, but that doesn't alter this deeper truth. Understanding this tempers the poison arrow of single-pointed hatred. Certainly, if the Nazis had contemplated this, there never would have been a Holocaust. If Mao had contemplated this, there never would have been a Cultural Revolution, with its continuing trail of blood. If we contemplate this, we will contribute to the causes of peace, and not war, in the world. We will see our shared humanity, even with those who hate us and seek to destroy everything we hold dear.

Profound Similarity

The Dalai Lama begins almost every public address by saying that every living being shares the wish to have happiness and avoid suffering. He says this with such regularity that it is easy to dismiss it as simple and trite, a mere platitude not worth thinking about too deeply. But it actually represents a profound insight worth contemplating again and again. In fact, if this were all the Dalai Lama ever said, this and nothing more, we would have more than enough material to work with for a very long time. Instead of attending to the obvious differences between people, we need to "cultivate an awareness of the more subtle but ethically more significant similarities that ordinarily go unnoticed."[47]

If we look beyond common distinctions and prejudices, "we will be able to appreciate fully that everyone, without exception, wants and deserves to be happy and wishes to avoid even the slightest suffering."[48] All beings both wish for and deserve happiness and freedom from suffering, although these goals continually elude them. The key word here is "deserves." It is also the point of resistance and difficulty. It is much easier to accept that all beings wish for happiness than to truly believe that they all deserve happiness. All beings do deserve happiness, however, because every being has a pure nature that is innately capable of awakening to freedom and joy. This nature is the true being within. Everything else, however reprehensible it may be, is a secondary characteristic.

Reflecting upon the fact that every one of us shares, and deserves to fulfill, this most fundamental desire establishes a foundation for the third level of equanimity: seeing the equality between ourselves and others, and generating the sincere wish to benefit ourselves and others equally. Gehlek Rimpoche describes equanimity at this level: "My commitment to help all sentient beings and my commitment to help myself . . . has the same priority. It is equal."[49] Through universal equanimity, "we will be able to cultivate universal love, compassion and eventually the full realization of bodhicitta: the open heart dedicated totally to the ultimate benefit of all."[50]

Modern life has brought increasing isolation, and many feel estranged from their own neighbors. We may live in a neighborhood for years and yet not know the person down the street. Differences in religion, values, race, or politics reinforce these feelings of distance. We come to believe others are so different from ourselves that we don't know them or understand them; yet, on a deeper level, we know them quite well. Every single one of them is like you and me, wanting happiness and wishing to avoid suffering. This is no mere superficial similarity; it is the deepest urge we all share. Despite all differences, if we "cut right through the surface," we "recognize a kindred soul at the core."[51] This is why, when the Dalai Lama says he feels a closeness with everyone he meets, it is true, and people sense it is true.

Because of our profound similarity to others, "it is a mistake to wish some well and others harm."[52] When developing equanimity at the prior stage, we observed the transitory, and therefore unreliable, nature of attachment, anger, and indifference as a basis for compassion. At this stage of equanimity, we recognize that "all of us, including the most despicable of people, do all that we do because we're seeking happiness and want to be free of suffering."[53] Miserly or generous, benevolent or cruel, through good times and bad, high and low, each of us yearns for and seeks happiness. In this quest for happiness, myriad beings, including ourselves, act obsessively and with great confusion. Can we develop equanimity toward ourselves and others in the face of the turmoil we continually create? This is the challenge before us.

Recognizing your similarity with others "does not mean that you consider other's *ways* of getting happiness suitable and thus affirm them. Quite the opposite: you become more astute at not affirming them."[54] Equanimity does not mean that you ignore cruelty in others. You see the fact that others go about seeking happiness in ways that cause harm for what it is, but this knowledge gives rise to compassionate action rather than judgment, vengeance, and further alienation. When you see deeply that others are just like yourself, desiring happiness and yet habitually driven to create the conditions for further suffering, you open your heart to the predicament of being addicted to self-centered life. Self-centeredness creates every problem. It blinds you to the real causes of happiness and binds you to the real causes of misery. What painful predicament is more worthy of compassion than this?

Feeling Ourselves and Seeing Others

We don't generally place a great priority on the happiness of others. We are, however, thoroughly concerned with whether others serve our quest for satisfaction. We habitually fall into perceiving others in terms of how they might be vehicles or obstacles to our own goals and ambitions. Jeffrey Hopkins observes that, "We're all so similar, yet somehow it's so easy to cross that line and use other people for one's own happiness—in ways we would never want to be used ourselves." He suggests that perhaps we do this so easily because "we use radically different modes [of perception] for self and others."[55] We primarily *see* others with our eyes, whereas we *feel* ourselves. We are acutely aware of our own hunger, thirst, illness, health, pleasure, or pain, but we don't, as a rule, feel into the experience of others. We see the people around us, but their thirst doesn't make us thirsty and their hunger doesn't deprive us of a meal. The illness, suffering, or death of another seems quite different, and separate, from our own. As a result, our own experience, with which we are so intimately acquainted, feels more real. Seeming more real to ourselves than others do, we also feel more important to ourselves than others do. Our own happiness becomes paramount, and the well-being of others secondary or irrelevant.

This sense of self-importance can take a particularly disturbing turn in relation to those we despise and fear. In these instances, we not only feel removed from their pain, we may actually rejoice at their pain, thinking, "Oh good, they're finally getting what they deserve." When our enemies suffer, we may celebrate. Television, movies, cartoons, and even comic books reinforce the view that our enemy's pain is our victory. But, as Trungpa points out, "happiness that is built on pain is spurious and only leads to depression in the long run."[56] Genuine happiness simply cannot flourish on the limbs of someone else's sorrow—even our enemy's. Furthermore, although we may take momentary pleasure at seeing our enemy suffer, if we felt that enemy's suffering as our own, we would find no pleasure in their pain.

Worthy of Love

In my earlier discussion of Freud, I elaborated on the objections he had to the injunction to love your neighbor as yourself. Freud vigorously defended his stance that this was both an absurd concept and a guilt-inducing ideal. He felt it was absurd because people could never live up to it, and guilt-inducing because they believed they should be able to do so. But far more disturbing to me is Freud's vehemence that, even if it were possible to generate such feelings, strangers were not worthy of his love. Strangers have done nothing to deserve love. In fact, Freud claimed that they have "more claim to my hostility and even my hatred."[57]

Freud advanced a two-fold criterion for worthiness. In order for people to be worthy of your concern or care, they must fulfill at least one of these criteria. Either they must be like you, so you can see yourself in them and therefore love them as yourself; or they must possess traits you admire, so you will then love them as an exemplar of the ideals to which you aspire. I trust it is clear by now that, through reasoned analysis and contemplation, you can come to see that all living beings fall within the very categories Freud outlines here.

The equanimity we cultivate depends upon recognizing the profound likeness between ourselves and others. Loving others becomes a natural expression of our relationship with them, and likeness to them. We love others because we share an intimate bond with them. Knowing them at the deepest level, they cease to be strangers; they become fellow sufferers and fellow travelers. This realization is the ground of universal compassion, because, as your equanimity encompasses more and more beings, the force of love and compassion can also increase exponentially.

Developing equanimity is a humanizing activity. Conversely, in order to hurt others, we actively de-humanize or de-soul them. We imagine they are not living beings like ourselves, and therefore not worthy of the care and kindness that those who are like us deserve. Having separated ourselves from others in this manner, it is much easier to ignore or harm them. Labeling others as less than human, or less than persons, makes it acceptable to do whatever we please with them. When equanimity is cultivated and stabilized, we can no longer exclude others from the ranks of humans or persons. It is, then, not so easy to hurt or neglect them. If we lack equanimity, this unfortunately is what we inevitably do.

It is even easier to justify excluding from the ranks of "all beings" those whose behavior is profoundly evil. We see absolutely no purpose in having compassion for such demonic individuals. Our own hatred is often incited in response to their heinous deeds. But stop and consider for a moment: If some of the truly despicable and monstrous beings on the planet were freed from the blinding effect of their hatred and the psychic pain that causes and accompanies it, they would quite naturally be kinder. They would be far less likely to inflict suffering upon others. We inflict suffering when we ourselves are suffering. When our own minds are at ease, we have no need or desire to harm others. So, wishing for all inconceivably cruel individuals to be free of suffering is automatically wishing for the conditions in which they would no longer inflict suffering on others. When we generate such a compassionate mind, we become capable of taking strong action without succumbing to hatred ourselves.

At bottom, we are left with the incontrovertible truth that every being, whether friend, foe, or stranger, wishes for happiness and wishes to be free of suffering, just as we do. We all share this wish. It needs no further elaboration. We all wish for pleasure and we all wish to avoid pain; it is as basic as that. It is our nature to be this way, just as it is the nature of fire to burn and the nature of bees to make honey. This is simply the way things are. The Buddhist path does not suggest that we forego or deny our natural urge to happiness, but that we pursue it in a way that makes its attainment possible.

Chapter 6

ANSWERING THE CALL:
THE ALCHEMY OF THE HEART

■   ■   ■

No better love than love with no object.

−RUMI

T he entire lojong text is encapsulated instruction. Each aphorism is like a mnemonic device stimulating recall and disclos-
ing variegated layers of meaning. Some aphorisms make
such bold statements about the nature of reality and the causes of happiness and sorrow that they threaten the foundations of our worldview.
They challenge many of our most basic assumptions about life and liberty. We are not meant simply to accept or reject these ideas on impulse,
but to wrestle with them, as there is nothing abstract or theoretical
about these teachings. They are truly food for thought, meant to be
gradually ingested and incorporated, and ultimately to make a lasting
impression on our heart and mind, and a difference in the way we live in
the world. Over time, as the practice takes root, every individual who
practices lojong develops a unique and personal relationship to the
material.

The lojong is designed to help individuals, one by one, identify the
obstacles to happiness and cultivate the conditions in which their fundamental well-being may flourish. Such well-being "is not simply a happy
feeling; it is a state of being that underlies and suffuses all emotional

states, that embraces all the joys and sorrows that come our way."[1] As deeply as we long for this well-being, it is exceptionally difficult to bring about, because the process of achieving it goes against the grain of our deepest instinctive conditioning. Instincts, we discover, may lead us astray. The voice of our instincts, continually affirming the solidity and separateness of self and other, has long been a trusted advisor but, in truth, "sometimes our instincts are not wise."[2]

Through repeated contemplation and increasing familiarity, simply recalling or reading any one of the aphorisms can cut through, or at least put a dent in, our intractable habitual tendencies on the spot. After a time, they begin to arise unbidden in the midst of life. You hear yourself blaming your partner for ruining the dinner, when to your surprise, "Drive all blames into one," pops up in your mind. All blame may not drop away, but a shift occurs, and with it comes another crack in your ancient armor.

Doing this practice requires us, as one of the last of the aphorisms instructs, to train wholeheartedly. The wholeheartedness spoken of here is steadfast, ardent, and gentle, because softening our hard edges and opening to ourselves fully is a lifelong process. It requires a balance of constancy, determination, and relaxation. It is like we are trying to grow seeds in earth that hasn't seen rain for 100,000 years. Although it is earth's nature to receive water, the rain must fall in harmony with the conditions of the earth below. If rain is sporadic, it will not be sufficient to soften the hard, parched earth. If the downpour is too heavy, the earth will repel the excess water, causing destructive flash floods. But if the rain falls gently and persistently, day after day, the earth will soften to welcome it, and the once-inhospitable earth will become a moist and fertile ground, capable of producing a bountiful harvest.

The Message of Lojong

The lojong practice identifies the obstacles to compassion and love as two-fold. The first of these is self-centeredness or selfishness—the habit of seeing ourselves as most important and always placing ourselves and our wishes ahead of others. This attitude puts us at odds with virtually everyone we encounter, because everyone else is also dominated by self-centeredness. Demanding that life centralize into ourselves undermines our happiness, because it contradicts the way things actually are. Self-centeredness is a breeding ground for personal unhappiness, as well as of all the strife and disharmony in the world. According to lojong logic, all our troubles arise because we are slaves to our self-importance. Simply put, this "selfish mind is the worst disease."[3]

The second obstacle to developing love and compassion is our habit of grasping at an intrinsic, independently existing self. Our self-grasping, or self-habit, is a master deceiver; it is the poisonous root of the tree of suffering. The Dalai Lama explains why it is so critical to see through this wrong knowing of self.

> The reason so much emphasis is placed on the rejection of an eternal soul or self in the Buddhist teachings is that much of our confusion and suffering is seen to arise from a false sense of self, and in particular from a belief in some kind of eternal independently existing self at the core of our being.[4]

Self-grasping is the deeper of the two obstacles, giving rise to the selfish mind. Belief in a solidly existing "me" automatically creates "mine." What is mine belongs to me; without me, mine will not arise at all. The self-centered or selfish mind protects and serves the interests of the self-grasping mind. Together, these pretenders to the throne perpetually lead us astray and let us down.

> Every trouble you are going through . . . all of them are connected with this idea. If you find one which is not caused by the "me" idea, I will bow to you ten times. But you're not going to find it—I guarantee you, you're not going to find it . . . You don't even have to think about life after life—that is a long shot. Think yesterday, or the day before yesterday.[5]

Through the practice of lojong, we gradually attenuate both selfishness and self-grasping and replace them with great compassion and the wisdom of emptiness, respectively. We do this by cultivating relative and absolute bodhimind. The achievement of a fully developed, seamlessly unified compassion and wisdom is Buddhahood, and its realization marks the fulfillment of our evolutionary potential. "A buddha is the butterfly that finally emerges from the cocoon of the human life form."[6] Although the lojong practice highlights the cultivation of compassion, it is a complete practice that also includes instructions for the development of wisdom. Wisdom is the heart of compassion, and compassion is the heart of wisdom. Each is inside the other. Without wisdom, compassion is incomplete. It resembles a bird with one wing—flapping and flapping, but never able to take off in flight. Not unlike Psyche and Eros, compassion and wisdom require each other in order to fully become themselves.

Relative Bodhimind

The second point of the lojong constitutes its main practice: Cultivate relative and absolute bodhimind. Traditionally, either the relative or the absolute bodhimind aphorisms can be introduced first, and there are merits to each approach. However, in keeping with teachings I have received, I will begin with the relative bodhimind aphorisms.

The first of these aphorisms is: "Drive all blames into one," or "Banish the one object of every blame." These statements push us into the deep end of the pool. We are no longer dipping our toes at the water's edge; we're in up to our eyeballs. Who is to blame for all our problems? What is getting in the way of our happiness? Where is the one on whom we can pin the cause of our dissatisfaction? Wanting to untangle the web of suffering in which we are caught, it is natural for us to search for the culprit. The good news is that the mysterious thwarter of our joy is finally going to be exposed. But we may not be prepared for the revelation. Such is the nature of apocalypse. It may not be at all what we expect. There is no dragon out there to slay, no evil demon to destroy. The culprit will not be found anywhere outside ourselves, and, truly speaking, neither will the savior. Rather, we find that all our troubles can be boiled down to one source alone: our persistent selfishness. Glimpsing the culprit of selfishness is the beginning of salvation and liberation, although it seems utterly foreign and strange. Like Ivan spotting the hut of Baba Yaga turning on a chicken leg, or Dorothy landing in Oz, we are being drawn beyond the borders of our familiar world.

"Drive all blames into one" can feel like pretty miserable advice. Here we are, embarking on a path of compassion, and the first instruction is to drive all blames into ourselves. This is not what we expected, and we may bristle upon hearing it. It may sound more like a guilt-inducing reproach than sage advice for developing love and compassion. This, however, is not the intended meaning at all. It is not our selves we are blaming. Blaming the "one" does not mean we literally blame ourselves. It is the dictatorship of a self-centered "I" controlling our lives and never giving us a moment's rest at which we point the proverbial finger. We are blaming the "I" that separates itself from the rest of the world and sees itself and its concerns as most important. This self-centeredness is the enemy of our happiness. It is so easy to confuse selfishness with self-love, wrongly concluding that, if we want to develop compassion, we are not supposed to care for ourselves.

We need to make a very clear distinction between doing the bidding of our imperious "I" and caring for ourselves. The problem is that we are in the habit of confusing the two and, consequently, we cling to the belief that protecting the egoic "I" is protecting ourselves when, in fact, the opposite is true. This confusion keeps us scurrying to and fro, frantically going nowhere on the painful treadmill of samsara. "We have allowed self-centeredness to exhaust us in the past, and in return we have received very little good and a lot of anxiety."[7] Blaming this "one" pulls the rug out from under the false god we worship.

Caring for ourselves is the reason we bring our habitual selfishness under scrutiny. And when we do, we discover we have been conned. We have been tricked by the illusory appearance of a separate and independent self, and unwittingly, we serve that illusion twenty-four hours a day. "Every day, we wake up in the morning and are hit by the biggest intuitive lie known to human consciousness. The lie goes like this: 'It's me, it's me, I'm it. I'm the center of the universe. I come first. I hold it all together.'"[8] Clinging to and protecting this lie is our deepest compulsion, and freeing ourselves from the ravages of this addiction is the unsurpassed key to liberation.

Addicted to Self

As with other addictions, we need to begin by acknowledging the power our addiction to self has over our lives. The etymology of the word "addict" refers to a condition of slavery.[9] Marion Woodman adds to the enslaving aspect of addiction her view that addiction is "a distorted religion."[10] Considering that the Latin etymology of the word "religion" means binding or tying oneself to a greater good, it is easy to see how addiction can be conceived of as a slavish distortion of the religious impulse. Addiction binds us as does religion, but it doesn't yoke us to the greater good; it makes us the slaves of empty promise.

Addiction is an act of surrender, of faithfully and habitually giving oneself over. It is the act of delivering ourselves body and soul to a ruling principle or master. Our addiction to the image of an independently existing self, and to the importance of this self, is pervasive; it cannot be reduced to either a physical condition or a psychological state. It cannot be classified strictly as a disease, or as a behavior disorder, or as a moral failing—it defies such classification. Unlike other addictions, addiction to self-importance is not experienced as a choice, but as an ontological fact. Many, perhaps most, believe that taking up life and focusing it through the lens of "me, me, me," and "mine, mine, mine" is not an addiction at all—it is simply the way things are.

Viktor Frankl is among those who have challenged this assumption. He recalls Freud's conviction that exposing a diverse group of people to hunger would blur all individual differences and reveal the "one unstilled urge." Frankl counters that, whereas Freud came to these conclusions on the basis of analyzing wealthy patients in a lavish Victorian setting, his observations were made in the burning hell of Auschwitz. "There, individual differences did not 'blur' but, on the contrary, people became more different; people unmasked themselves, both the swine and the saints." Freud's conclusions are speculative; Frankl speaks from direct experience. And to those who would upbraid him for suggesting that humanity strive to model itself upon the few "saints," Frankl gives this response:

> You may be prone to blame me for invoking examples that are exceptions to the rule. "*Sed omnia praeclaratam diffilia quam rara*

sunt" (but everything great is just as difficult to realize as it is rare to find) reads the last sentence of the *Ethics* of Spinoza. . . . I see therein the very challenge to join the minority. For the world is in a bad state, but everything will become worse unless each of us do our best.[11]

Every adept in the unbroken lineage of teachers tracing back to the Buddha has rejected as erroneous the belief that, because a majority expresses certain tendencies, we can draw sound conclusions regarding human nature. The Buddha himself, and every advanced contemplative who has followed thereafter, affirms the presence of an indestructible, pure nature within each living being. Gehlek Rimpoche offers this concise reply to those who maintain that self-addiction is synonymous with human nature: "You may say it is human nature, but it is not . . . It is a terrible addiction that we bring in within our life."[12]

Addicted to the self and its protection, we are propelled by a yearning that forever eludes satisfaction. We are driven by our addictive clinging to self, and spent by the empty bowl of our craving. Shantideva called this addiction to self "a great ghost" whose spectral presence causes "all the injury, fear and pain in the world."[13] Unlike most other addictions, this one doesn't display any of the usual markers. We won't find our addiction to self on street corners; we won't walk past it in alleys or see it winking at us from behind a slot machine. There is no bottle concealed in a paper bag, no money exchanged, no needle tracks, no fleshless skin hanging on vacant bones, no secret rendezvous; there are no outer signs to be seen. The addiction to self is everywhere and, because it is everywhere, it is exceptionally well hidden. It is an open secret.

Unless we turn and look at ourselves, we can easily live our whole lives without noticing our enslavement to a tyrannical "I" manipulating our every move. We have surrendered our volition so completely that we believe this is just the way things are. Unless we realize we have a choice, nothing can alter the influence this addiction to self has over our lives. The selfish mind will continue to be sent out like a whore to work the streets, all the while keeping her pimp and master (self-grasping) protected and prosperous. She is controlled by him, but he depends on her. This is our misery. This is where the blame belongs. This is the arrangement we must mutiny against. This is the place for revolution and uprising. This is the task of transformation. "Freeing ourselves from negative emotions, freeing ourselves from samsara, means nothing less than this. Free from our ego's spell. That's what it is."[14] The spell of ego must be broken if love and compassion are to have room to grow.

Dropping the Object of Blame

"Drive all blames into one" also encourages us to look at the blame game itself. "It's not that there isn't anything to be concerned or upset about. People have plenty of reasons to be angry. We have to acknowledge this. We are angry. But blaming the other doesn't solve anything."[15] If we take a close look at blame, we will see it for the problem it is. There is simply nothing to be gained by blaming, and there is so much to be lost. For one thing, it keeps us stuck in old rage and resentment. John F. Kennedy spoke to the American people about the need to let go of blame when he said, "Our task is not to fix the blame for the past, but to fix the course for the future." Blame is a way of holding onto hurt and injustice, and this holding on is like a knot in our heart. The more clearly we recognize that the painful contraction in our heart is caused by holding on to blame, the stronger our commitment to abandoning it becomes.

Yesterday, I was in the office of a friend and noticed a poster on her wall advertising a book called, *Don't Shoot Yourself in the Foot*. The poster listed two types of behavior, those that are self-defeating and those leading to success. The very first item in the column listing self-defeating behaviors was: Blaming others. The antidote, or counterpart, on the list of behaviors leading to success was: Taking responsibility. Even if we are seeking worldly success, blaming others is still counterproductive. Even if we are single-pointedly focused on fulfilling our selfish objectives, blame will undermine our efforts. "Blame is a way in which we solidify ourselves."[16] The more we solidify ourselves, the more stuck we remain.

Not blaming means getting past our tendency to see ourselves as either victim or victor. It suggests a middle way. But we need to stop blaming long enough to figure out what that middle way is, and that means feeling things we are accustomed to pushing away. It means learning to sit with pain and disappointment instead of plotting a strategy of retaliation. Instead of using blame as a defense and distraction, we drop our defensive reactivity and feel the soft flesh beneath. Pema Chodron advises that, if we want to stop the cycle of blaming, "Instead of throwing the snowballs out there, just put the snowball down."[17]

"Putting the snowball down" means that, when we're angry, fed up, jealous, or anxious, we actually feel it. Instead of acting out or repressing, we move closer to the feeling. We shed our heavy coat of armor and risk exposing our tender, vulnerable, skin. If we do, we may discover to our surprise "that vulnerability is compassion."[18] When we practice not blaming, we practice nonaggression. Instead of reinforcing the impenetrable fortress around our heart and shooting out poison arrows from behind its protective wall, we let the wall come down and let the world come in. When the wall comes down and the world comes in, the feared thing, the bulging-eyed, three-headed monster, transforms.

One of the greatest and most beloved yogis of Tibet was Milarepa. He lived a hermit's life for many years, devoting himself entirely to meditation. One evening he returned to his cave after gathering firewood and found it had been take over by demons. They were everywhere, and Milarepa was determined to get rid of them. First, he tried asking them to go, but they did not even seem to hear him. Then he tried taking his seat and teaching them about wisdom and compassion, and still nothing happened. In frustration, he lunged at the demons, but they were unfazed. They laughed at him. Finally giving up, Milarepa sat down and said it looked as if they would all live in the cave together. Upon hearing this, all the demons left. Except one. The biggest demon stayed behind, and Milarepa, not knowing what else to do, put himself in the mouth of the demon and said, "Go ahead and eat me, if that will satisfy you." At that moment, the last demon bowed low to Milarepa and disappeared.

The compassionate mind transcends the closed fist and clenched jaw of the blaming mind. Compassion is not concerned with whom to blame; it is concerned with the alleviation of suffering. No matter how justified our blame might be, we suffer its presence in our hearts and minds, and others suffer its presence as well. If we care about alleviating our own suffering we won't hold onto blame. And as for others, Henry Wadsworth Longfellow spoke to this eloquently when he said, "If we could read the secret history of our enemies we should find in each man's life sorrow and suffering enough to disarm all hostility." Not blaming begins with feeling what we feel. Then, perhaps, we will be able to feel what others feel as well.

Cultivating Our Capacity to Feel

Most of us have never been encouraged to feel what we feel, and we don't know how to do it. We recoil from our feelings because they seem too raw, too piercing and bare. Such direct contact with ourselves makes us want to jump out of our skins. We don't know how to hold our seat amid tempest and storm. Instead, we opt for locking our feelings up behind five deadbolts in the basement, or we act out, hoping to get rid of them.

Acting out is an attempt to seek relief by targeting an object of blame on which we can dump our heavy load. Inflicting pain on ourselves or others can provide short-lived relief, but in the end, we are left with the original problem and the additional consequences of our acting out. Moreover, we add to the growing cloud of free-floating anger and blame in the world.

Violence is a language of blame. For those lacking skill in other forms of communication, or who lack confidence in other forms of communication, or who are simply habituated to it, violence is often their messenger. I recently saw a television program in which a man who was a former gang leader in his community spoke about this. One day, Ted Koppel, of *Nightline*, showed up in his town and spent a great deal of time getting to know him and some other gang members. Koppel was genuine in his desire to understand gangs. The young man was so moved by Koppel's sincerity that it changed his life. He is now a spokesperson traveling to different parts of the country, trying to help young African American men find other ways to express themselves. He said that, before meeting Koppel, he had never appreciated the power of language. He never knew that expressing himself in words could actually transform his feelings and effect change. Violence was the only form of communication he had ever known or believed in.

Emotions and frustrations are so powerful that we want to *do* something with them. Sometimes we want to do something to the person we blame for the hurt. Sometimes we take it out on a third party or a stranger. Other times we direct those feelings toward ourselves. Hurting ourselves is also a form of communication. It is a communication of rage, fear, powerlessness, and pain. The hurt we feel courses through our body, churning our emotions until they become intolerable. At that point, anything seems better than feeling the way we do, so we take action against ourselves.

A woman I have been working with walks into the office and assumes her usual position at the farthest end of the couch. I have been seeing her once a week for about six months; she is twenty-four years old—an articulate, friendly, talented young woman. She never misses a session. Considering the struggles she brings into the room, there may be many reasons for her perfect attendance record. I draw no conclusions here. One thing is clear. She is highly intuitive, and fiercely protective of her pain. She is exceptionally vigilant, and has so mastered her vigilance that I may not notice—but I do.

While writing this, I glance out my window and see a beautiful deer—a doe—looking in at me from only a short distance away. I see many deer near my home, but this is the first time one has looked directly in the window at me. I watch the supremely sensitive doe, her ears attuned to the slightest signals in the environment, ready to disappear into the green. The appearance of the deer punctuates my feelings about the intuitive, anxious, and vigilant qualities of the young woman I am describing.

Recently, this woman nonchalantly mentioned that she often got stomach aches in advance of our meetings. Today, she tells me she suffered from alternating bulimia and anorexia for seven years, beginning in junior high. An episode she shares from that time in her life sears my imagination. On one day, as on countless other days, she locked herself in the bathroom to throw up. Her parents were on the other side of the door. This day, she was unable to stimulate vomiting with her finger, so, undeterred, she put a butter knife down her throat.

The knife got stuck in her throat and she couldn't get it out; blood gushed out of her mouth and the knife was too slippery for her to grip with bare hands. She lay down on the floor, and using a towel was able to catch hold of the knife and remove it. The incident terrified her and she never spoke of it—until now. It did not end her bulimia. Years later, she tells me she knows the feelings of that time are still with her. Although no longer actively bulimic or anorexic, all the emotions fueling her illness are still troubling her and she doesn't know what to do with them. Can I help?

Men and women who suffer eating disorders submit to a daily ritual of bingeing, purging, or militantly controlling their intake. They are acting out. Every day, young women cut themselves with razor blades, not to kill themselves but to bleed. They are acting out. Acting out goes on all the time. Acting out is a fitting term for the dramatic enactment of our pain. We are acting, not only in the sense of taking action; we are also acting as actors on a stage. We assume a role in relationship to our feelings, because we don't know how to feel them directly and authentically—without "acting." We've all done it, and much of the time we have no idea what we are doing. That's part of acting out. We feel compelled, as if by a mysterious force to do something, to act. Why? It distracts us from difficult and confusing feelings—feelings like sadness, yearning, desperation, emptiness, inadequacy, loneliness, and fear.

I recall a harmless, but graphic, early childhood experience of acting out. I was in New York with my parents and they went into Manhattan for the evening, leaving me with my aunt. I was so hurt and angry that they didn't take me with them. How could they leave me? Why didn't I get to go out with them? My fury grew by the minute, whipping up like a thundercloud. And then, I spotted the relief to my surging frustration. There it was, calling to me from a shelf in the bathroom. A shiny tube of Brylcreem. I grabbed the greasy gel and squirted the whole thing in my hair. It was a good-size tube and my hair stuck out in thick wads of slick and spike all over my head. It was so thrilling to act, to take control and not feel like a helpless victim. But soon after, I had another problem. I had all this Brylcreem in my hair, and no way to get it out. My aunt found me in this condition.

The next thing I remember is looking up at her impassive face for a seeming eternity, my head hanging over the sink as she vigorously shampooed me for what seemed like a lifetime. She kept washing and washing and washing. It went on and on, and still my hair was a shiny mass of goo. The whole action drama is recalled, all these years later, with much laughter by all of us who were there. I certainly got my point across and, as a young girl, I knew no other way. But there is another way. We can stem the tide of reactivity, and move closer to ourselves.

There is no real relief to be found in blame, whatever form it takes. Blaming ourselves or blaming others perpetuates a vicious cycle of pain. It stokes the fire of aggression and alienation. And it adds more padding to our prison walls. Instead of blaming, we can reach below the porcupine quills, beneath the coat of mail, and experience the quivering flesh beneath. We can train in the middle of the fire. When old rage surfaces or fresh insults are heaped upon us, we can cultivate the courage, compassion, and honesty to find the middle way through. The middle way not only frees us from the rabid assault of blame, it benefits our hearts immeasurably. My father told me of a Hebrew prayer he often says before sleep:

Master of the Universe, I hereby forgive anyone who angered or antagonized me or who sinned against me—whether against my body, my property, my honor, or against anything of mine—whether accidentally, willfully, or purposely; whether through speech, deed, thought, or notion; whether in this transmigration or another transmigration—I forgive everyone. May no man or woman be punished because of me.

At the time he told me about this prayer, he said, "This is one of the greatest things you can come across. It gives me such a good feeling every time I say it." Hearing him express such genuine pleasure in practicing the radical release of blame, I felt encouraged. If my father could endure and survive the horror of the Holocaust and remain inspired by a path of open-heartedness, surely many more could be inspired to let go of far smaller offenses.

If we don't feed the fire of blame, it will burn for a while, but then go out. If we keep fueling the blaze, we will be swept up in a sea of flame. And if we imagine that blaming our mother, or our sixth grade teacher, is different from America and her current foes blaming each other, or the blame between Arab and Israeli, we are mistaken. The blame found in our families, in our neighborhood, at work, in the parking lot, in our local city council, in our government, is the same blame used to justify every conflict and atrocity in the world. Unless we slow the momentum of our own blaming minds and develop some compassion for self and others, there is no chance of relief on a larger scale. But, it takes time. We won't succeed in driving all blames into one the first, or even the thousandth time; but, with repeated effort, the habit of blaming others or harming ourselves simply because we know no other way will slowly subside.

The Kindness of Others

The next aphorism takes us a step further: "Be grateful to everyone," or "Meditate on everyone as kind." Every opportunity we have is because of others, including the opportunity to cultivate love and compassion. "If people aren't there, where are you going to get your compassion; upon whom?" Truly speaking, there isn't "one pleasure in our life where people are not involved," so "do not appreciate only what the Buddhas and God and enlightened beings have done, give credit to people."[19] Instead of focusing upon all the ways we have done good and have not been properly acknowledged, we reflect on all the ways others have done good and we are grateful for that. An ancient prayer, still commonly recited by Tibetan Buddhist practitioners today, puts it this way:

> *Cherishing beings and securing their happiness*
> *Is the gateway leading to infinite excellence.*
> *Inspire me to hold others more dear than my life,*
> *Even when I see them as my enemies.*[20]

If we stop and think about it, we will come to see that our comfort and survival have depended on the kindness of other beings. First of all, "each one of us owes our life and breath to a woman."[21] Every man, woman, and child—every one of us—is here because a woman shared her body and nourished us through her bloodstream. And it simply continues from there. Watching as a baby has its diaper changed, it is easy to forget that, not so long ago, we were that baby. We couldn't feed ourselves, clean ourselves, clothe ourselves, even move ourselves. Once we gained the ability to move on our own, someone saved our lives an incalculable number of times. We were saved from walking into traffic, and falling off of high places. We were saved every day from threats to our lives. We could not have survived the first years of life without the watchful eye of another.

Beggars on the streets of Calcutta know they depend on the kindness of others for their survival. We don't feel that way. As adults, most of us have enough money to buy our clothes, stock our refrigerators, and put a roof over our heads, and this gives us a false sense of autonomy. Individuals often insist, "I've achieved all that I have through my own hard work and sacrifice." This narrow view fosters an illusion of self-sufficiency. "Be grateful to everyone" encourages you to look at your life through a different lens.

Stop for a moment and think of the clothes you are wearing. Did you grow the cotton, shear the sheep, wash the wool, or weave the threads? Did you dye the fabric, stitch the cloth, or ship the garment to your local store? How about the leather you wear? Did it come off of your body? Everything you wear is due to the kindness of others—both human and animal. Everything you eat is due to the kindness of others. The house you live in and the car you drive, or the bike you ride, are due to the kindness of others. You are surrounded by the kindness of others. When you attend to the subtle presence of others in every sphere of life, you begin to perceive the interdependent nature of your existence. Your sure belief in a solid and independently existent self will begin to waver.

Seated in front of my computer and writing, instead of imagining I am alone with my work, which is how it appears at this moment, I reflect upon the numerous people who have contributed to computer technology, making the writing of such a large document so much easier for me. Looking at the stack of books surrounding me, I think of those whose written words have so enriched my own understanding. I think of family, friends, ancestors, adversaries, and people I have seen on the street, and all the ways they are part of this moment. I think of the profound teachings I have received on the vast subject of love and compassion. I think about the chair I sit on and the table holding my computer and all the invisible others who were responsible for making them, or overseeing their manufacture. The threads of connection are endless. At each moment, there is an opportunity to reflect upon the kindness of others, to be grateful to everyone. Meditating on the kindness of others is central to the cultivation of relative bodhimind, because, when you are grateful to others, your heart naturally softens toward them.

Unconditional Gratitude

Those who insult and irritate us are the most difficult subjects for gratitude, and the most fruitful. From the perspective of the lojong, those whom we consider adversaries are especially helpful. "It's true . . . if there's somebody criticizing you, it's always helpful because it's an opportunity."[22] Gratitude for the kindness of others does not mean we imagine all other beings as having kind intentions. We don't turn a blind eye to wrongdoing, and we don't become a Pollyanna chirping senselessly about how kind and wonderful everyone is. There are those who wish to harm us, and those who succeed in harming us. We don't brush this reality aside for some illusion about the kindness of others. Contemplating the kindness of others means that, whatever their intentions, we can still benefit from whatever others do. Rather than submitting to resentment or hatred, rather than nursing a grudge or denying a problem, we opt for a way to further open our heart.

Instead of perseverating over how others have sacrificed us to serve their greed or ambition, we see how we can benefit, even from injustice and betrayal, and we are grateful for that. The Dalai Lama often refers to the "kindness" of the enemy, in his case meaning the Communist

Chinese. Why are they kind? Certainly not because of any intention on their part. When he says things like "the time of greatest gain in terms of wisdom and inner strength is often that of greatest difficulty,"[23] he is not speaking in the abstract. He includes himself and the benefit he has derived from his forced exile. Though our tendency is to want to forcefully rid ourselves of any situation that doesn't suit us, the point the Dalai Lama is making is that we can actually benefit from it instead.

Normally, we think that the best thing we can do is try to free our lives of irritation and adversity. We want to oust them like unwelcome guests. The lojong radically departs from such views. It tells us that difficulties and frustrations are inevitable, so when they strike, find the opportunity within them. "Neurotic attitudes and environmental frustrations are the means of transcending such conditions."[24] Instead of running away from or fighting against adversity, we work with our mind. Our suffering can be like "the sandpaper which makes us smooth."[25] We can use negativity to soften, and ultimately destroy, the grip of our negative emotions. "When adversity becomes an ally in the fulfillment of our deepest aim, the cultivation of wisdom and compassion, it is no longer adversity."[26] "Be grateful to everyone" tells us to be grateful for situations that push our buttons, because, at these moments, we discover our limits and have the chance to stretch ourselves further. When we reach our limit with a person or circumstance, rather than submitting to the habit of lashing out or withdrawing, we may find the situation has something to teach us.

More than a century ago, the enlightened nomad Patrul Rinpoche was wandering the mountains as an anonymous mendicant. He heard about a renowned hermit who had spent many years in seclusion, and stopped by unannounced to visit with him. The ascetic humbly invited him in. Soon after entering his cave, the anonymous visitor inquired, "Tell me, what brought you to live in this remote cave?" The hermit replied, "I have come here to devote myself to meditation. In recent years I have been meditating on patience." The visitor looked at him, a gleam in his eye, "There is no need for pretense here. A couple of frauds like us could never really accomplish such a difficult thing. But I do know how good it feels to receive the admiration of others." The hermit turned red in the face, but the visitor continued, "I bet you get a lot of gifts too!" At this the hermit exploded, "Liar! Why do you torment me with these harsh words? Why don't you just leave me in peace?" Getting up to leave, Patrul Rinpoche turned to the hermit and said, "Friend, where is your patience now?" Patience cannot be cultivated without irritation. When we are comfortable, it is easy to be patient and serene. Those who challenge and provoke provide us with the best opportunity to practice. The wise ones know this, and embrace the difficulties from which most run.

The great Indian master Atisha is among the wise. When he left India and made the long journey to Tibet, where he spent the last seventeen years of his life, he brought along a Bengali tea boy who was an ill-tempered, irascible fellow. Atisha had heard the Tibetan people were so sweet and good-natured, and was concerned he would not experience sufficient irritation. The Tibetans were mystified as to why a great being like Atisha would have such a disagreeable attendant. Finally, someone asked Atisha why he had brought the boy with him and he replied, "Well, to tell you the truth, once I came to Tibet I realized I didn't need him because there are plenty of irritants here! But I didn't know that before coming and didn't want to risk losing an opportunity to deepen my practice of patience."

Most of us experience difficulties as insults, rather than opportunities. When life hands us a bowl of lemons, we don't want to make lemonade. We want what we want, and that's all there is to it. We want to be comfortable, and we certainly don't want people interfering with our lives, making them more difficult. We don't want to transform ourselves; we want the world to change. Be grateful to someone for insulting us? If we don't think about it carefully, it sounds truly ludicrous. If we do, then, maybe not. After all, a pearl comes into being through the intrusion of sand.

An ancient story told by the Christian Desert Fathers tells of a novice who receives the following instruction from his master. "For three years you are to give money to everyone who insults you." After the passing of three years, the master is satisfied with the young man's progress, and tells him he is ready to go to Alexandria and travel further along the path of wisdom. As he approaches Alexandria, the student encounters an old man sitting at the gate. The old man insults and humiliates everyone who comes and goes. As a matter of course, he insults the student, who laughs in response. The old man inquires, "Why do you laugh when I insult you?" "Because," the student says, "for years I have been paying the people who've insulted me, and now you give it to me for free!" Upon hearing this, the old man responds, "Enter the city, it is yours." If we wait for the world to change, nothing happens, but if we transform ourselves, the gates to the city of wisdom open wide.

Shantideva used the analogy of a warrior to inspire those who commit to awakening.[27] The bravest warriors are those who, upon seeing their own blood spilled in battle, become even more courageous and determined. Warriors of awakening do not lose heart in the face of insults or difficulties. Instead of submitting to fear, they ride, heads held high, into the center of it. "Enlightenment is accomplished by being voracious, by transforming all of life, the good, the bad, and the weird, into the path."[28] If we work with all conditions in our lives, gradually our mind will become a trusted friend, helping us in good times and bad.

"Be grateful to everyone" is a complete reversal of our usual attitude. Instead of looking for what is right and what is wrong, we consider: How do I make the best use of this situation? What jewel might be buried in this debris? When somebody runs off with your wallet or you arrive at a hotel and they've given away your reservation, it's not easy to think about the kindness of others. You don't want to be grateful to the person who steals your parking place; you don't want to consider the kindness of others who embarrass or degrade you. Seeing all beings as kind does not, however, mean that we passively accept injustice. We do all we can to address injustice in our lives, and in the world, but with a heart that is open, not closed.

Choosing to meditate on all beings as kind, and driving all blames into one, have nothing to do with whether or not we take action; they have everything to do with our inner attitude. The Dalai Lama takes action every day, trying to regain freedom for the Tibetan people.

Mahatma Gandhi took action in order to help liberate the Indian people from the rule of the British. It is up to each one of us, every day, to look at our lives and choose how to respond to the difficulties and wrongdoing we encounter. We can choose the middle way, or we can continue to live life, in the words of James Hillman, as "a vast defensive arrangement against psychic realities, a manic propitiation to keep Hades at bay."[29]

Persephone's dark light shines here. This myth is a fine illustration of the movement from defense against the unwanted intrusion—in this case Hades—to love for it. Persephone, still unravished, walks in a field of spring flowers. Spotting a particularly lovely and alluring flower, she reaches out to pluck it and, in that instant, the Earth opens up and Hades, extending his mighty hand out from the Underworld, forcefully brings Persephone into the labyrinth of the great below. The innocent virgin becomes queen of the Underworld and willing consort to Hades through an initially unsought and unwanted abduction. It strikes me how true this is for most of us. There are few among us who would volunteer for the difficulties in our lives. They fall upon us, they seize us from below like the powerful hand of Hades, and our inclination is to resist. But this pull overpowers all resistance. The following dream illustrates the universal theme of descent in another way.

I am in the wilderness. I see some snakes and point them out to a friend who doesn't see them. In that moment, the snakes disappear from view and reappear on the other side of a perilously steep gorge. There are five snakes, each one a different color—white, yellow, red, blue, and green. I point them out to her again and say, "Those are the five Buddha families." Then I am alone, sitting on the ground, and a lioness comes by. She sniffs me, circles me, and leaves me be. A moment later, I am sitting at the edge of the gorge. The drop looks impossibly steep, and I don't see how to get across. I see a man and a redheaded woman easily ascending on the other side. The lioness comes back, but this time she scratches me with her paw. I feel the warm trickle of blood and turn to see if I can retreat, but I cannot. I know she will devour me if I don't descend.

I begin talking to my teacher, although he is not physically present, saying I don't see a way over this gorge; it looks impossibly treacherous. The next thing I know, a man and woman are taking me down. I don't see them, but I know they are the man and woman I saw earlier. We are descending into greater and greater depths. The upper world falls away and, after quite some time, we are traveling underwater in what seems to be a cave. I feel relaxed underwater, despite not knowing how long I will be submerged. We emerge on the other side.

It can take the hand of Hades, or the paw of a lion, to bring us over our edge. We resist the defeat of our in-charge, egoic sensibility. And yet, paradoxically, we often find our greatest strength, renewal, and even inspiration in facing our fears, accepting the unacceptable, or by coming to terms with loss. Just as the rocks in the river give greater power to the water rushing over them, the difficulties we encounter can propel us to greater depths. Adversity can take us down—beneath anger, confusion, and retribution; beneath hopelessness, despair, and loneliness—until we touch our soft, infinitely tender heart. It can open the way to wholeness. Nevertheless, no matter how often we emerge transformed by the dark, unknowing moments, some inclination to resist remains with us for as long as our belief in an independent self persists. This can be a very long time. So abduction remains a necessary portal to surrender. Christine Downing speaks to this:

> I also see now why being taken to those depths is always an abduction. For we—or, at least, I—never feel quite whole enough, quite courageous enough, quite mature enough, to go *there* on our own. We are always still virginal before the really transformative (killing) experiences.[30]

Gratitude opens the way—gratitude for a necessary abduction, and gratitude for a return to the upperworld. These are the gifts of Persephone. Being grateful to everyone means also being grateful for everything. It means just being grateful—unconditionally. Be grateful for the difficulties, and be grateful for the relief of those difficulties. Just as Persephone comes to love Hades, we can come to love the dark moments, the disappointments and desolations of our lives. Finding the treasures amid the darkness, the hidden wealth of the Underworld, we love the soft breeze, the blessed sunshine, and the subtle fragrance of a rose no less.

Exchange

There are methods for developing great love and compassion within the Tibetan Buddhist tradition that do not specifically target the selfish mind or involve exchanging self and other. This method is unique to lojong. The great yogi Langri Tangpa summed up the pith instruction of lojong this way: "Of all the profound teachings I have read, this only have I understood: that all harm and sorrow are my own doing and all benefit and qualities are thanks to others. Therefore all my gain I give to others, all loss I take upon myself."[31]

Traditional Tibetan teachings liken those who practice the lojong to the peacock that is able to eat poison. "If crows tried to copy the peacock, and eat the poison they will die."[32] The peacock, on the other hand, is at home in the poison grove. Eating freely of the poison that other birds shun, its feathers become even more beautiful and lustrous. The self-centering, ego-logical view sanctioned by the collective and assented to by the masses tells us we are like crows that must vigilantly protect themselves from the poison around them. Lojong logic says we can be like the peacock; we "can absorb the poison—then the rest of the situation becomes medicine."[33]

The practice of exchanging self and others is the reason the lojong was kept secret for so long. Because this instruction is so easily mistaken for a strange form of masochism or martyrdom, or at best held out as an impossible ideal, it was passed on in secrecy for generations. It just seemed too wild and unorthodox a method for most to understand. Geshe Chekawa, who eventually recorded the text and began teaching the lojong more openly, started by teaching the practice to lepers. Leprosy was widespread in Tibet at the time, and there was no cure for it. By practicing mind-training techniques, many lepers were actually cured of their disease. Hence the teaching became affectionately known among Tibetans as the "Dharma for leprosy."

Chekawa's brother, a hardened skeptic, overheard these instructions being given privately to some lepers and decided to try them out for himself. Chekawa noticed a change for the better in his brother and realized he was practicing these methods. He decided that, if even his brother could benefit, it was time to make these teachings more widely available. Although it is true that the practice is difficult, it is not impossible. There are many who have successfully navigated its steep terrain. And we can do the same. Starting where we are and working with the instruction to whatever degree we are capable, we can gradually soften our hard shell of self-absorption. And although the vision of lojong is panoramic, the process is moment-to-moment. Somehow, putting one foot in front of the other, we move steadily along.

Five points enumerated in the lojong help us identify the stages of practice. The first is to recognize that self and other all share in the wish for happiness and the wish to avoid suffering—a part of the development of the third level of equanimity discussed earlier. The second is to recognize the faults of self-centeredness—an outcome of working with the aphorism "Drive all blames into one." The third is to think about the benefits of cherishing others—accomplished when we meditate on the kindness of all. Once we have contemplated the pitfalls of self-absorption and the benefits of gratitude, we are ready for the fourth step: exchanging self and other.

Exchanging self and other does not mean that you become the other. Rather it means "that the position I occupy in my mind, and the position other people occupy in my mind is exchanged. The . . . priority that I give myself, I give to others instead."[34] This type of exchange is also the deepest level of equanimity. This is the attitude most mothers have toward their children; they would gladly take on the pain or illness of their children in order to relieve it. The attitude of a mother toward her precious child is like a seed cultivated until fully grown at the level of exchange, where it includes not only our children or dear ones, but all other beings. At that level, we generate a commitment to work for the benefit of all.

Although our primary concern up until now has been with our own interests and the interests of those we consider close, we resolve to overturn that habit. When the attitude of exchange begins to establish itself, we realize that our happiness and suffering is in reality no more important than anyone else's. On this basis, we are equal to all other beings. It may seem difficult to imagine that anyone could genuinely feel this way, but there are many who have and do. And while they may be relatively rare, they are not limited to Tibetan adepts cloistered for centuries in the remote and protected Himalayas. Etty Hillesum is an inspiring example. Describing her feelings about the massive deportations of Jews and other "unwanted social elements," she writes, "People often get worked up when I say it doesn't really matter whether I go or somebody else does, the main thing is that so many thousands *have* to go."[35] Exchange is the foundation of the fifth step: the practice of tonglen.

The Practice of Tonglen

Dropping the scales from our eyes, we see, perhaps for the first time, that fixation on ourselves, on "me" and "mine," has never brought us the happiness we so yearn for. It hasn't worked so far, and there is no reason to believe it will work now. Nevertheless, old habits die hard. Although a lot is said about the pain of samsara and the possibility of freedom, we don't often hear about how painful and difficult the journey to freedom can be. We don't really know what the caterpillar undergoes while enduring what must seem an eternity of darkness before emerging as a butterfly. The truth is that it requires no less than everything to really undertake this practice of inner alchemy, because the selfish mind will do everything in its power to maintain its sovereignty in our lives. It will try to persuade and coax us in every possible way not to abandon it.

In the practice of tonglen, both selfishness and self-grasping are offered as the dark *prima materia* to be transformed. "The alchemists taught that soul work is an *opus contra naturam,* a work against nature."[36] Tonglen practice ignites an alchemical fire that fuels this process. It moves us from nature to soul, which is, in truth, our deeper nature. This alchemy undermines the habitual mechanism of self by "transmuting the metaphorical lead of impure selfish desire into the gold of purified desire."[37]

Practicing tonglen feels risky, because we relinquish the familiar and well-worn self-centered way and opt for the unknown, open way. It so directly and so radically targets the root of our suffering that it is especially suited to those who don't have time to waste. In reality, this means all of us. It is as if we have just been diagnosed with a fatal disease and discover that conventional medicine has nothing to offer us. The doctors know of no cure for our illness, so they advise us to go home, settle our affairs, and prepare to die. Because we have nothing to lose, we begin looking into unconventional treatment options. We are willing to try things we never would have considered, because the orthodoxy in which we normally put our faith has nothing to offer.

This is the realization we have when confronted with the intractable illness of our selfish mind and the ever-nearing sickle of death. We need drastic measures, because our customary efforts to achieve well-being don't deliver, and we don't want to waste our precious lives. We have no time to waste. But the radical alternative offered by tonglen isn't just any garden-variety alternative. It is a perennial, tried-and-true medicine specifically designed to help suffering beings like ourselves heal. If our hearts are brave, tonglen will be a soothing balm for our souls.

The practice of tonglen utilizes the breath as a vehicle for transformation. There are many types of mindfulness practice that use the breath as an object of concentration, a path to stabilized awareness, or a grounding touchstone. The tonglen uses the breath in a different way. "In tonglen practice we replace the mindfulness of the breath that doesn't have any contents with the mindfulness of the breath that does."[38] And because we use the breath as the medium, tonglen is also a practice that synchronizes our body and mind.

The basic instruction of tonglen is to breathe in the bad and breathe out the good. In essence, when anything is unwanted or painful, we breathe it in. And when anything is pleasurable, delightful, and desirable, we breathe it out. We give it away. As Trungpa remarked, "The practice of tonglen is very simple. We do not have to sort out our doctrinal definitions of goodness and evil. We simply breathe out any old good and breathe in any old bad."[39] Instead of grasping at good feelings and hoarding any happiness we may experience, we send it out to everyone else. Our timeworn habit is to push away pain and grasp at pleasure. The practice of tonglen deftly overturns this tendency. Inhalation and exhalation become a Möbius strip in which one side seamlessly becomes the other. Either way, whether breathing in or out, we relax further into openness.

Tonglen is not theoretical, and the suffering we breathe in is not abstract. It is absolutely necessary to touch our own experience of suffering in a real sense and to experience compassion for ourselves, in order to feel compassion for the suffering of others. As we sit with our own pain and despair, we come to realize that we are also sitting with the universal experience of suffering. Our own intimate knowledge of suffering and its many textures allows us actually to connect with the suffering of flesh and blood others. We come to realize that we are not only sitting with our pain, we are sitting with *the* pain. Thoughts such as "This is what it feels like to suffer," or "This is what people experience when they suffer" herald a subtle, but significant, shift in our awareness from the personal to the universal.

One of the beauties of this practice is that it cuts through all the ways we keep ourselves apart from others. Whatever our differences— rich or poor, black or white, liberal or conservative—everybody feels pain. The causes may be different, and we may express it differently, but people everywhere experience anger, jealousy, loneliness, fear. Beneath the stories of our lives we find this universal truth.

Tonglen is a method for gradually awakening the compassion within our heart, no matter how sealed off it may be. The continual effort to shield and protect our heart causes us so much suffering. When we begin to let our heart be touched, we discover that even in the midst of pain, openness and tenderness for life are ever-present.

The practice of tonglen is a practice of responding from the heart and awakening the heart via the breath. Sensing the world and breathing in the world are not divided in the heart. "The word for perception or sensation in Greek was *aisthesis,* which means at root a breathing in or taking in of the world."[40] Taking in or breathing in the world is the heart's mode of perception. Aisthesis is how we know the world through our heart.

The practice of tonglen can be done anywhere, anytime. It can be done in the moment we encounter suffering, as well as during a formal sitting practice. The formal sitting meditation is done in order for the practice to infuse the rest of our lives, but tonglen is not meant to be limited to the meditation cushion. An introduction to the meditation follows.

S IT QUIETLY AND OPEN TO THE SPACIOUS QUALITY OF YOUR MIND. Open to the wellspring of love and compassion within you, and let it fill every part of your being. Now bring to mind as vividly as possible someone you care about who is suffering. Try to imagine every aspect of his or her pain. Look through this person's eyes. Sense the intensity of distress, and feel your heart respond. Let yourself deeply wish for this person to be free of suffering. Then imagine collecting all of his or her suffering in the form of hot, grimy smoke. Breathe it in—a dark, sticky substance of pain—and bring it into the core of self-grasping at your heart. There, it dissolves every trace of self-centeredness, as though vaporizing a dense black knot.

Now, your boundless radiant heart is fully revealed. From your true heart, breathe out the brilliant light of happiness and joy. This light completely fills that person with well-being. With each cycle of breath, the hot, grimy smoke comes in and the clear, brilliant light goes out. Begin with one person. Breathe in the suffering of that person or animal, and breathe out relief from all manner of pain and misery. Breathe in the illness, unhappiness, fear, or poverty and breathe out freedom and release. Imagine that the person is completely relieved of suffering and suffused with joy.

Expand your scope. Allow that one person who is suffering to remind you of the numberless others who are suffering in just the same way—the millions who are unhappy, fearful, hungry, ill, or impoverished. Let the one open you to the many. Open to all of them. Think of the old man you passed on the street with loneliness in his eyes, and all the rest just like him. Think of your mother's fatal alcoholism and the millions who suffer the same. Think of the child you saw in the cancer ward. Think of your own relentless chronic illness, and all those who are struggling with illness themselves. Breathe it all in. From the bottom of your heart, wish them to be free of their pain. Take the dark cloud of suffering into the very core of your resistance. Watch it dissolve the ancient knot of self-centeredness at your heart, and then breathe out relief.

In your mind's eye, see these numberless beings relieved of the pain they are experiencing. Imagine that, from your inexhaustible heart, you are sending out the brilliant light of joy and ultimate well-being to completely relieve the suffering of countless others. Your whole body is none other than a radiant jewel, a magic lamp. From every pore, limitless light radiates in all directions, fulfilling the wishes of all beings, providing the complete satisfaction of their every need. Feel a firm conviction in the cleansing of their pain and its causes, and in their establishment in everlasting joy. If at any time you feel overwhelmed, simply return to focusing on one person, and focus on that one person until you are ready to expand your scope further.

■   ■   ■

Tonglen practice is the practice of exchanging your joy for the suffering of others. The more misery, sickness, and cruelty there is in the world, the more others can benefit from your practice of tonglen. The essence of the "giving" part of this practice was beautifully articulated by the peerless Shantideva more than a thousand years ago, when he said:

May I be a protector for those without one,
A guide for travelers on the way;
May I be a bridge, a boat and a ship
For all those who wish to cross the water.

May I be an island for those who seek one
And a lamp for those desiring light,
May I be a bed for those who wish to rest
And a slave for all who want a slave.

May I be a wishing jewel, a magic vase,
Powerful mantras and great medicine,
May I become a wish-fulfilling tree
And a cow of plenty for the world.

Just like space
And the great elements such as earth,
May I always support the life
Of all the boundless creatures.

And until they pass away from pain
May I also be the source of life
For all the realms of varied beings
That reach until the ends of space.[41]

As for the "taking" part of the practice, we may worry about breathing in all this bad air and giving away our precious goodness. We may worry that we are going to harm and impoverish ourselves. Or we may feel we are too confused and burdened with suffering ourselves to open to anyone else's. We fear breathing in the bad; we fear its pollution and contamination. But these are precisely the feelings we need to explore.

I recall having a conversation with Ribur Rinpoche a number of years back about tonglen. He told me that, if tonglen practice frightened me, I should welcome my fear as I would welcome an important guest. The arising of fear meant that my practice was bringing my self-grasping mind out into the open. This may be unsettling, but actually it is a very good sign. If I felt no resistance to breathing in another's pain, I probably hadn't really allowed myself to think of it as real. Then he laughed and said, "Who is it that you fear harming? See if you can find the one you are trying to protect."

Sogyal Rinpoche addresses this concern as well, saying, "The one thing you should know for certain is that the only thing that Tonglen could harm is the one thing that has been harming you the most: your own ego, your self-grasping, self-cherishing mind."[42] Allan Wallace adds this important point: "The practice of tonglen may actually alleviate the suffering of another person, but the true criterion of success . . . is the attenuation of our own self-centeredness and the growth of love and compassion in our own hearts."[43]

The target of our in-breath is our illusory, self-grasping self, the one pretending since beginningless time to be the real me, and the selfishness this mistaken view fosters. Each inhalation threatens to undermine the continued domination of this impostor. Of course, it feels as if the real you is being threatened, and herein lies the unique genius of the tonglen. It constellates an alchemical encounter between self-grasping with its web of fallacies, and the subtle, but indestructible, pure nature of your being. Ordinary individuals can undertake such alchemy because of our true inner nature, our luminous soul, the hidden light, the primordially pure being that remains forever undefiled and indestructible within our hearts. Robert Thurman describes the nature of our deepest being in this way:

> The luminous soul is described in Buddhist texts as like fine gold that never tarnishes, a new moon ever on the increase, a fire that grows ever more intense, an inexhaustible treasury for others' prosperity, an ocean unruffled by winds of complications, an immovable king of mountains, a miracle medicine, the greatest friend, a fountain pouring forth undiminished the meaning of liberating Truth, and a great cloud from which rains the source of life and wealth of all beings.[44]

Compassion for Self

Compassion for others and compassion for ourselves are interdependent. As Erich Fromm insightfully remarked, "Anyone who loves his neighbor but does not love himself shows that the love of his neighbor is not genuine," because "love is based on an attitude of affirmation and respect, and if this attitude does not also exist towards oneself . . . it does not exist at all."[45] Likewise, whatever we reject in ourselves we will reject in others, and whatever we reject in others we also reject in ourselves. Breathing in our own suffering helps strengthen our love and compassion. The more pained, wretched, and discouraged we feel, the more we can benefit from tonglen. Moreover, the idea of breathing in our own suffering won't scare us as much as breathing in somebody else's suffering. If we are able to breathe in our own revulsion, vengefulness, arrogance, oppression, or fear, we will, over time, be able to open our hearts to the millions of others who suffer these as well. On the other hand, "if we are unable to take even our own problems upon ourselves, obviously we will be unable to take others' suffering."[46]

The value of relating to unwanted and split-off parts of ourselves was discussed in some depth in our earlier exploration of the shadow. Jung states unequivocally that those seeking wholeness must be willing to assimilate, rather than condemn, rejected shadow elements, saying that, "condemnation does not liberate, it oppresses."[47] We gain nothing by vilifying ourselves, no matter how sinister a darkness our shadow casts. Furthermore, the things we reject in ourselves we project onto others and eject into the world around us. Ejecting our shadow is like throwing our garbage out the car window. And the practice of tonglen is like picking up that garbage and putting it to good use.

In India, I learned that a lot of what I considered garbage was valued by others. If I discarded a bent paper clip, someone might use it to repair a shoe. A bottle cap could fill a hole in a wall. A tossed orange peel might be eaten by a cow roaming the city streets. Returning to the United States, it took a while for me to stop throwing my banana peels and apple cores on the street. As I made the transition between these two worlds, I realized that garbage, like everything else, is relative. It depends, just as beauty does, on the eye of the beholder. Breathing in pain and bringing everything to the path means there is no garbage, because everything is good for something. Whether we experience blue skies or storms, whether we are in the groove or in a ditch, whether we have difficulty or delight, all that we encounter can be fuel for awakening the heart of compassion.

Robert Bly referred to the creative engagement of our dark side as "eating the shadow." If we don't eat our shadow, we "contribute to the danger of nuclear war, because every bit of energy that we don't actively engage . . . is floating somewhere in the air above the United States."[48] Tonglen practice is a method for unconditionally eating the shadow. We breathe in every bit of darkness, but we don't stop with our own. We don't just clean up after ourselves; we clean up the trash someone else threw out the window as well. We don't draw a line in the sand and say, "That's not my garbage, so I'm not going to touch it." We breathe in worlds of darkness, no matter whose it is, no matter where it originates. But we begin by extending kindness toward ourselves. The practice of self-tonglen is as follows:

B EGIN BY MOMENTARILY OPENING TO THE SPACIOUSNESS of your mind and the wellspring of compassion within you. Now let yourself feel whatever unhappiness and pain you are feeling at this moment. You may be disappointed by a friend, or you may have disappointed a friend. You may be angry at your boss, physically ill, alienated from the world, or feeling ugly, ashamed, or inadequate. You may be gripped by envy, depression, or fear. You may be feeling arrogant or smug. Don't blame yourself and don't blame anyone else either. Instead, bring your awareness to whatever painful feelings are present, and then wish for yourself to be free from the suffering you are experiencing. Imagine your suffering in the form of hot, grimy, smoke and bring that smoke into the core of self-grasping at your heart. There, it dissolves every trace of self-centeredness, as though vaporizing a dense black knot. Now, your boundless, radiant heart is fully revealed. From your true heart, breathe out the brilliant light of happiness, joy, and ultimate well-being to yourself.

You may expand this practice to include the suffering you have not yet experienced—your future suffering. Breathe in the suffering you may experience this evening, tomorrow, next month, or next year. Breathe in the suffering you may experience the rest of your life. Imagine the suffering of future illness, loss, disappointment, and death, and breathe these into your heart now. Take into yourself the suffering of this moment and the suffering that awaits you. Then breathe out tender-hearted relief.

■　　■　　■

It doesn't matter if you begin with yourself and are unable for a time to breathe in or out on behalf of others. The important thing is not to fake it. Start with what's real. If the only thing that seems real to you is your own pain in this very moment, begin with that. As you open to yourself, you will naturally open to others. Let your circle of compassion grow with your heart. Through repeated practice of tonglen, you begin to move closer to whatever you're feeling, to breathe it in rather than run away from it or blame it on someone else. You start doing what Chögyam Trungpa called "leaning into the sharp points."

Machig Labdrön, one of the most renowned and beloved of Tibet's mystic women, and one of my great inspirations, was given this instruction over one thousand years ago by her teacher:

> Confess all your hidden faults!
> Approach that which you find repulsive!
> Whoever you think you cannot help, help them!
> Anything you are attached to, let go of it!
> Go to places that scare you, like cemeteries!
> Sentient beings are as limitless as the sky,
> Be aware!
> Find the Buddha inside yourself![49]

The most despised and repellent things, those we normally turn from in disgust, are the very things we must turn toward with compassion. As Oscar Wilde said, "It's not the perfect but the imperfect that is in need of our love." This is one of the many special qualities of this practice. Suffering becomes a gift when it brings us to love and compassion. There is a story with roots in Africa that so splendidly communicates the message of this teaching that I include it here, as story medicine and a more than fitting summation for the instruction on developing relative bodhimind.

In an African village a group of young women banded together to humiliate one of them who was different, and of whom they were envious. They were especially envious because she wore a necklace of beads more beautiful than any necklace any of them owned. One day, when the envied and despised one joined them by the banks of the river, they hid their necklaces and told her they had thrown them into the river as an offering to the river god. The young woman, being of generous heart, immediately removed her necklace and threw it into the river as well, whereupon the young women retrieved the necklaces they had hidden and went off jeering and laughing at the naive young woman whom they had so easily duped.

The young woman sat down by the river, heavy with grief. She had been tricked, and now she prayed fervently for a way to retrieve her necklace. After some time, she heard the voice of a god bidding her to jump in the river. Without a moment's hesitation, she plunged in and found herself on the riverbed, where an old woman sat waiting. This old one was ugly beyond imagination. Just the sight of her repulsed, and the stench of her was sickening and nauseating. Her flesh was covered with open, weeping sores. Upon sighting the young woman, she called out, "Lick my sores!" The young woman, touched by the old woman's plight, moved toward the revolting hag and licked her oozing sores. Then the old woman said to her, "Because you have done as I asked, I will protect you when the demon that devours the flesh of young women hunts you down." At that very moment, the young woman heard a bone-chilling roar, and out came a terrifying monster in search of her. But he soon left, cursing because the old woman had hidden her away.

The old woman turned once more to the young woman saying, "Here is your necklace"—and she placed around her neck a strand of beads far more beautiful than any she had ever seen. "Go back to your village," the old woman advised, "but when you have gotten a few yards from the water's edge, you will see a stone. Throw it in the pool and, without looking back, return to your ordinary life." The girl did as instructed. She found the stone, threw it in the water, and proceeded without a backward glance.

The other young women, noticing her return, begged to know where she had obtained a necklace of such rare beauty. The girl told them of the old woman at the bottom of the pool, but before she had a chance to say any more, they all proceeded to jump in the river. There they found the revolting, old woman who did as she had done before. "Lick my sores," she called out to them. But they laughed at such a preposterous request. None of them would dream of doing something so disgusting—and useless. They demanded their necklaces, but before the old woman could reply, there came a ferocious roar and a ghastly monster lunged out from the shadows and made a mighty meal of them.

Absolute Bodhimind

The first of the absolute bodhimind aphorisms is: "Having gained stability, let the mystery be revealed," or "Having gained stability, be shown the secret." The stability referred to here is the stability of our compassion. "When that becomes stable . . . then we talk about absolute bodhimind, which is wisdom."[50] Stability is necessary because, of all the Buddha's teachings, emptiness is the most difficult to understand. And emptiness is so easy to misunderstand. This can have serious and far-reaching consequences, because as Nagarjuna, founder of the Madhyamika school of the Middle Way, said, "Viewing emptiness mistakenly, like grabbing a poisonous snake incorrectly, brings ruin to those of little intelligence."[51] Therefore, "we should learn the secret, the meaning of emptiness, and then meditate on it until we realize it."[52]

Even the term "emptiness" is confusing, but there seem to be none that are less confusing. The "void," the "absolute," the "truth" are all terms that fall prey to our habit of reifying, of absolutizing relative truths. But emptiness is not a fixed, transcendent truth divorced from conventional reality. "Emptiness is the central path that leads not beyond this reality but right into its heart."[53] Because all phenomena, including ourselves, exist in a way that contradicts appearances, teachings on emptiness are described as the revelation of a secret, or a mystery.

We cannot know emptiness by looking around us, because the ultimate mode of our existence is not evident to the senses. You may rightly ask, "If it is so difficult to understand, and even more difficult to realize, why is it so important to contemplate emptiness at all?" Realizing emptiness exposes the deception of our instinctive self-habit and uproots the grasping at a self that is the cause of all our suffering. This is why it is worth doing. Although many may concede that, despite conventional appearances to the contrary, things don't exist independently and alone, "nonetheless, most of us still feel deeply that whatever we perceive . . . exists by itself."[54]

For example, when holding a piece of paper, I automatically perceive its existence independent of any other object. All the unseen elements present in this paper remain unseen unless I stop to think about them. I don't see the wood, or the tree, or the logger who cut the tree. I don't see the sun or soil that nourished the tree. Nowhere to be seen are the clouds that released the necessary rainfall, or the mother who raised the child who ultimately chopped down the tree, nor those who processed the wood and made it into paper. If I begin looking at the intricate web of relationships appearing to my mind as a single piece of paper, it is endless. Furthermore, I feel myself to be "in here" and perceive the paper standing on its own "out there." In reality, my consciousness is linked with this paper through my perceiving of it. Where do I draw the line? Where do I begin and where does the paper end?

Through close observation, we come to see that, despite the appearance of independent self-existence, phenomena simply do not exist that way. Because phenomena—including ourselves—exist as dependently related events, they are empty of intrinsic identity. We find that all phenomena depend upon three things: Our mind and mental designations (we see something and say "This is paper, or that is a tree, a star, a jug, a lamp."); causal conditions (the paper depends on trees, and clouds, and people, and so forth); and its parts (the paper is composed of diverse elements, such as wood pulp and water, coming together and becoming paper).

Likewise, a chair depends on its legs and its seat, without which it is not a chair. There is no "chairness" to be found in a chair separate from the collection of parts upon which we sit. There is no single part we can hold up and say, "Here is the chair." There is no ultimate, essential thingness to be discovered. It is as though all phenomena were an infinite set of nesting dolls. No matter how many you open, there is always another inside. There is no point of indivisibility, no singular "this is it" to be revealed. Phenomena are truly point-less. This reality only becomes apparent to us by searching for the way in which things exist. If we look for emptiness, we find nothing. But if we look into the nature of phenomena, we find they are empty of intrinsic existence. "If we thoroughly search for the underlying mode of existence—the actual nature of reality—then the appearance of things as independent entities gradually loses its clarity until it finally disappears."[55] Still, parts do come together and we do sit on chairs, and write on paper, and rest in the shade of a tree.

As a human being, I differ in many ways from a piece of paper or a chair, but I am similarly dependent on an unrepeatable matrix of causes and conditions. I am composed of ever-changing features and characteristics. Searching every stratum of existence, I can find no essential me apart from the flow of a unique collection of conditions and processes. Still, I know I am here. I smell the flowers outside my window, and if someone were to pinch me, I would certainly feel it.

Herein lies the most difficult paradox: the self may not be something, but neither is it nothing. Its being and non-being co-exist. The more deeply I look to find myself, the more I find there is no end to me, and no beginning either. I am drilling into infinity. No homunculus of a transcendent self will be found hiding in my body or my mind, even though on the surface of things—and quite far below the surface of things—it appears otherwise. "Eventually we are persuaded by our experience . . . that there is no *thing* that resides at the core of our being; there is only the ongoing function of engaging with others around us and the task at hand."[56]

Sacrifice or Revelation, Dreaming or Waking

At the end of his life, Jung concluded that the goal of life was to discover our "empty center." If Jung had fully grasped the implications of this insight earlier on, he might have founded a very different depth psychology. For many of us, feeling our empty center is synonymous with depression and alienation and is certainly not the goal of life. Mark Epstein reflects upon the opportunities that are lost because we "pathologize a feeling that in Buddhism serves as a starting place for self-exploration."[57] The hope and expectation are that a good analysis can heal feelings of emptiness or unreality. The resolution of these feelings is believed to come about through identifying early causes and strengthening the ego's capacity to digest painful events without regressing or splitting—or by integrating split-off psychic elements such as the shadow, and the anima or animus.

In Buddhism, the approach is quite different. Of course, we need to cultivate the capacity to digest the pain of life's traumas, as well as integrate the shadow and the contra-sexual elements. But this will never be enough. Our sense of emptiness, of unreality, of being cut off from life, cannot be explained by particular events in early life. It is much deeper and more pervasive than particular events or split-off elements. Healing this level of self-alienation comes about when we see the relative construct of the ego for the relative construct that it is, and experience the liberating truth of selflessness. This realization of emptiness or selflessness does not, however, eradicate the ego as a conventionally existing truth. It shatters the fiction of an absolute, self-existent "I" functioning under its own power.

> Thus the fear of many psychoanalysts—that egolessness sounds like a forerunner of psychosis, paralysis or decompensation—is unfounded. For egoless awareness does not mean losing sight of the conventional boundaries of where this mind/body leaves off and other mind/bodies begin. Rather, these conventional self-boundaries are seen as just that—conventional constructions—rather than as absolute demarcations that fence off a solidly existing, separate territory.[58]

It is worth noting here that, although some discussion has taken place in the field of psychology concerning the ego and its relationship to both self and selflessness, I believe our sense of self or "intrinsic reality instinct"[59] actually more closely resembles the "instinctual strength of the id"[60] than the mediating, administrative, and self-representational function of the ego to which it is often likened. In either case, whether we link our sense of an intrinsic self with the ego or with the id does not critically impact our apprehension of selflessness. It is crucial, however, to understand that selflessness does not destroy or sacrifice something that actually exists. Selflessness destroys our confusion, not anything else.

In the West, widespread misunderstanding of this vital point extends to the field of psychology. Lionel Corbett's depiction of those who achieve a relativized self illustrates the problem well.

> Such a person is able to transcend by means of a process of radically decentring, or relativizing the self. That is, he or she no

longer needs to see the self as the necessary centre of the universe, requiring all available attention and resources in the service of its own needs . . . . This kind of behaviour always requires a conscious sacrifice of the self, which is possible without bitterness or resentment only if the self is strong. We then transcend in the sense of going beyond the limits of strict individuality, realizing our essential unity with others. But this level of attainment—so beloved of Eastern thought—is only possible when true selfhood is achieved, because a fragile self would collapse under the strain.[61]

The realization of selflessness does not relativize and decentralize the self; it exposes the fiction of a truly existent self. The self never existed in the way we imagine, and seeing emptiness means we see the way things are. The self is not being relativized; it is, and always has been, relative. We release our hold on an absolute self, not as a transcendent act of conscious sacrifice, but because we finally realize it is false. The true self, a subject of great interest among Western analysts, is paradoxically empty of any true self-existence. The erosion of our false self does not expose a truer self hiding within. It reveals the emptiness of the self altogether.

This realization is as shattering as it is liberating. The world will never look the same, or be the same, for those who have encountered emptiness. A path of transformation takes on an entirely different meaning in the light of this revelation. Everything takes on a different meaning. "To experience emptiness is to experience the shocking absence of what normally determines the sense of who you are and the kind of reality you inhabit."[62] Such transformation

> . . . does not fortify the separate self, but utterly shatters it—not consolation but devastation, not entrenchment but emptiness, not complacency but explosion, not comfort but revolution—in short not a conventional bolstering of consciousness but a radical transmutation and transformation at the deepest seat of consciousness itself.[63]

Initially, our insight into emptiness may only last a moment, a fleeting glimpse, but in that glimpse we see ourselves and the world as infinitely open and inextricably interconnected. The early Indian master Dharmakirti said that even one such moment is enough to tear the fabric of our samsara into shreds.

Emptiness, contrary to what we may have thought, is found not to be empty at all. It is full. It is full of eyes and ears and touch and smell; it is full of radiant Buddhas and downcast beggars; full of black holes, stars, moons, galaxies, and universes; full of grains of sand, and saxophones, and traffic jams. Emptiness is full of infinite existence. "The moment I say 'emptiness' . . . think of full . . . . It is full, full, it is totally full! It is not empty, it is full. But the fullness is empty."[64] Introduction to emptiness is the springboard for the remaining absolute bodhimind aphorisms, beginning with: "Regard all dharmas as dreams" or "Consider the world as dreamlike."

Despite appearances to the contrary, both ourselves, and all other phenomena lack even an atom of independent self-existence. Nothing independently exists. Dreams arise in relation to dreamers and are real while they last; so does life. "Through examination we see the concrete rigid ego dissolve into fiction, and the solidity of our world turns fluid."[65] The ultimate truth status of ourselves and phenomena begins to soften, and the stubborn solidity we have so long attributed to things begins melting away. "Regarding all dharmas as dreams does not mean that you become fuzzy and woolly"; it "means that although you might think that things are very solid, the way you perceive them is soft and dreamlike."[66]

When you regard the world as dreamlike, you see that both life and death are like dreams. Life and death are not dreams, but they are like dreams. Vivid, clear, and intense, they are capable of arousing every kind of passion and fury, but they, nevertheless, lack intrinsic reality. They arise and pass away in dependence on causes and conditions, and not on their own power. They are real. They are also dreamlike. As the Diamond Sutra states so well: "So you should view all this fleeting world; A star at dawn, a bubble in the stream; A flash of lightning in a summer cloud; A flickering lamp, a phantom, and a dream." Seeing the world as dreamlike, we may also see it as story or as mytho-poetry, because "the language of storytelling and poetry is the powerful sister of the dream language."[67]

We notice that life is more slippery than we thought, and the more closely we look, the more slippery it gets. Where is yesterday's rain against the windowpane, or the walk I took last evening among the hyacinths and lilacs? The green of spring leaves, the wet earth, and the scent of flowers in the air are easily conjured in my mind. They were so real, but where are they now? And where is this past winter with its cold tentacles reaching into my flesh, its sparkling snow and its bare, skeletal branches black against a moonlit sky? They are all story, memory, and imagination. Memory infuses images with memorability. The Greeks honored humanity's infinite collection of images, personifying it as the goddess Mnemosyne, mother to the Muses. She is the keeper of the treasure of *memoria*.

> *Memoria* was described as a great hall, a storehouse, a theatre packed with images. And the only difference between remembering and imagining was that memory images were those to which a sense of time had been added, that curious conviction that they had once happened.[68]

Yesterday's walk among the lilacs and hyacinths and my childhood walks to the corner store are now images in the theatre of memoria. They are like sweet dreams. The taunting of children on the school bus is like a bad dream. As Pema Chödrön says, "Every situation is a passing memory."[69] Understanding this is the beginning of wisdom.

Once there was a king who assembled his counselors and gave them the following task: "I have little time for philosophy and contemplation, my life is taken up with the needs of my kingdom and my subjects. Therefore, I ask you to gather your wisdom as one and bring to me a basic but essential truth to help me rule wisely." He continued, "I need a simple method to help me maintain an even mind despite the pull of two strong currents—the lion of arrogance and pride, and the thief of despair and depression." With this, he released his counselors to their task. After many days and nights of soulful introspection and lively conversation, it came to them. "This will certainly serve the king," they declared with one voice and, sending for the finest calligrapher in the land, they instructed him to inscribe with gold on parchment, "This too shall pass."

Discovering that our life is like a dream is waking up to see life as it is. This is also what happens when we wake up in a dream while still dreaming. Rather than waking in the morning and realizing we have been in a dream, we recognize we are dreaming while dreaming. We call this experience lucid dreaming. "Regard all dharmas as a dream" instructs us in lucid living. We wake up to life while living it. During lucid dreaming, dreams intensify and creative possibilities multiply. Everything seems almost hyper-real. Situations are more transparent and more alive at the same time. We take more risks, are more fearless, and become more playful. Similarly, when we become lucid in life, we become more adventuresome and creative. Previously unthought possibilities can become manifest realities.

Appearances suggest that phenomena exist out there, independent of our perception. It certainly looks that way, and, for most of us, that is good enough to make it true. We collectively honor the adage "seeing is believing." But when we dream, we see things too. We touch people, we climb mountains, we fall off cliffs, we give birth. But none of this happens outside of a relationship to the dreamer. There is a view in physics today that "whether a photon is a particle or a wave is determined by what the instrument measures. Reality doesn't exist independently of the system of measurement and interpretation."[70] Dream and dreamer are similarly interdependent, and this is equally true when we are awake. To be fully awake is to be a Buddha, for the word "Buddha" means "one who is awake." For a Buddha, being awake means waking up to the dream of life and participating in it to the fullest. Regarding all phenomena as dreamlike is a strong tonic, but it is not to be taken alone. It needs to be taken in combination with the next aphorism: "Examine the nature of unborn awareness."

With this slogan, we begin to see that each of the absolute bodhimind aphorisms both uphold and dismantle the one preceding. If you get too comfortable regarding phenomena as a dream, go deeper. Who is experiencing the dream of life? Who realizes or perceives anything?

Where does your awareness of life and dream come from? This aphorism shines a laser beam right through our monolithic "I." Where exactly is the mind that is dreaming this dream? Instead of nailing things down, the nails begin dissolving in your hands. "We are moving further and further away from concretizing and making things so solid and always trying to get some ground under our feet."[71] First we notice the dreamlike nature of things, and then we notice that the dreamer is remarkably transparent as well. The dreamer is no more solid than the dream.

This aphorism instructs us to observe the observer. When we do, we see that myriad things come and go, but awareness is ever-present; it neither comes nor goes. "The mind has not come from somewhere like a guest who has come into a room, nor does it go anywhere. It has no form or color and does not abide in any definite place."[72] It is nowhere to be found, and it is everywhere pervasive. Because awareness does not arise, it also doesn't pass away. Awareness is unborn and undying. "Mind arises and passes, yet in the midst of its ongoing flux there is unborn awareness . . . . To ascertain and dwell in the nature of unborn aware-ness is to achieve the deathless state."[73]

According to the experiential reports of great adepts in the Tibetan Buddhist tradition, consciousness continues after the breath has stopped. Therefore, it can be said that, "there is no such thing as a dead person, only a dead body."[74] After the senses have completely with-drawn and the brain no longer functions, an accomplished meditator begins the deepest level of meditation. There are many accounts of adepts remaining in meditation anywhere from days to weeks following clinical death. It happened hundreds of years ago; it still happens today. Gehlek Rimpoche reports that his father, "who died at the end of the Cultural Revolution in Tibet, remained in that state for fifteen days."[75] The sixteenth Karmapa, who died in a Chicago hospital in the early 1980s, is another example. Although scientific instruments confirmed that he was clinically dead, his skin remained supple, warmth could be detected at his heart, and rigor mortis did not set in until the period of meditation had passed several days later. For those who witnessed this marvel, everything they had previously believed about life and death came into question. As Wallace points out, "The materialist view that when the brain dies, consciousness vanishes, and the Buddhist view of continuity of consciousness from one lifetime to another are mutually exclusive."[76] Medically speaking, your mind ceases at the time of death; Buddhist adepts agree in part with this assessment. *A* mind has ceased. The mind that is uniquely characterized by the life you just lived ceases to be when you die. But a stream of continual consciousness exists beyond that mind. It has been with you throughout life, and it remains after death; it is your "unborn awareness."

> Unborn awareness is awareness in its primordial state, unstructured by experience or by a human brain or nervous system. The primordial nature of awareness is not structured by a sense of subject versus object. Unborn awareness is also not conditioned by being a good or bad person or even by being human.[77]

Every one of us will die, and every one of us will experience our primordial, unborn awareness. When everything else—body, breath, and mind—falls away, this most subtle consciousness remains. The question is whether or not we will have the ability to recognize it, and the contemplative skills to make use of it. For most of us, our unborn awareness remains as cloaked as the inner workings of a computer in the hands of an infant—a mysterious black box with a blank screen. This is the reason for training throughout life. We train so that when our most subtle consciousness dawns it will not pass us by unnoticed. We will recognize it, perceive its empty nature, and merge with it. And to preclude our tendency to reify unborn awareness or emptiness, the next aphorism reminds us to: "Self-liberate even the antidote" or "The remedy itself is released in its own place."

The remedy of emptiness is released through its realization. In other words, emptiness itself keeps us from absolutizing emptiness. If we remain too absorbed in the dreamlike nature of phenomena, or too inclined to reify unborn awareness, this aphorism instructs us to go further into the understanding of emptiness we have cultivated up until now. We must stave off our tendency to conclude wrongly that consciousness, or even emptiness, exists independently, as the one "real" thing. If we don't, we are in peril of falling into the extremes of eternalism or nihilism. Emptiness is not the one thing, and it is not no-thing. Like phenomena, emptiness is empty of independent existence.

Emptiness is not separate from phenomena. This is what is meant by the Heart Sutra's stunning proclamation, "Form is emptiness and emptiness is form. Form is no other than emptiness, and emptiness is no other than form." The insight that form is emptiness "challenges materialism and the realistic conception of the universe by establishing that phenomena—from the tiniest particle to the Buddha's omniscience—ultimately do not possess any existence of their own."[78] Conversely, "emptiness is form" affirms relative truth, and refutes nihilistic formulations. Lama Tsong Kapa, a great adept of the 14th century, advised those striving to realize emptiness to "strive to understand dependent origination."[79] Rather than looking for emptiness, look instead for how things exist and you will find emptiness.

Approaching emptiness via phenomena and dependent origination is called the "Royal Reason of Relativity." Tsong Kapa described the supreme method of apprehending emptiness in this way:

> Appearance as inevitably relative,
> And emptiness as free of all assertions—
> As long as these are understood apart,
> The Victor's intent is not yet known.
> But, when they are simultaneous without alteration,
> The mere sight of inevitable relativity
> Becomes sure knowledge rid of objective habit-patterns,
> And the investigation of authentic view is complete.[80]

By continually deepening our insight into emptiness, we come to "Rest in the nature of Alaya, the essence," or "Establish the nature of the path in the sphere of the foundation of all." Before taking sides, before deciding whether phenomena exist this way or that way, before submitting to our habitual certainty over being or non-being, we return repeatedly to the contemplation of emptiness. Don't confuse resting in the empty nature of reality with the spaced-out, dull state that commonly occurs when our mind is relaxed, however. The mind rests in its open nature—without tension, but with limpidity. By resting the mind in the sphere of the foundation of all, we unite tranquility and lucidity without allowing one factor to overtake the other. This blend of acute awareness and total relaxation is often likened to a fish gliding through the water. The fish moves through the water, yet the water remains undisturbed.

We need to keep recalling our understanding of emptiness, because we chronically misconstrue reality. A mere glimpse of emptiness is not enough to free us, because we are instinctively prone to absolutizing relative truths. This is our deepest affliction; in order to heal the mind of it, we must continually return to the meditation on emptiness, to the sphere of the foundation of all. We need to steep our minds in it, until our minds and our realization of emptiness become inseparable.

The last of the absolute bodhimind aphorisms speaks to the ongoing challenge of maintaining the openings and glimpses experienced during meditation amid the frenzy and flurry of daily life. When we are not engaged in a formal contemplation of emptiness, we are told: "Between sessions, be an illusionist" or "In post-meditation, be a child of illusion."

Walking into a dimly lit room, you freeze in fear as your eyes fall upon a coiled snake in the corner. Turning on the light, you see that it is a rope and not a snake after all. Your fear vanishes; you have seen the truth. As long as you see the snake and not the rope, you are afraid. When you see the true situation, you are free from fear. Likewise, when you see the true reality of emptiness, fear of existence and non-existence are transcended. Being a child of illusion relieves us of literalistic and absolutist fantasies, and encourages us to see the illusory nature of appearances.

We find an analogy in the magician's creation of illusion. In India, magicians conjure deceptive appearances by using the power of mantric spells. Fierce illusory tigers, bountiful magical feasts, phantasms of beautiful men and women all arise and appear real to the enthralled audience. They seem to exist in actuality. The apparitions are seen by the magicians as well, but are known to be illusions of their own creation. Having generated these visions, the magician is not tricked into thinking of them as real. Likewise, we mustn't be tricked by the appearance of ourselves and of phenomena as solidly and independently existing. Our separate bodies, and the seeming privacy of our minds, make a convincing argument for the existence of a separate self, but we need not be deceived. Recall how illusory the magician's creations are, despite how real they appear to be. Things need not exist absolutely in order for them to exist. In fact, their relative existence *is* their infinite existence.

I appear, and I function as an individual. This is true. I act, I think, I speak, I die, I create. Yet, I am not any one of these things. I am not my body or my mind. I am also not separate from my body and mind. I cannot be found in a single physical or mental trait, but neither do I exist independent of these traits. I cannot be reduced to any single time, place, or space. My existence is utterly and completely dependent and irreducible. This aphorism reminds me of the empty center of things. Appearances seem solid, but I can see through them. Things appear and they are empty, simultaneously. When I hold a glass in the palm of my hand, I can see the glass and my palm in the same moment. One view does not obstruct the other.

As a child of illusion, you walk lightly through the world. There is no dogma to which you can cling, no single truth behind which you can rally, no absolute self to uphold, no righteous war to wage.

> Instead, all images and doctrines are seen as essentially mythic, that is to say, neither true nor false, but sacred. As sacred stories . . . doctrines, images, and symbols should be evaluated on the basis of their utility. Do they promote human wholeness or do they promote alienation and oppression?[81]

Indeed, life is fleeting, precious, and vulnerable—fragile, yet essentially indestructible. Emptiness is a resounding affirmation, not a negation, of our infinite existence. Its realization brings about a transformation in our deepest heart. Because phenomena are empty of intrinsic existence, we can touch and be touched, influence and be influenced. Because existence is empty, there is room for creation and destruction; there is room for renewal and transformation. The essence of life, and of all existence, is revealed upon awakening to the reality of emptiness. The ultimate expression of this reality is in a heart embracing all of existence with compassion.

Chapter 7

DISTILLING THE ESSENCE

■ ■ ■

The quality of mercy is not strained,
It droppeth as the gentle rain from heaven
Upon the place beneath; it is twice bless'd;
It blesseth him that gives, and him that takes.

—WILLIAM SHAKESPEARE

T he enigma known as language is constituted as much by silence as by sound. It arises out of a gestural bodily field; it is a living fabric woven between those who speak and those who listen. Words carry us to a place beyond their domain, offering themselves in order to illuminate a threshold they do not cross. They create a space they don't enter. Words are a bridge transporting us back and forth between body and mind, between self and world, braiding phenomena into a five-colored radiance that is neither physical nor mental, yet not entirely other than these. There is a vastness and a timeless call from which words seem first to take shape, as though nature itself had arisen as a sacred syllable on a mount of breath.

The speaking body is the generative site from which a vast matrix is spun out of the silence of the flesh. Language is continually created and recreated out of the silent, poetic depths of an animated, interconnected world. Written words are a more recent innovation of language. The separation of the body and its ideas through writing is a matter of profound significance in the evolution of human life. Once written, words can be revisited and contemplated any time we choose, independent of the time they were first recorded, and independent of the breathing, speaking body that first recorded them. Reader and writer may share neither time nor space, but they are held together, nevertheless, in an imaginal field crossing both. The written word creates a relationship and a continual motion between writers and their own inscriptions, and ultimately between reader and text.

The written word persists through time like ancient stone sentinels or enduring petroglyphs. Text is not bound by time; it transcends the fleeting world of the body. We can read Shakespeare or Shantideva although they are long gone. We can study them thousands of years later because their words remain inscribed on paper. This astonishing feat has made many things possible, but it has its drawbacks. The written word lacks breath. It lacks fluidity. It stands stark on a page, looking sure, definite, unchanging. It enlists the eye and not the ear, and is therefore more likely to be held absolutely and literally, and not understood contextually and synthetically.

By contrast, the oral traditions, including Tibetan Buddhism, know that a living tradition depends on a transmission via the breath, because written words cannot transmit the living spark of realization. They can, however, serve other notable purposes. They can open the mind to a new world of possibilities; they can stimulate new thought; they can act as a reminder of things already known, but easily and habitually forgotten; they can help deepen insight and understanding; they can be an invaluable source of inspiration and support; they can help us come to know things by heart. These are but a few of the gifts of the written word. Words both spoken and written have a potent, natural magic. The word "spell," with its double meaning of putting letters together in a particular order and magic formulae or incantations are further evidence of this.

Recognizing the power of words, the Tibetan tradition makes an important distinction between those who write or speak about a path of transformation on the basis of scholarship alone, and those who communicate on the basis of direct experience. A scholar is fit to inform others, but only one with lived experience is fit to guide another. No amount of book learning can take the place of this. The ability to guide another depends upon realization that is embodied. Such a guide may also be a scholar or a wordsmith, but not necessarily.

Those who embody the way to freedom and joy are considered equal to the Buddha who lived 2500 years ago, whatever their religious affiliation or lack of it. As guides, they are, in fact, more precious. They are living emissaries, mentoring those today who wish for the timeless realizations of love and compassion rooted in wisdom. I have had the supreme good fortune to receive instruction and guidance from such adepts. The words written here on the subject of compassion in general, and on the lojong in particular, have derived much support from the many wise and worthwhile books referenced. But at the heart of all I have endeavored to communicate is the inspiration received through a living transmission, and whatever small understanding I have gained through working with these teachings in my life.

This book is written as a call to compassion. I have worked to demonstrate the centrality of compassion and love, and particularly the ways in which this has been both acknowledged and ignored by depth psychologists. In the works of Freud and Jung, we discovered that the insights of depth psychology derive primarily from listening to the suffering soul and its pathologies. Mental health is far less explored, and less understood. There is, within our practice of psychology, a limit placed on how mentally healthy, how free of suffering, and how compassionate we can be.

Buddhism, on the other hand, derives its insights from the Buddha's realization of optimal mental health, a state free from suffering and full of joy. The Buddha spoke a great deal about suffering for the purpose of helping individuals understand and uproot its causes. He spoke of it in order to guide them to freedom. The realization of indwelling freedom is the starting point for the Buddha's therapy. It is his lion's roar. The difference in the origin of these two traditions influences every theoretical twist and turn thereafter.

Freud and Jung both thought deeply about the place of love in human life. They both acknowledged that love is indispensable to personal well-being and social harmony. But neither paid more than fleeting attention to the ways we can intentionally cultivate the transformative power of love and compassion. Jung did, however, acknowledge the need for a methodology to cultivate what he called higher self-development, as well as the "insufficiency of Western culture as compared with that of the East"[1] when it came to providing such methodology.

Whereas teaching about love and compassion has been largely neglected in the field of psychology, it has been the main theme of study and practice in Tibetan Buddhism for over a thousand years. The Tibetan tradition is replete with instruction and methodology, because while the rest of the world was focused on outer progress, Tibet was focused on inner development. And since love and compassion are understood in this tradition to be both the engine and elixir of transformation, enormous emphasis was placed on their cultivation.

The instructions on love, compassion, and wisdom introduced in this book are tried-and-true medicine for the afflictions of self-grasping and selfishness, the two culprits undermining our happiness and plaguing our lives. This approach to love and compassion does not view caring for the soul as another way of catering to "the ego in drag."[2] It is a visionary and revolutionary approach to transforming instinct and habit. As Lama Yeshe remarked in one of the last teachings he gave in 1983, a year before he died, bodhimind is "like atomic energy to transform your mind."[3]

For centuries, an attitude has persisted in our society that Euro-American civilization is the most advanced on the planet. The field of psychology is, unfortunately, not immune to this view. A great deal can be gained by opening to the possibility that cultures other than our own have much to teach us about inner transformation and optimizing psychological health. It is true that we have been the pioneers of remarkable advances in the physical world. Our innovations in science, technology, and medicine are truly astonishing. We have a rich heritage in the arts, in music, in literature and philosophy, and in the Western spiritual traditions. And of course, we have also gained far-reaching insights into psychic life in the first hundred years of depth psychology. Perhaps we can feel secure enough in our considerable strengths and in the great strides we have made exploring the psyche and its logos to open our hearts and minds to the places where we lag behind, places that remain less developed. Alan Wallace asks, "Have Indian and Tibetan civilizations made any great discoveries of their own that we have not, and might they have anything to teach us?"[4] I believe the answer is "Yes."

The lojong teachings come from another time and another world. But the essence of these teachings transcends labels of ancient or modern. They are neither culture-bound nor dated. The thousand-year-old collection of aphorisms comprising the lojong is a timeless and sacred technology cutting across cultural differences and speaking universally to the human experience. It is easily adapted to address both the individual and particular conditions of our contemporary lives and the larger context of our collective experience. It is this intersection of the current and personal with the timeless and universal that makes the lojong as potent today as ever.

I find there are four major points to be distilled from the essential actions and principles of these teachings. I enumerate them here as a simple way for all of us to remember the heart of the lojong and the ingredients for inner alchemy:

- Compassion for self

- Compassion for others

- Exchanging self and others

- No self and no other

If we unite the contemplation of these four essentials with the practice of tonglen, we will have a sound basis for both psychological health and genuine transformation.

THE ROOT VERSES OF
SEVEN POINT MIND TRAINING
BY
GESHE CHEKAWA

■   ■   ■

(Excerpted from *Becoming a Child of the Buddhas*, by Gomo Tulku)

Homage to Great Compassion.

These instructions are the essence of nectar.
They have been passed down from Serlingpa.
They are like the diamond, the sun, and a medicinal tree.
Understand the purpose and so forth of these texts.
When the five degenerations are flourishing,
transform them into the path to enlightenment.

1. Preliminary Supporting Dharma Practices
Initially train in the preliminaries.

2. Training the Mind in the Path to Enlightenment
Put all the blame on the one.
Meditate on everyone as kind.
Train alternately in the two, taking and giving.
Begin taking with yourself.
Mount the two upon the breath.
There are three objects, three poisons, and three roots of virtue.
These in brief, are the instructions for the post-meditation period.

Be mindful in order to admonish yourself.
Train yourself with the verses during all activities.
Having attained stability, be shown the secret.
Consider phenomena to be like a dream.
Analyze the nature of ungenerated awareness.
Even the antidote itself is naturally free.
Focus on the nature of the basis of all, the entirety of the path.
Between sessions be an illusionist.

3. Bringing Unfavorable Conditions into the Path to Enlightenment

When the vessel and its contents are filled with negativities,
Transform these unfavorable conditions into the path to
enlightenment.
Immediately apply whatever you meet to meditation.
Possess the four preparations, the supreme method.

4. Integrating the Practices in a Single Lifetime

In brief, the essence of the instructions is to apply the five forces.
The Great Vehicle instructions on transference are those very five
forces; cherish this behavior.

5. The Measure of a Trained Mind

Combine all dharmas into one intention.
Of the two witnesses, rely on the primary one.
Always rely on mental happiness alone.
The measure of being trained is to no longer regress.
To be trained is to possess the five signs of greatness.
You are trained when able even if distracted.

6. The Commitments of Mind Training

Constantly train in the three general points.
Change your attitude but remain natural.
Do not mention other's impaired limbs.
Do not think about others' affairs.
Initially purify whatever affliction is the strongest.
Give up all hope of reward.

Avoid poisoned food.

Do not hold a grudge.

Do not respond to malicious talk.

Do not lie in ambush.

Do not strike to the core.

Do not put the load of a *dzo* on an ox.

Do not aim to win the race.

Do not use perverse means.

Do not turn a god into a demon.

Do not seek others' suffering as a means to your own happiness.

7. Advice Regarding Mind Training

Perform all yogas with the one.

Apply the one to all perverse oppressors.

Do the activities, one at the beginning and one at the end.

Be patient whichever of the two occurs.

Guard the two at the risk of your life.

Train in the three difficult ones.

Obtain the three principal causes.

Cultivate the three without deterioration.

Possess the three without separation.

Train in purity and impartiality with respect to objects.

Cherish all of the encompassing and profound trainings.

Meditate constantly on the special causes.

Do not look for other conditions.

Practice the most important right now.

Avoid the distorted understandings.

Do not be erratic.

Train continuously.

Attain liberation with the two, investigation and analysis.

Do not boast.

Refrain from retaliating.

Do not act impetuously.

Do not wish for gratitude.

NOTES

Introduction

1. Robert Romanyshyn, *Technology as Symptom and Dream* (New York: Routledge, 1989), p. 90.
2. C. G. Jung, "The Transcendent Function," in *The Collected Works of C. G. Jung, Volume 8: Structure and Dynamics of the Psyche* (Princeton: Princeton University Press, 1960), p. 75.
3. Sigmund Freud, "Recommendations to Physicians Practicing Psycho-analysis" (1912) in J. Strachey, ed. and trans., *The Standard Edition of the Complete Psychological Works of Sigmund Freud*, vol. 12 (London: Hogarth Press, 1958), p. 115. Further references to this work will be cited as *The Standard Edition*.
4. Roger Lewin, *Compassion: The Core Value That Animates Psychotherapy* (Northvale, NJ: Jason Aronson, 1996), p. 68.

Chapter 1

1. Stephen Batchelor, *Alone with Others* (New York: Grove Press, 1983), p. 72
2. C. G. Jung, *Two Essays on Analytical Psychology* (Princeton: Princeton University Press, 1977), p. 155.
3. Rimpoche Nawang Gehlek, *Love and Compassion, a Weekend Course*, unpublished Jewel Heart transcript (Ann Arbor, MI: Jewel Heart, 1992), p. 15.
4. His Holiness the Dalai Lama, *Ethics for the New Millennium* (New York: Riverhead Books, 1999), p. 237.
5. Quoted in Diane Osbon, ed., *Reflections on the Art of Living: A Joseph Campbell Companion* (New York: HarperCollins, 1991), p. 24.
6. C. G. Jung, "The Transcendent Function," in *The Collected Works of C. G. Jung, Volume 9* (Princeton: Princeton University Press, 1960), p. 90.
7. Erich Fromm, *Psychoanalysis and Religion* (New Haven, CT: Yale University Press, 1950), p. 6.
8. Bruno Bettelheim, *Freud and Man's Soul* (New York: Random House, 1982), p. 102.

9. Sigmund Freud, "Thoughts for the Times on War and Death," originally published 1915. In J. Strachey, ed. and trans., *The Standard Edition*, vol. 14 (London: Hogarth Press, 1957).

10. C. G. Jung, *Modern Man in Search of a Soul* (Orlando, FL: Harcourt Brace Jovanovich, 1933), p. 117.

11. C. G. Jung, *Memories, Dreams, Reflections*, Aniela Jaffé, ed., and R. and C. Winston, trans. (New York: Vintage, 1989. Originally published New York: Pantheon, 1961), p. 269.

12. Robert A. F. Thurman, *Inner Revolution: Life, Liberty, and the Pursuit of Real Happiness* (New York: Riverhead Books, 1998), pp. 34–35.

13. James Hillman, *Re-Visioning Psychology* (New York: Harper Perennial, 1975), p. 55.

14. L. Ladner, *The Psychodynamics of Compassion: Psychological Reflections on the Tibetan Buddhist Stages of the Path of Literature*, unpublished doctoral dissertation (Carpinteria, CA: Pacifica Graduate Institute, 1997), p. 30.

15. Roger Walsh and Frances Vaughan, *Paths Beyond Ego: The Transpersonal Vision* (New York: Putnam, 1993), p. 49.

16. Jung, *Modern Man in Search of a Soul*, p. 54.

17. Richard Palmer, *Hermeneutics* (Evanston, IL: Northwestern University Press, 1969).

18. Otto Rank, *Beyond Psychology* (New York: Dover, 1941), p. 291.

19. Sogyal Rinpoche, *Tibetan Book of Living and Dying* (New York: HarperCollins, 1993), p. 188.

20. John Welwood, *Toward a Psychology of Awakening* (Boston: Shambhala, 2000), p. 163.

21. Pabongka Rinpoche, *Liberation in the Palm of Your Hand*, M. Richards, trans., Trijang Rinpoche, ed. (Boston: Wisdom Publications, 1991).

22. His Holiness the Dalai Lama, quoted in Gyalwa Druppa and Glenn H. Mullin, *Training the Mind in the Great Way* (Ithaca, NY: Snow Lion, 1993), p. 13.

23. Gomo Tulku, *Becoming a Child of the Buddhas* (Boston: Wisdom Publications, 1998), p. vii.

24. Druppa and Mullin, *Training the Mind in the Great Way*, p. 14.

25. Thurman, *Inner Revolution*, p. 195.

26. Chögyam Trungpa, *The Heart of the Buddha* (Boston: Shambhala, 1991), p. 121.

27. Thurman, *Inner Revolution*, p. 187.

28. Ken Wilber, *Sex, Ecology, Spirituality* (Boston: Shambhala, 1995), pp. 252–253.

Chapter 2

1. C. G. Jung, *Psychology and Alchemy*, R.F.C. Hull, trans. (Princeton: Princeton University Press, 1993), p. 32. Originally published in 1944.

2. Melanie Klein, *Envy and Gratitude and Other Works: 1946–1963* (London: Hogarth Press, 1975), p. 269.

3. James Hillman, *Inter Views: Conversations Between James Hillman and Laura Pozzo on Therapy, Biography, Love, Soul, Dreams, Work, Imagination and the State of the Culture* (New York: Harper and Row, 1983), p. 178.

4. His Holiness the Dalai Lama and H. Cutler, *The Art of Happiness* (New York: Riverhead Books, 1998), p. 114.

5. Chögyam Trungpa, *Cutting Through Spiritual Materialism* (Boston: Shambhala, 1973), p. 213.

6. Pabongka Rinpoche, *Liberation in the Palm of Your Hand*, M. Richard, trans., Trijang Rinpoche, ed. (Boston: Wisdom Publications, 1991), p. 34.

7. Quoted in Ken Wilber, *Sex, Ecology, Spirituality* (Boston: Shambhala, 1995), pp. 292–293.

8. Pabongka Rinpoche, *Liberation in the Palm of Your Hand*, p. 583.

9. Trungpa, *Cutting Through Spiritual Materialism*, p. 101.

10. Pabongka Rinpoche, *Liberation in the Palm of Your Hand*, p. 34.

11. Quoted in Diane Osbon, *Reflections on the Art of Living: A Joseph Campbell Companion* (New York: HarperCollins, 1991), p. 53.

12. Compare Sigmund Freud, "Recommendations to Physicians . . . " (1912) in J. Strachey, ed., *The Standard Edition*, vol. 12, p. 115, with "On Beginning the Treatment," (1913), in *The Standard Edition*, vol. 12 (London: Hogarth Press, 1958), pp. 139–140.

13. Ron Leifer, *The Happiness Project* (Ithaca, NY: Snow Lion, 1997), p. 125.

14. Emma Jeanette and Ludwig Edelstein, *Asclepius* (Baltimore: Johns Hopkins Press, 1998), p. 139.

15. Edelstein, *Asclepius*, p. 141.

16. Leifer, *The Happiness Project*, p. 28.

17. Leifer, *The Happiness Project*, p. 126.

18. Sigmund Freud, *The Future of an Illusion* (1927), J. Strachey, ed. and trans. (New York: W. W. Norton, 1961), p. 43.

19. Freud, *The Future of an Illusion*, p. 31.

20. Freud, *The Future of an Illusion*, p. 55.

21. Sigmund Freud, *The Question of Lay Analysis* (1927), J. Strachey, ed. and trans. (New York: W. W. Norton, 1959), pp. 217–219.

22. Freud, *The Question of Lay Analysis*, pp. 93–94.

23. Erich Fromm, *Psychoanalysis and Religion* (New Haven, CT: Yale University

Press, 1950), p. 7.

24. Freud, *The Question of Lay Analysis*, pp. 119, 121.

25. Franz Brentano, *Psychology from an Empirical Standpoint*, A. C. Rancurello, D. B. Terrell, and L. L. McAllister, trans. (New York: Humanities Press, 1973), p. xv.

26. Bruno Bettelheim, *Freud and Man's Soul* (New York: Random House, 1982), pp. 12–13.

27. Sigmund Freud, *Beyond the Pleasure Principle*, J. Strachey, ed. and trans. (New York: W. W. Norton, 1961), p. 61. Original work published in 1920.

28. Otto Rank, *Psychology and the Soul* (Baltimore: Johns Hopkins University Press, 1998), p. 63.

29. Otto Rank, *Beyond Psychology* (New York: Dover Publications, 1941), p. 191.

30. Rank, *Beyond Psychology*, p. 63.

31. Sandor Ferenczi, *The Clinical Diary of Sandor Ferenczi*, J. Dupont, ed., and M. I. Balint and N. Zaraday Jackson, trans. (Cambridge, MA: Harvard University Press, 1988), p. xx.

32. Ferenczi, *Clinical Diary*, p. 61.

33. Andre Haynal, *Controversies in Psychoanalytic Method: From Freud to Ferenczi to Michael Balint* (New York: New York University Press, 1989), p. 32.

34. Ferenczi, *Clinical Diary*, p. 56.

35. Jung, *Psychology and Alchemy*, p. 119.

36. Jung, *Psychology and Alchemy*, p. 120.

37. C. G. Jung, *The Psychology of the Transference*, R.F.C. Hull, trans. (Princeton: Princeton University Press, 1992), p. 34.

38. C. G. Jung, *Memories, Dreams, Reflections*, Aniela Jaffé, ed., R. and C. Winston, trans. (New York: Vintage, 1989), p. 354.

39. C. G. Jung, *The Vision Seminars*, vol. 1 (Zurich, Switzerland: Spring Publications, 1976), p. 215.

40. Jung, *Psychology and Alchemy*, pp. 53–54.

41. Jung, *Psychology and Alchemy*, p. 52.

42. Edward Edinger, *Anatomy of the Psyche* (Chicago: Open Court, 1985), p. 223.

43. James Hillman, *Inter Views*, p. 183.

44. James Hillman, *The Myth of Analysis* (New York: Harper Collins, 1972), p. 88.

45. Hillman, *The Myth of Analysis*, p. 283.

46. Hillman, *Inter Views*, p. 183.

47. James Hillman, *A Blue Fire* (New York: Harper and Row, 1989), p. 164.

48. Helen Luke, *The Way of Women* (New York: Doubleday, 1995), pp. 199–200.

49. Wilhelm Dilthey, *Selected Writings*, H. P. Rickman, trans. and ed. (New York: Cambridge University Press, 1976), p. 105.

50. Dilthey, *Selected Writings*, p. 181.
51. Martin Buber, *I and Thou* (New York: Charles Scribner's Sons, 1937), p. 11.
52. Martin Buber, *Between Man and Man* (Boston: Beacon Press, 1955), p. 168.
53. Richard Hycner, *Between Person and Person* (Highland, NY: The Gestalt Journal, 1988), p. 84.
54. Hycner, *Between Person and Person*, p. 53.
55. Hans Trub, "Healing through Meeting," in M. Friedman, ed., *The Worlds of Existentialism* (New York: Random House, 1964), p. 503.
56. Trub, "Healing through Meeting," p. 499.
57. Hycner, *Between Person and Person*, p. 60.
58. Maurice Friedman, *Religion and Psychology* (New York: Paragon House, 1992), p. 50.
59. Buber, *Between Man and Man*, p. 70.
60. Buber, *Between Man and Man*, p. 60.
61. Heinz Kohut, *The Restoration of the Self* (Madison, CT: International Universities Press, 1977), p. 304.
62. Heinz Kohut, *How Does Analysis Cure?* (Chicago: The University of Chicago Press, 1984), p. 82; Kohut, *Restoration of the Self*, p. 306.
63. Kohut, *Restoration of the Self*, p. 302.
64. Kohut, *Restoration of the Self*, pp. 252, 254.
65. Quoted in Allen Siegel, *Heinz Kohut and the Psychology of the Self* (New York: Routledge, 1996), p. 186.
66. Quoted in Siegel, Heinz Kohut, p. 191.
67. His Holiness the Dalai Lama, *Ethics for a New Millennium* (New York: Riverhead Books, 1999), p. 130.
68. Dalai Lama, *Ethics*, p. 11.
69. Dalai Lama, *Ethics*, p. 12.
70. Dalai Lama, *Ethics*, p. 9.
71. Dalai Lama, *Ethics*, p. 234.
72. Dalai Lama, *Ethics*, p. 17.
73. Dalai Lama, *Ethics*, p. 23.
74. Dalai Lama, *Ethics*, p. 123.
75. Dalai Lama, *Ethics*, p. 81.
76. Trungpa, *Cutting Through Spiritual Materialism*, p. 208.
77. Geshe Rabten, *Treasury of Dharma* (London: Tharpa, 1988), p. 70.
78. Rabten, *Treasury of Dharma*, p. 70.
79. Trungpa, *Cutting Through Spiritual Materialism*, p. 98.
80. Thubten Yeshe, *Introduction to Tantra* (Boston: Wisdom Publications, 1987), p. 58.
81. Trungpa, *Cutting Through Spiritual Materialism*, p. 99.

82. Robert A. F. Thurman, "A Tibetan Perspective," in D. Goleman and R.A.F. Thurman, eds., *MindScience: An East-West Dialogue* (Boston: Wisdom Publications, 1991), p. 108.

83. Dalai Lama and Cutler, *Art of Happiness*, p. 240.

84. Dalai Lama, *Ethics*, p. 83.

85. Dalai Lama, *Ethics*, p. 83.

86. Dalai Lama, *Ethics*, p. 70.

87. Dalai Lama, *Ethics*, p. 71.

88. Chögyam Trungpa, *Illusions Game* (Boston: Shambhala, 1994), p. 29.

89. Trungpa, *Cutting Through Spiritual Materialism*, p. 210.

90. Chögyam Trungpa, *The Heart of Buddhism* (Boston: Shambhala, 1991), p. 126.

91. Sogyal Rinpoche, *Tibetan Book of Living and Dying* (New York: HarperCollins, 1993), p. 189.

92. Chögyam Trungpa, "Becoming a Full Human Being," in J. Welwood, ed., *Awakening the Heart: East/West Approaches to Psychotherapy and the Healing Relationship* (Boston: Shambhala, 1983), p. 127.

93. Trungpa, "Becoming a Full Human Being," p. 126.

94. Trungpa, "Becoming a Full Human Being," pp. 130, 127.

95. Trungpa, "Becoming a Full Human Being," p. 127.

96. Chögyam Trungpa, *The Myth of Freedom* (Boston: Shambhala, 1976), p. 92.

97. Trungpa, "Becoming a Full Human Being," pp. 128–129.

98. Tarthang Tulku Rinpoche, "Tibetan Buddhism, the Way of Compassion," in J. Needleman and D. Lewis, eds., *On the Way to Self Knowledge* (New York: Alfred Knopf, 1976), p. 84.

99. Dalai Lama and Cutler, *Art of Happiness*, pp. 40, 41.

100. Dalai Lama and Cutler, *Art of Happiness*, p. 122.

101. Dalai Lama, *Ethics*, p. 131.

Chapter 3

1. Sigmund Freud, *Beyond the Pleasure Principle*, J. Strachey, ed. and trans. (New York: W. W. Norton, 1961), pp. 63–64. Original work published 1920.

2. Bruno Bettelheim, *Freud and Man's Soul* (New York: Random House, 1982), p. 107.

3. Freud, *Beyond the Pleasure Principle*, pp. 45, 46.

4. Freud, *Beyond the Pleasure Principle*, p. 42.

5. Freud, *Beyond the Pleasure Principle*, p. 47.

6. Freud, *Beyond the Pleasure Principle*, p. 73.

7. Sigmund Freud, *An Outline of Psychoanalysis*, J. Strachey, ed. and trans.

(New York: W. W. Norton, 1949), p. 5. Original work published 1940.

8. Freud, *Beyond the Pleasure Principle*, pp. 60–61.

9. Christine Downing, "Sigmund Freud's Mythology of Soul," in D. Slattery and L. Corbett, eds., *Depth Psychology: Meditations in the Field* (Einsiedeln, Switzerland: Daimon Verlag, 2000), pp. 65, 66.

10. Bettelheim, *Freud and Man's Soul*, p. 109.

11. Downing, "Sigmund Freud's Mythology of Soul," p. 62.

12. Bettelheim, *Freud and Man's Soul*, p. 110.

13. Freud, *Beyond the Pleasure Principle*, p. 77.

14. Erich Neumann, *Amor and Psyche* (Princeton: Princeton University Press, 1969), p. 53.

15. Sigmund Freud, "Introductory Lectures on Psycho analysis," in J. Strachey, ed. and trans., *The Standard Edition*, vols. 15 and 16 (London: Hogarth Press, 1963), p. 416. Original work published 1916–1917.

16. Sigmund Freud, *The Basic Writings of Sigmund Freud*, A. A. Brill, ed. and trans. (New York: Random House, 1938), p. 876.

17. Sigmund Freud, *The Ego and the Id*, J. Strachey, ed., J. Rivière, trans. (London: Hogarth Press, 1962), p. 36.

18. Freud, *An Outline of Psychoanalysis*, p. 8.

19. Sigmund Freud, "On Narcissism," in *The Standard Edition*, vol. 14, p. 82. Original work published in 1914.

20. Freud, "On Narcissism," p. 85.

21. Bettelheim, *Freud and Man's Soul*, p. 102.

22. Karen Horney, *New Ways in Psychoanalysis* (New York: W. W. Norton, 1939), p. 89.

23. Horney, *New Ways in Psychoanalysis*, p. 100.

24. Horney, *New Ways in Psychoanalysis*, p. 90.

25. Horney, *New Ways in Psychoanalysis*, p. 98.

26. Horney, *New Ways in Psychoanalysis*, p. 99.

27. Horney, *New Ways in Psychoanalysis*, p. 99.

28. Mark Epstein, *Thoughts Without a Thinker: Psychotherapy from a Buddhist Perspective* (New York: Basic Books, 1995), p. 4.

29. Downing, "Sigmund Freud's Mythology of Soul," p. 70.

30. Sigmund Freud, *Civilization and Its Discontents*, J. Strachey, ed. and trans. (New York: W. W. Norton, 1961), p. 42. Original work published 1930.

31. Freud, *Civilization*, p. 73.

32. Freud, *Civilization*, p. 82.

33. Freud, *Civilization*, p. 25.

34. Freud, *Civilization*, p. 104.

35. Freud, *Civilization*, pp. 49-50.

36. Freud, *Civilization*, pp. 20-21.
37. Freud, *Civilization*, p. 50.
38. Freud, *Civilization*, p. 56.
39. Freud, *Civilization*, p. 56.
40. Freud, *Civilization*, p. 57.
41. Freud, *Civilization*, p. 58.
42. Freud, *Civilization*, p. 57.
43. Freud, *Civilization*, p. 67.
44. Freud, *Civilization*, p. 81.
45. Freud, *Civilization*, pp. 68–69.
46. Freud, *Civilization*, p. 69.
47. Horney, *New Ways in Psychoanalysis*, p. 126.
48. Horney, *New Ways in Psychoanalysis*, pp. 127, 129.
49. Horney, *New Ways in Psychoanalysis*, pp. 130, 131.

Chapter 4

1. C. G. Jung, *The Psychology of the Transference*, R.F.C. Hull, trans. (Princeton: Princeton University Press, 1992), p. 8. Original work published 1946.
2. Jung, *The Psychology of the Transference*, p. 13.
3. Jung, *The Psychology of the Transference*, p. 24.
4. Jung, *The Psychology of the Transference*, p. 57.
5. Jung, *The Psychology of the Transference*, p. 34.
6. Jung, *The Psychology of the Transference*, p. 7.
7. Jung, *The Psychology of the Transference*, p. 12.
8. Jung, *The Psychology of the Transference*, p. 18.
9. C. G. Jung, "The Transcendent Function," in *The Collected Works of C. G. Jung*, Vol. 8, R.F.C. Hull, trans. (Princeton: Princeton University Press, 1960), p. 74.
10. Jung, *The Psychology of the Transference*, p. 161.
11. Jung, *The Psychology of the Transference*, pp. 3, 5.
12. C. G. Jung, *Modern Man in Search of a Soul* (Orlando, FL: Harcourt Brace Jovanovich, 1933), p. 49.
13. Jung, *The Psychology of the Transference*, p. 35.
14. Jung, *Modern Man*, p. 53.
15. Jung, *Modern Man*, p. 50.
16. Jung, *The Psychology of the Transference*, p. 73.
17. Jung, *The Psychology of the Transference*, pp. 82–83.
18. Jung, *The Psychology of the Transference*, pp. 71–72.

19. C. G. Jung, *Memories, Dreams, Reflections*, Aniela Jaffé, ed., and R. and C. Winston, trans. (New York: Vintage, 1989), p. 359. Original work published 1961.

20. Jung, "The Transcendent Function," p. 69.

21. Jung, "The Transcendent Function," p. 89.

22. C. G. Jung, *Two Essays on Analytical Psychology* (Princeton: Princeton University Press, 1977), p. 99.

23. Jung, *Two Essays*, p. 358.

24. Jung, "The Transcendent Function," p. 74.

25. Jung, "The Transcendent Function," p. 91.

26. Jung, *Memories*, p. 358.

27. Jung, *The Psychology of the Transference*, p. 24.

28. Ginette Paris, *Pagan Grace* (Woodstock, CT: Spring Publications, 1990), p. 110.

29. Jung, *The Psychology of the Transference*, p. 28.

30. Jung, *Modern Man*, p. 41.

31. C. G. Jung, *Answer to Job*, R.F.C. Hull, trans. (Princeton: Princeton University Press, 1991), p. 97. Original work published 1952.

32. Jung, *Modern Man*, p. 238.

33. Jeremiah Abrams and Connie Zweig, *Meeting the Shadow* (Los Angeles: Jeremy Tarcher, 1991), p. xvii.

34. Jung, *Answer to Job*, p. 106.

35. Jung, *The Psychology of the Transference*, p. 157.

36. Jung, *Memories*, p. 227.

37. Jung, *Memories*, pp. 87–88.

38. Jung, *The Psychology of the Transference*, p. 57.

39. Jung, *The Psychology of the Transference*, p. 69.

40. Jung, *Modern Man*, p. 234.

41. Jung, *Modern Man*, p. 235.

42. C. G. Jung, *Psychological Reflections*, Jolande Jacobi and R.F.C. Hull, eds. (Princeton: Princeton University Press, 1978), p. 249.

43. His Holiness the Dalai Lama, *Transforming the Mind* (London: Thorsons, 2000), p. 117.

44. Jung, *Modern Man*, pp. 116–117.

45. Jung, *Two Essays*, p. 148.

46. Jung, *Modern Man*, p. 197.

47. Jung, *Modern Man*, p. 198.

48. Jung, *The Psychology of the Transference*, p. 72.

49. Jung, *Two Essays*, p. 125.

50. Jung, *Answer to Job*, p. 98.
51. Jung, *Answer to Job*, p. 97.
52. Jung, *Two Essays*, pp. 5, 152–153.
53. Jung, *Two Essays*, p. 4.
54. Jung, *Two Essays*, p. 118.

Chapter 5

1. Robert Bly and Marion Woodman, *The Maiden King* (New York: Henry Holt, 1998), p. 54.
2. M. Ventura, "The Inevitable and the Unpredictable," in *Salt Journal* 3, no. 3 (2001):43.
3. Chögyam Trungpa, *The Myth of Freedom* (Boston: Shambhala, 1976), p. 149.
4. Pema Chödrön, *The Wisdom of No Escape* (Boston: Shambhala, 1991), p. 3.
5. James Hillman, *Re-Visioning Psychology* (New York: HarperPerennial, 1975), p. 223.
6. Gyalwa Gendun Druppa and Glenn H. Mullin, trans., *Training the Mind in the Great Way* (Ithaca, NY: Snow Lion, 1993), p. 17.
7. Sermey Khensur Lobsang Tharchin, *Achieving Bodhicitta* (Howell, NJ: Mahayana Sutra and Tantra Press, 1999), p. 5.
8. Rimpoche Nawang Gehlek, *Lojong: Seven Point Mind Training*, unpublished Jewel Heart transcript (Ann Arbor, MI: Jewel Heart, 1999), p. 2.
9. Druppa and Mullin, *Training the Mind*, p. 13.
10. Lama Yeshe in Druppa and Mullin, *Training the Mind*, p. 25.
11. Chödrön, *Wisdom of No Escape*, p. 97.
12. Gehlek, *Lojong*, p. 20.
13. Geshe Rabten and Geshe Dhargyey, *Advice from a Spiritual Friend* (Boston: Wisdom Publications, 1996), p. 70.
14. Chödrön, *Wisdom of No Escape*, p. 99.
15. Stephen Batchelor, *Buddhism without Beliefs* (New York: Riverhead Books, 1997), p. 29.
16. Sogyal Rinpoche, *Tibetan Book of Living and Dying* (New York: HarperCollins, 1993), p. 29.
17. Sigmund Freud, "On Transience," in *The Standard Edition*, vol. 14, pp. 305–306.
18. Freud, "On Transience," p. 306.
19. Robert Romanyshyn, *The Soul in Grief* (Berkeley, CA: North Atlantic, 1999), p. 8.
20. Sogyal Rinpoche, *Tibetan Book of Living and Dying*, p. 16.

21. Trungpa, *Myth of Freedom*, p. 13.
22. Sogyal Rinpoche, *Tibetan Book of Living and Dying*, p. 95.
23. His Holiness the Dalai Lama and H. Cutler, *The Art of Happiness* (New York: Riverhead Books, 1998), p. 7.
24. Rimpoche Nawang Gehlek, *Good Life, Good Death* (New York: Riverhead Books, 2001), p. 17.
25. Tarthang Tulku, *Path of Heroes* (Oakland, CA: Dharma Publishing, 1995), p. 109.
26. Jack Kornfield, *A Path with Heart* (New York: Bantam, 1993), p. 276.
27. Tulku, *Path of Heroes*, p. 133.
28. Sogyal Rinpoche, *Tibetan Book of Living and Dying*, p. 20.
29. Gehlek, *Lojong*, p. 47.
30. Yeshe, *Introduction to Tantra*, p. 63.
31. Marion Woodman, *Conscious Femininity* (Toronto: Inner City, 1993), p. 122.
32. Marie-Louise von Franz, *Alchemy* (Toronto: Inner City, 1980), p. 222.
33. Yeshe, *Introduction to Tantra*, p. 66.
34. James Hillman, *Inter Views: Conversations between James Hillman and Laura Pozzo on Therapy, Biography, Love, Soul, Dreams, Work, Imagination and the State of the Culture* (New York: Harper and Row, 1983), p. 111.
35. Robert A. F. Thurman, trans., *The Holy Teachings of Vimalakirti* (University Park, PA: Pennsylvania State University Press, 1976), pp. 18–19.
36. Robert Romanyshyn, lecture given at the Pacifica Graduate Institute, Carpinteria, CA, October 16, 1998.
37. Yeshe, *Introduction to Tantra*, p. 64.
38. Tharchin, *Achieving Bodhicitta*, p. 22.
39. Karen Horney, *Our Inner Conflicts* (New York: W. W. Norton, 1945), p. 47.
40. B. Alan Wallace, *Boundless Heart* (Ithaca, NY: Snow Lion, 1999), p. 102.
41. Etty Hillesum, *An Interrupted Life and Letters from Westerbork* (New York: Henry Holt, 1996), p. 256.
42. Hillesum, *Interrupted Life*, p. 256.
43. Geshe Rabten, *Treasury of Dharma* (London: Tharpa, 1988), p. 138.
44. Rabten, *Treasury of Dharma*, p. 138.
45. Jeffrey Hopkins, *Cultivating Compassion* (New York: Broadway Books, 2001), p. 63.
46. Wallace, *Boundless Heart*, p. 159.
47. Anne Carolyn Klein, *Meeting the Great Bliss Queen* (Boston: Beacon Press, 1995), p. 95.
48. Yeshe, *Introduction to Tantra*, p. 66.
49. Gehlek, *Lojong*, p. 47.
50. Yeshe, *Introduction to Tantra*, p. 66.

51. Wallace, *Boundless Heart*, p. 155.
52. Klein, *Meeting the Great Bliss Queen*, p. 93.
53. Wallace, *Boundless Heart*, p. 155.
54. Hopkins, *Cultivating Compassion*, p. 38.
55. Hopkins, *Cultivating Compassion*, p. 31.
56. Chögyam Trungpa, *Training the Mind and Cultivating Loving-Kindness* (Boston: Shambhala, 1993), p. 188.
57. Sigmund Freud, *Civilization and Its Discontents*, J. Strachey, ed. and trans. (New York: W. W. Norton, 1961), p. 67. Original work published 1930.

Chapter 6

1. B. Alan Wallace, *Buddhism with an Attitude* (Ithaca, NY: Snow Lion, 2001), p. 13.
2. Rachel Remen, *Kitchen Table Wisdom* (New York: Riverhead Books, 1996), p. 75.
3. Sermey Khensur Lobsang Tharchin, *Achieving Bodhicitta* (Howell, NJ: Mahayana Sutra and Tantra Press, 1999), p. 74.
4. His Holiness the Dalai Lama, *Transforming the Mind* (London: Thorsons, 2000), p. 99.
5. Rimpoche Nawang Gehlek, *Lojong: Seven Point Mind Training*, unpublished Jewel Heart transcript (Ann Arbor, MI: Jewel Heart, 1999), p. 63.
6. Robert A. F. Thurman, *Inner Revolution: Life, Liberty and the Pursuit of Real Happiness* (New York: Riverhead Books, 1998), pp. 62–63.
7. B. Alan Wallace, *Passage from Solitude* (Ithaca, NY: Snow Lion, 1992), p. 69.
8. Thurman, *Inner Revolution*, p. 68.
9. Joyce McDougall, *The Many Faces of Eros* (New York: W. W. Norton, 1995).
10. Marion Woodman, *Conscious Femininity* (Toronto: Inner City, 1993), p. 127.
11. Viktor Frankl, *Man's Search for Meaning* (New York: Simon and Schuster, 1984), p. 154.
12. Gehlek, *Lojong*, p. 71.
13. Shantideva, *A Guide to the Bodhisattva's Way to Life*, Stephen Batchelor, trans. (Dharamsala, India: Library of Tibetan Works and Archives, 1979), p. 125.
14. Gehlek, *Lojong*, p. 73
15. Pema Chödrön, *Start Where You Are* (Boston: Shambhala, 1994), p. 46.
16. Chödrön, *Start Where You Are*, p. 81.
17. Chödrön, *Start Where You Are*, p. 52.
18. Chögyam Trungpa, *Training the Mind and Cultivating Loving-Kindness* (Boston: Shambhala, 1993), p. 17.

19. Gehlek, *Lojong*, pp. 75, 82.
20. L. C. Gyaltsan, *Lama Chopa*, unpublished Jewel Heart transcript (Ann Arbor, MI: Jewel Heart, 2000), p. 23.
21. Linda Chrisman, "Birth," in Lenore Friedman and Susan Moon, eds., *Being Bodies* (Boston: Shambhala, 1997), p. 59.
22. Gehlek, *Lojong*, p. 75.
23. His Holiness the Dalai Lama, *Ethics for a New Millennium* (New York: Riverhead Books, 1999), p. 139.
24. Keith Dowman, *Buddhist Masters of Enchantment* (Rochester, VT: Inner Traditions, 1988), p. 23.
25. Tenzin Palmo, "Tuning the Mind to Make a Sweet Melody," in *Mandala Magazine* (March, 2001):38.
26. Wallace, *Buddhism with an Attitude*, p. 235.
27. Shantideva, *A Guide to the Bodhisattva's Way of Life*, Stephen Batchelor, trans. (Dharamsala, India: Library of Tibetan Works and Archives, 1979).
28. Wallace, *Buddhism with an Attitude*, p. 194.
29. James Hillman, *Re-Visioning Psychology* (New York: HarperPerennial, 1975), p. 208.
30. Christine Downing, *The Goddess: Mythological Images of the Feminine* (New York: Continuum, 1981), p. 45.
31. Dilgo Khyentse, *Enlightened Courage* (Ithaca, NY: Snow Lion, 1993), p. 50.
32. Gehlek, *Lojong*, p. 1.
33. Trungpa, *Training the Mind*, p. 83.
34. Gehlek, *Lojong*, p. 65.
35. Etty Hillesum, *An Interrupted Life and Letters from Westerbork* (New York: Henry Holt, 1996), p. 177.
36. Thomas Moore, *Care of the Soul* (New York: HarperCollins, 1992), p. 123.
37. Caroline Casey, *Making the Gods Work for You* (New York: Harmony Books, 1998), p. 44.
38. Trungpa, *Training the Mind*, p. 57.
39. Trungpa, *Training the Mind*, p. 47.
40. James Hillman, *The Thought of the Heart and the Soul of the World* (Dallas: Spring Publications, 1981), p. 107.
41. Shantideva, *Guide to the Bodhisattva's Way of Life*, p. 25.
42. Sogyal Rinpoche, *Tibetan Book of Living and Dying* (New York: HarperCollins, 1993), p. 207.
43. Wallace, *Buddhism with an Attitude*, p. 184.
44. Thurman, *Inner Revolution*, p. 188.
45. Erich Fromm, *Psychoanalysis and Religion* (New Haven, CT: Yale University Press, 1950), p. 87.

46. Tulku, *Becoming a Child of the Buddhas*, p. 28.
47. C. G. Jung, *Modern Man in Search of a Soul* (Orlando, FL: Harcourt Brace Jovanovich, 1933), p. 234.
48. Robert Bly, *A Little Book on the Human Shadow* (San Francisco: Harper and Row, 1988), p. 43.
49. Tsultrim Allione, *Women of Wisdom* (Boston: Routledge and Kegan Paul, 1984), pp. 160–161.
50. Gehlek, *Lojong*, p. 105.
51. Geshe Rabten and Geshe Dhargyey, *Advice from a Spiritual Friend* (Boston: Wisdom Publications, 1996), p. 80.
52. Tulku, *Becoming a Child of the Buddhas*, p. 31.
53. Stephen Batchelor, *Buddhism without Beliefs* (New York: Riverhead Books, 1997), p. 82.
54. Rabten and Dhargyey, *Advice*, p. 81.
55. Rabten and Dhargyey, *Advice*, p. 82.
56. Polly Young-Eisendrath, *The Resilient Spirit* (New York: Addison-Wesley, 1996), p. 118.
57. Mark Epstein, *Going to Pieces without Falling Apart* (New York: Broadway Books, 1998), p. 16.
58. John Welwood, *Toward a Psychology of Awakening* (Boston: Shambhala, 2000), p. 46.
59. Mark Epstein, *Going on Being* (New York: Broadway Books, 2001).
60. Sigmund Freud, *Civilization and Its Discontents*, J. Strachey, ed. and trans. (New York: W. W. Norton, 1961), p. 108. Original work published 1930.
61. Lionel Corbett, *The Religious Function of the Psyche* (New York: Routledge, 1996), p. 172.
62. Batchelor, *Buddhism without Beliefs*, p. 80.
63. Ken Wilber, *One Taste* (Boston: Shambhala, 1999), p. 27.
64. Gehlek, *Lojong*, p. 12.
65. Thurman, *Inner Revolution*, p. 60.
66. Trungpa, *Training the Mind*, p. 30.
67. Clarissa Pinkola Estés, *Women Who Run with the Wolves* (New York: Ballantine, 1992), p. 471.
68. James Hillman, *Inter Views: Conversations between James Hillman and Laura Pozzo on Therapy, Biography, Love, Soul, Dreams, Work, Imagination, and the State of the Culture* (New York: Harper and Row, 1983), p. 41.
69. Chödrön, *Start Where You Are*, p. 12.
70. Wallace, *Buddhism with an Attitude*, p. 103
71. Chödrön, *Start Where You Are*, p. 18.

72. Rabten and Dhargyey, *Advice*, p. 86.

73. Wallace, *Buddhism with an Attitude*, p. 118.

74. Rimpoche Nawang Gehlek, *Good Life, Good Death* (New York: Riverhead Books, 2001), p. 32.

75. Gehlek, *Good Life, Good Death*, p. 30.

76. Wallace, *Buddhism with an Attitude*, p. 227.

77. Wallace, *Buddhism with an Attitude*, p. 111.

78. Jérôme Edou, *Machig Labdrön and the Foundations of Chöd* (Ithaca, NY: Snow Lion, 1996), p. 26.

79. Geshe Wangyal, *The Door of Liberation* (New York: Lotsawa, 1978), p. 129.

80. Robert A. F. Thurman, ed., *Life and Teachings of Tsong Kapa* (Dharamsala, India: Library of Tibetan Works and Archives, 1982), p. 58.

81. Rita Gross, *Soaring and Settling* (New York: Continuum, 1998), p. 174.

Chapter 7

1. C. G. Jung, *Modern Man in Search of a Soul*, (Orlando, FL: Harcourt Brace Jovanovich, 1933), pp. 53–54.

2. Ken Wilber, *One Taste* (Boston: Shambhala, 1999), p. 36.

3. Thubten Yeshe, "Bodhicitta: The Perfection of Dharma," *Mandala Magazine* (March, 2001): 31.

4. B. Alan Wallace, *Buddhism with an Attitude* (Ithaca, NY: Snow Lion, 2001), p. 9.

BIBLIOGRAPHY

Abrams, Jeremiah, and Connie Zweig. *Meeting the Shadow*. Los Angeles: Jeremy Tarcher, 1991.

Allione, Tsultrim. *Women of Wisdom*. Boston: Routledge and Kegan Paul, 1984.

Batchelor, Stephen. *Alone with Others*. New York: Grove Press, 1983.

———. *Buddhism without Beliefs*. New York: Riverhead Books, 1997.

Bettelheim, Bruno. *Freud and Man's Soul*. New York: Random House, 1982.

Bloom, Pamela, ed. *Buddhist Acts of Compassion*. Berkeley, CA: Conari Press, 2000.

Bly, Robert. *A Little Book on the Human Shadow*. San Francisco: Harper and Row, 1988.

Bly, Robert, and Marion Woodman. *The Maiden King*. New York: Henry Holt and Company, 1988.

Brentano, Franz. *Psychology from an Empirical Standpoint*. A. C. Rancurello, D. B. Terrell, and L. L. McAllister, trans. New York: Humanities Press, 1973.

Buber, Martin. *Between Man and Man*. Boston: Beacon Press, 1955.

———. *I and Thou*. New York: Charles Scribner's Sons, 1937.

———. *The Knowledge of Man*. Highlands, NJ: Humanities Press International, 1988.

Capra, Frank. *It's a Wonderful Life*. Liberty Film, 1946.

Casey, Caroline. *Making the Gods Work for You*. New York: Harmony Books, 1998.

Chödrön, Pema. *Start Where You Are*. Boston: Shambhala, 1994.

———. *When Things Fall Apart*. Boston: Shambhala, 1997.

———. *The Wisdom of No Escape*. Boston: Shambhala, 1991.

Chrisman, Linda. "Birth," in Lenore Friedman and Susan Moon, eds. *Being Bodies* (pp. 59–64). Boston: Shambhala, 1997.

Corbett, Lionel. *The Religious Function of the Psyche*. New York: Routledge, 1996.

Dalai Lama, H. H. *Ethics for the New Millennium*. New York: Riverhead Books, 1999.

————. *Transforming the Mind*. London: Thorsons Books, 2000.

Dalai Lama, H. H. and H. Cutler. *The Art of Happiness*. New York: Riverhead Books, 1998.

Dilthey, Wilhelm. *Selected Writings*. H. P. Rickman, trans. and ed. New York: Cambridge University Press, 1976.

Dowman, Keith. *Buddhist Masters of Enchantment*. Rochester, VT: Inner Traditions, 1998.

Downing, Christine. *The Goddess: Mythological Images of the Feminine*. New York: Continuum Publishing, 1981.

————. "Sigmund Freud's Mythology of Soul," in D. Slattery and L. Corbett, eds. *Depth Psychology: Meditations in the Field* (pp. 59–72). Einsiedeln, Switzerland: Daimon Verlag, 2000.

Druppa, Gyalwa Gendrun and Glenn H. Mullin, trans. *Training the Mind in the Great Way*. Ithaca, NY: Snow Lion Publications, 1993.

Edelstein, Emma Jeanette Levy and Ludwig. *Asclepius*. Baltimore: Johns Hopkins Press, 1998.

Edinger, Edward. *Anatomy of the Psyche*. Chicago: Open Court Publishing, 1985.

Edou, Jérôme. *Machig Labdrön and the Foundations of Chöd*. Ithaca, NY: Snow Lion Publications, 1996.

Epstein. Mark. *Going on Being*. New York: Broadway Books, 2001.

————. *Going to Pieces without Falling Apart*. New York: Broadway Books, 1998.

————. *Thoughts without a Thinker: Psychotherapy from a Buddhist Perspective*. New York: Basic Books, 1995.

Ferenczi, Sandor. *The Clinical Diary of Sandor Ferenczi*. J. Dupont, ed., and M. I. Balint and N. Zarday Jackson, trans. Cambridge, MA: Harvard University Press, 1988. Original work published 1932.

Frankl, Viktor. *Man's Search for Meaning*. New York: Simon and Schuster, 1984.

Freud, Sigmund. *The Basic Writings of Sigmund Freud*. A. A. Brill, ed. and trans. New York: Random House, 1938.

———. *Beyond the Pleasure Principle*. J. Strachey, ed. and trans. New York: W. W. Norton, 1961. Original work published 1920.

———. *Civilization and Its Discontents*. J. Strachey, ed. and trans. New York: W. W. Norton, 1961. Original work published 1930.

———. *The Ego and the Id*. J. Strachey, ed., J. Rivière, trans. London: Hogarth Press, 1962. Original work published 1923.

———. "Further Recommendations in the Technique of Psycho-Analysis: Observations on Transference-Love" In Strachey, J., ed. and trans. *The Standard Edition of the Complete Psychological Works of Sigmund Freud*, vol. 12, pp. 159–171. London: Hogarth Press, 1958. Original work published 1915.

———. *The Future of an Illusion*. J. Strachey, ed. and trans. New York: W. W. Norton, 1961. Original work published 1927.

———. "Introductory Lectures on Psychoanalysis." In Strachey, J., ed. and trans. *The Standard Edition of the Complete Psychological Works of Sigmund Freud*, vols. 15 and 16. London: Hogarth Press, 1963. Original work published 1916–1917.

———. "On Beginning the Treatment." In Strachey, J., ed. and trans. *The Standard Edition of the Complete Psychological Works of Sigmund Freud*, vol. 12, pp. 121–144. London: Hogarth Press, 1958. Original work published 1913.

———. "On Narcissism." In Strachey, J., ed. and trans. *The Standard Edition of the Complete Psychological Works of Sigmund Freud* vol. 14, pp. 67–104. London: Hogarth Press, 1957. Original work published 1914.

———. "On Transience." In Strachey, J., ed. and trans. *The Standard Edition of the Complete Psychological Works of Sigmund Freud*, vol. 14, pp. 305–307. London: Hogarth Press, 1957. Original work published 1916.

———. *An Outline of Psychoanalysis*. J. Strachey, ed. and trans. New York: W. W. Norton, 1949. Original work published 1940.

———. *The Question of Lay Analysis*. J. Strachey, ed. and trans. New York: W. W. Norton, 1959. Original work published 1927.

———. "Recommendations to Physicians Practicing Psycho-Analysis." In Strachey, J., ed. and trans. *The Standard Edition of the Complete Psychological Works of Sigmund Freud*, vol. 12, pp. 109–120.

London: Hogarth Press, 1958. Original work published 1912.

―――. "Thoughts for the Times on War and Death." In Strachey, J., ed. and trans. *The Standard Edition of the Complete Psychological Works of Sigmund Freud*, vol. 14, pp. 272–302. London: Hogarth Press, 1957. Original work published 1915.

Friedman, Maurice. *Religion and Psychotherapy*. New York: Paragon House, 1992.

Fromm, Erich. *Psychoanalysis and Religion* New Haven, CT: Yale University Press, 1950.

Galland, China. *The Bond between Women*. New York: Riverhead Books, 1998.

Ginsberg, Allen. *Howl*. San Francisco: City Lights Books, 1956.

Goleman, Daniel, ed. *Healing Emotions*. Boston: Shambhala, 1997.

Goodchild, Veronica. *Eros and Chaos*. York Beach, ME: Nicolas-Hays, 2001.

Gross, Rita. *Soaring and Settling*. New York: Continuum, 1998.

Gyaltsan, L. C. *Lama Chopa*. Jewel Heart, trans. Unpublished Jewel Heart transcript. Ann Arbor, MI: Jewel Heart, 2000.

Haynal, Andre E. *Controversies in Psychoanalytic Method: From Freud to Ferenczi to Michael Balint*. New York: New York University Press, 1989.

Hillesum, Etty. *An Interrupted Life and Letters from Westerbork*. New York: Henry Holt, 1996.

Hillman, James. *A Blue Fire*. New York: Harper and Row, 1989.

―――. *Inter Views: Conversations between James Hillman and Laura Pozzo on Therapy, Biography, Love, Soul, Dreams, Work, Imagination and the State of the Culture*. New York: Harper and Row, 1983.

―――. *The Myth of Analysis*. New York: Harper Collins, 1972.

―――. *Re-Visioning Psychology*. New York: Harper Perennial, 1975.

―――. *The Thought of the Heart and the Soul of the World*. Dallas: Spring Publications, 1981.

Hopkins, Jeffrey. *Cultivating Compassion*. NY: Broadway Books, 2001.

Horney, Karen. *New Ways in Psychoanalysis*. New York: W. W. Norton, 1939.

―――. *Our Inner Conflicts*. New York: W. W. Norton, 1945.

Hycner, Richard. *Between Person and Person*. Highland, NY: The Gestalt Journal, 1988.

Jung, Carl Gustav. *Answer to Job*. R.F.C. Hull, trans. Princeton: Princeton University Press, 1991. Original work published 1952.

———. *Memories, Dreams, Reflections*. Aniela Jaffé, ed.; Richard and Clara Winston, trans. New York: Vintage Books, 1989. Original work published 1961.

———. *Modern Man in Search of a Soul*. Orlando, FL: Harcourt Brace Jovanovich, 1933.

———. *Psychological Reflections*. Jolande Jacobi and R.F.C. Hull, eds. Princeton: Princeton University Press, 1978.

———. *Psychology and Alchemy*. R.F.C. Hull, trans. Princeton: Princeton University Press, 1993. Original work published in 1944.

———. *The Psychology of the Transference*. R.F.C. Hull, trans. Princeton: Princeton University Press, 1992. Original work published in 1946.

———. "The Transcendent Function." In *The Collected Works of C. G. Jung, Vol. 8*. R.F.C. Hull, trans. Princeton: Princeton University Press, 1960.

———. *Two Essays on Analytical Psychology*. Princeton: Princeton University Press, 1977.

———. *The Vision Seminars*, vol. 1. Zurich, Switzerland: Spring Publications, 1976.

Khyentse, Dilgo. *Enlightened Courage*. Ithaca, NY: Snow Lion, 1993.

Klein, Anne Carolyn. *Meeting the Great Bliss Queen*. Boston: Beacon Press, 1995.

Klein, Melanie. *Envy and Gratitude and Other Works: 1946–1963*. London: Hogarth Press, 1975.

Kohut, Heinz. *How Does Analysis Cure?* Chicago: The University of Chicago Press, 1984.

———. *The Restoration of the Self*. Madison, CT: International Universities Press, 1977.

Kornfield, Jack. *A Path with Heart*. New York: Bantam Books, 1993.

Ladner, L. *The Psychodynamics of Compassion: Psychological Reflections on the Tibetan Buddhist Stages of the Path Literature*. Unpublished doctoral dissertation. Carpinteria, CA: Pacifica Graduate Institute, 1997.

Langs, R., ed. *Classics in Psychoanalytic Technique*. Northvale, NJ: Jason Aronson, 1990.

Leifer, Robert. *The Happiness Project*. Ithaca, NY: Snow Lion, 1997.

Lewin, Roger. *Compassion: The Core Value that Animates Psychotherapy*. Northvale, NJ: Jason Aronson, 1996.

Luke, Helen. *The Way of Women*. New York: Doubleday, 1995.

Maslow, Abraham. *Religion, Values, and Peak Experiences*. New York: Viking Press, 1970.

McDougall, Joyce. *The Many Faces of Eros*. New York: W. W. Norton, 1995.

McGuire, William, ed. *The Freud/Jung Letters*. Abridged and edited. R. Mannheim and R.F.C. Hull, trans. Princeton: Princeton University Press, 1974.

Moore, Thomas. *Care of the Soul*. New York: HarperCollins, 1992.

Neumann, Erich. *Amor and Psyche*. Princeton: Princeton University Press, 1956.

Osbon, Diane, ed. *Reflections on the Art of Living: A Joseph Campbell Companion*. New York: HarperCollins, 1991.

Ovid. *Metamorphoses*. A. D. Melville, trans. London: Oxford University Press, 1998.

Palmer, Richard. *Hermeneutics*. Evanston, IL: Northwestern University Press, 1969.

Palmo, Tenzin. "Tuning the Mind to Make a Sweet Melody." In *Mandala Magazine* (March, 2001): 36–39.

Paris, Ginette. *Pagan Grace*. Woodstock, CT: Spring Publications, 1990.

Pinkola Estés, Clarissa. *Women Who Run with the Wolves*. New York: Ballantine Books, 1992.

Plato. *The Philosophy of Plato*. I. Edman, ed. and B. Jowett, trans. New York: The Modern Library, 1956.

Rabten, Geshe. *Treasury of Dharma*. London: Tharpa Publications, 1988.

Rabten, Geshe, and Geshe Dhargyey. *Advice from a Spiritual Friend*. Boston: Wisdom Publications, 1996.

Rank, Otto. *Beyond Psychology*. New York: Dover Publications, 1941.

———. *Psychology and the Soul.* Baltimore: Johns Hopkins University Press, 1998.

Remen, Rachel. *Kitchen Table Wisdom.* New York: Riverhead Books, 1996.

Rilke, Rainer Maria. *Rilke on Love and Other Difficulties.* J. Mood, trans. New York: W. W. Norton, 1975

Rimpoche, Nawang Gehlek. *Good Life, Good Death.* New York: Riverhead Books, 2001.

———. *Lam Rim Teachings,* vol. 3. Unpublished Jewel Heart transcript. Ann Arbor, MI: Jewel Heart, 1993.

———. *Lojong: Seven Point Mind Training.* Unpublished Jewel Heart transcript. Ann Arbor, MI: Jewel Heart, 1999.

———. *Love and Compassion, a Weekend Course.* Unpublished Jewel Heart transcript. Ann Arbor, MI: Jewel Heart, 1992.

———. *Odyssey to Freedom.* Unpublished Jewel Heart transcript. Ann Arbor, MI: Jewel Heart, 1997.

Rinpoche, Pabongka. *Liberation in the Palm of Your Hand.* M. Richards, trans., Trijang Rinpoche, ed. Boston: Wisdom Publications, 1991.

Rinpoche, Sogyal. *Tibetan Book of Living and Dying.* New York: HarperCollins, 1993.

Rinpoche, Tarthang Tulku. "Tibetan Buddhism, the Way of Compassion." In J. Needleman and D. Lewis, eds., *On the Way to Self Knowledge* (pp. 84–113). New York: Alfred Knopf, 1976.

Romanyshyn, Robert. Lecture. Carpinteria, CA: Pacifica Graduate Institute, October, 16, 1998.

———. Lecture. Carpinteria, CA: Pacifica Graduate Institute, June, 11, 1999.

———. *The Soul in Grief.* Berkeley, CA: North Atlantic Books, 1999.

———. *Technology as Symptom and Dream.* New York: Routledge, 1989.

Shantideva. *A Guide to the Bodhisattva's Way of Life.* Stephen Batchelor, trans. Dharamsala, India: Library of Tibetan Works and Archives, 1979.

Siegel, Allen M. *Heinz Kohut and the Psychology of the Self.* New York: Routledge, 1996.

Spiegelman, J. Marvin and Mokusen Miyuki. *Buddhism and Jungian Psychology*. Phoenix, AZ: Falcon Press, 1985.

Sweet, M. J. and C. G. Johnson. "Enhancing Empathy: The Interpersonal Implications of a Buddhist Meditation Technique." In *Psychotherapy* 27 (1990): 19–29.

Tharchin, Sermey Khensur Lobsang. *Achieving Bodhichitta*. Howell, NJ: Mahayana Sutra and Tantra Press, 1999.

Thurman, Robert A. F. *Inner Revolution: Life, Liberty and the Pursuit of Real Happiness*. New York: Riverhead Books, 1998.

———. "A Tibetan Perspective." In Daniel Goleman and R. A. F. Thurman, eds., *MindScience: An East-West Dialogue*. Boston: Wisdom Publications, 1991.

Thurman, Robert A. F., ed. *Life and Teachings of Tsong Kapa*. Dharamsala, India: Library of Tibetan Works and Archives, 1982.

Thurman, Robert A. F., trans. *The Holy Teaching of Vimalakirti*. University Park, PA: Pennsylvania State University Press, 1976.

Trub, Hans. "Healing through Meeting." In M. Friedman, ed. *The Worlds of Existentialism* (pp. 499–505). New York: Random House, 1964.

Trungpa, Chögyam. "Becoming a Full Human Being." In John Welwood, ed. *Awakening the Heart: East/West Approaches to Psychotherapy and the Healing Relationship* (pp. 126–131). Boston: New Science Library, Shambhala, 1983.

———. *Cutting through Spiritual Materialism*. Boston: Shambhala, 1973.

———. *The Heart of the Buddha*. Boston: Shambhala, 1991.

———. *Illusions Game*. Boston: Shambhala, 1994.

———. *The Myth of Freedom*. Boston: Shambhala, 1976.

———. *Training the Mind and Cultivating Loving-kindness*. Boston: Shambhala, 1993.

Tulku, Gomo. *Becoming a Child of the Buddhas*. Boston: Wisdom Publications, 1998.

Tulku, Tarthang. *Path of Heroes*, (vol. 1). Oakland, CA: Dharma Publishing, 1995.

Ventura, M. "The Inevitable and the Unpredictable." In *Salt Journal 3*, no. 3 (2001): 42-49.

Von Franz, Marie-Louise. *Alchemy*. Toronto, Canada: Inner City Books, 1980.

Wachowski, Andy and Larry. *The Matrix*. New York: Warner, 1999.

Wallace, B. Alan. *Boundless Heart*. Ithaca, NY: Snow Lion Publications, 1999.

———. *Buddhism with an Attitude*. Ithaca, NY: Snow Lion Publications, 2001.

———. *A Passage from Solitude*. Ithaca, NY: Snow Lion Publications, 1992.

Walsh, Roger, and Frances Vaughan, eds. *Paths beyond Ego: The Transpersonal Vision*. New York: Putnam, 1993.

Wangyal, Geshe. *The Door of Liberation*. New York: Lotsawa, 1978.

Weisel, Elie. *All Rivers Run to the Sea: Memoirs*. New York: Albert Knopf, 1995.

Welwood, John, ed. *Awakening the Heart: East/West Approaches to Psychotherapy and the Healing Relationship*. Boston: New Science Library, Shambhala, 1983.

———. *Toward a Psychology of Awakening*. Boston: Shambhala, 2000.

Wilber, Ken. *One Taste*. Boston: Shambhala, 1999.

———. *Sex, Ecology, Spirituality*. Boston: Shambhala, 1995.

Wilde, Oscar. *The Picture of Dorian Gray and Other Writings by Oscar Wilde*. New York: Bantam Books, 1982.

Woodman, Marion. *Conscious Femininity*. Toronto: Inner City Books, 1993.

Yeshe, Thubten. "Bodhicitta: The Perfection of Dharma." In *Mandala Magazine* (March, 2001): 30–32.

———. *Introduction to Tantra*. Boston: Wisdom Publications, 1987.

———. *Light of Dharma*. Boston: Wisdom Publications, 1983.

Young-Eisendrath, Polly. *The Resilient Spirit*. New York: Addison-Wesley, 1996.

INDEX

ABOUT THE AUTHOR

AURA GLASER HOLDS A PH.D. in Clinical Psychology from Pacifica Graduate Institute, a M.A. in Clinical Psychology from the Center for Humanistic Studies, and a B.A. in Women's Studies from the University of Michigan. In the late 1970s, she traveled to India where she began to study and practice Tibetan Buddhism. One of the foremost students of Gehlek Rimpoche, she is a teacher and a co-founder of Jewel Heart, an international Buddhist organization. She maintains a private psy-chotherapy practice, and lives in Ann Arbor, Michigan. Readers may contact Aura at auraglaser@cittamani.org.